FINANCIAL T~~~~ ~~~~~~

Terminology Plain and Simple Explained

Revision 1.1

Thomas Herold
Evolving Wealth, LLC.
©2014 All rights reserved.

www.evolvingwealth.org

Table of Content

Table of Content

401K

401K's are retirement plan accounts. Contrary to what you may have heard, these accounts are not actually investments. They are specific purpose accounts that are funded using pre-taxed dollars taken out of your payroll. Wealth can be built up for retirement by purchasing assets in the plan that includes stocks, mutual funds, index funds, bond, and real estate investment trusts. These accounts do not get taxed on dividends, capital gains, or interest earned within them until such gains are later withdrawn.

A number of different kinds of 401K plans exist. All of them have their own specific purposes, drawbacks, and benefits. For example, those who work for not for profits or government agencies are not eligible for standard 401K accounts. They are offered 403B plans instead.

The Roth 401K is another type of 401K plan. It allows workers to put taxed dollars into their account. While they do not permit contribution tax write offs now, they do ensure that income taxes will never have to be paid on any of the account money, including dividends and capital gains earned, when it is withdrawn for retirement.

Another type of 401K plan is the Self Employed 401K. This new type of 401K account is ideal for people who work for themselves. It includes a number of different features that make it very appealing to the owners of small businesses.

Five main benefits comprise the advantages of 401K retirement plan investing. These include tax advantages, employer based match programs, portability, investment versatility, and hardship and loan withdrawal capabilities. The tax advantages of traditional 401K's center around the fact that your contributions are fully tax deductible, meaning that you only pay income taxes on the money as it is taken out.

Employer based match programs are like receiving free money for retirement. A number of employers offer this benefit of matching a certain percentage of a contribution of an employee as a benefit, for obtaining and keeping quality employees. These amounts can range up to a hundred and fifty percent of amounts contributed and even higher.

Portability of 401K's allows for you to take your account with you after leaving an employer. This is fitting since the account belongs to you and not the employer. You also have the option to leave an account with an employer's plan, if you prefer.

The investment versatility of 401K's means that many choices of investments are available for the funds placed in these accounts. Lower risk investors can choose to hold short term bonds. Higher risk investors might opt for equities and higher risk investments.

401K's also feature the ability to take loans against them. These are repaid according to terms set up with the plan administrators. When a family has medical expenses or other disasters to deal with, they may also take a hardship withdrawal from the plan. Pre-retirement age withdrawals include a ten percent plus tax rate penalty.

The maximum amounts that may be contributed every year in a 401K account vary with your salary, plan type, and government regulations. Typically, it is the lesser of either the most that your employer will allow you to put in as a percentage of your salary, such as four percent, or $16,500 plus the inflation index, as per 2010 government rules. This maximum dollar amount is increased with changes to the cost of living index each year.

Accountant

Accountants are professional financial personnel whose careers are centered on dealing with money and figures. Their responsibilities cover compiling financial records, certifying them, and recording them for businesses, individuals, government organizations, and not for profit organizations. As such, they track a company or individual's money through the development of reports.

Managers of companies and organizations and other individuals read these accounting reports. The managers learn the state and progress of their company from them. Governments utilize these reports to determine the taxes that companies are required to pay. Investors and other businesses look at them to determine if they wish to work with a company. Banks and others investigate these reports in their decisions of lending money to a company.

The majority of accountants are specialized. Four main types of accountants practice their trade. Management accountants follow the money that is both earned and spent by their employing companies.

Public accountants work at public accounting firms. Here, they perform auditing, accounting, consulting, and tax preparation work. These types of accountants perform numerous tasks for individuals who are clients of the accounting firm. Some public accountants have their own small business.

Government auditors and accountants ensure that the accounting records of government agencies are correct. Besides this, they double check the record of those individuals who transact business with the government. This helps to keep governments responsible.

Internal auditors are accountants who ensure that the accounting records of their company are correct. In this role, they are investigating to make certain that no person within the firm is stealing. Besides this, they investigate to make certain that no individual in the company is wasting the firm's capital.

Accountants perform their tasks in offices. Those accountants who work for public companies and government groups often travel to perform audits of their own company's other branches or outside companies. Regarding their hours, accountants typically work for a normal forty hours per week. Some accountants ply their trade for more than fifty hours each week. Especially in tax season that runs from January through April, tax accountants commonly work incredibly long hours.

The outlook for accountants is exceptionally strong. Their field of work is anticipated to grow substantially faster than the average occupation through at least 2018. The reasons for this have much to do with the complex nature of both income tax laws and mandatory financial reporting. Because of the nature of these laws and rules, the demand for accountants will always exist. Working as an accountant entails a wide variety of requirements and prerequisites. Some very important positions mandate advanced degrees. Other accountant positions only need an ability and compliance to learn the trade, along with the necessary patience to see the training through.

Adjustable Rate Mortgage

Adjustable Rate Mortgages, also known by their acronym ARM's, are those mortgages whose interest rates change from time to time. These changes commonly occur based on an index. As a result of changing interest rates, payments will rise and fall along with them.

Adjustable Rate Mortgages involve a number of different elements. These include margins, indexes, discounts, negative amortization, caps on payments and rates, recalculating of your loan, and payment options.

When considering an adjustable rate mortgage, you should always understand both the most that your monthly payments might go up, as well as your ability to make these higher payments in the future.

Initial payments and rates are important to understand with these ARM's. They stay in effect for only certain time frames that run from merely a month to as long as five years or longer. With some of these ARM's, these initial payments and rates will vary tremendously from those that are in effect later in the life of the loan. Your payments and rates can change significantly even when interest rates remain level. A way to determine how much this will vary on a particular ARM loan is to compare the annual percentage rate and the initial rate. Should this APR prove to be much greater than the initial rate, then likely the payments and rates will similarly turn out to be significantly greater when the loan adjusts.

It is important to understand that the majority of Adjustable Rate Mortgages' monthly payments and interest rates will vary by the month, the quarter, the year, the three year period, and the five year time frame. The time between these changes in rate is referred to as the adjustment period. Loans that feature one year periods are called one year ARM's, as an example.

These Adjustable Rate Mortgages' interest rates are comprised of two portions of index and margin. The index actually follows interest rates themselves. Your payments are impacted by limits on how far the rate can rise or fall. As the index rises, so will your interest rates and payments generally. As the index declines, your monthly payments could similarly fall, assuming that your ARM is one that adjusts down. ARM rates can be based on a number of different indexes, including LIBOR the London Interbank Offered rate, COFI the Cost of Funds Index, and a CMT one year constant maturity Treasury security. Other lenders use their own proprietary model.

Margin proves to be the premium to the rate that a lender itself adds. This is commonly a couple of percentage points that are added directly to the index rate amount. These amounts vary from one lender to the next, and are commonly fixed during the loan term. The fully indexed rate is comprised of index plus margin. When the loan's initial rate turns out to be lower than the fully indexed rate, this is referred to as a discounted index rate. So an index that sat at five percent and had a three percent margin tacked on would be a fully indexed rate of eight percent.

Agency Bonds

Agency bonds are those bonds that are actually issued by United States' government sponsored entities. This means that these bonds are not government guaranteed, as they are created by private companies. They are backed up implicitly by the United States government, since these organizations were created to permit some categories of individuals to have the ability to receive lower cost financing, in particular first time home buyers and students.

The biggest, best recognized names in Agency Bond issuers prove to be Sallie Mae, Freddie Mac, and Fannie Mae. These three large companies are different from government agencies in that they are not guaranteed by the United States' government's promise of full faith and credit. Instead, they are all privately held and run companies that are given government charters as a result of their critical activities that carry out government directed policies.

Agency bonds are used to raise money to help these companies offer farm loans, home loans, student loans, and international trade financing. As a result of the government deeming these activities to be significant enough to grant charters, the markets consider that the Federal Government will not permit these chartered firms to go under. This gives their agency bonds the implied government sponsored entity guarantee. As a result of this implicit guarantee, these agency bonds carry ratings and yields that are comparable to government issued debt.

As an example, Private Export Funding Corporation bonds prove to be backed up by actual collateral of United States government securities. Federal Farm Credit Banks' bonds are not, although it is a government sponsored entity. Despite the differences, the yield-to-maturity of the two bonds are 4.753% and 4.760% respectively. These two organizations' debt obligations are nearly priced the same, demonstrating once again the implicit guarantee in the government sponsored entity securities.

The issue of taxation is another important one to consider when you are looking at Agency Bonds. All agency bonds are taxable on Federal levels. Many are not taxed on state levels. This is critical if you are an investor who resides in a state that has its own taxes. The interest payments from the best known of these organizations like Freddie Mac and Fannie Mae can be taxed on a state level. The majority of others agency bonds avoid this taxation, making their rates more attractive for many investors.

The vast majority of all agency bonds outstanding, more than ninety percent, are issued by only the four largest government sponsored entities. By largest size, these are Federal Home Loan Banks, Federal Home Loan Mortgage Corporation, Federal National Mortgage Association, and Federal Farm Credit Banks. The Federal Home Loan Banks' and Federal Farm Credit Banks' agency bonds are not state income taxable.

AMEX (The American Stock Exchange)

The AMEX is the acronym for the American Stock Exchange. This exchange proves to be the third biggest such stock market in all of the United States when trading volume is considered, after the NYSE and the NASDAQ national exchanges. Located in the American financial center of New York, the AMEX carries around ten percent of every security that is listed within the United States. In the past, it had a much larger market share of traded securities.

The origins of the AMEX lie before it was called the American Stock Exchange. In 1953, the New York Curb Exchange became known as the AMEX. This exchange proved to be a mutual organization that the members owned. In decades past, the American Stock Exchange had an important position as a major competitor for the New York Stock Exchange. This role gradually fell to the rising NASDAQ stock exchange.

Back on the seventeenth of January in 2008, the NYSE Euronext exchange announced its intentions to buy out the American Stock Exchange in consideration of $260 million in NYSE stock. They completed the transaction on the first of October in 2008. NYSE originally intended to integrate the AMEX exchange into its Alternext European small cap exchange. They first renamed it the NYSE Alternext U.S. By March of 2009, NYSE had scrapped this plan and renamed it the NYSE Amex Equities exchange.

The overwhelming majority of AMEX trading these days is done in small cap company stocks, derivatives, and exchange traded funds. These are niches that the AMEX exchange carved out and maintained for itself despite the rising allure of the newer NASDAQ in the 1990's. The AMEX observes regular trading session hours running from 9:30 in the morning to 4:00 in the afternoon on Monday through Friday. The exchange is closed on Saturdays, Sundays, and all holidays that the exchange announces in advance.

Amortization

The word amortization is one that is commonly utilized by financial officers of corporations and accountants. They utilize it when they are working with time concepts and how they relate to financial statements of accounts. You typically hear this word employed when you are figuring up loan calculations, or when you are determining interest payments.

The concept of amortization possesses a lengthy history and it is currently employed in numerous different segments of finance. The word itself descends from Middle English. Here amortisen meant to "alienate" or "kill" something. This derivation itself comes from the Latin admortire that signified "plus death." It is loosely related to the derivation of the word mortgage, as well.

Amortization is literally the process of amortizing. This accounting principle is much like depreciation that diminishes a liability or asset's value over a given period of time through payments. Amortization covers the practical life span of a tangible asset. With liabilities, it includes a pre-set amount of time over which money is paid back. Like this, a certain amount of money is set aside for the loan repayment over its lifetime.

Even though depreciation is similar to amortization, they are not the same concepts. The main difference between them lies in what they cover. While depreciation is most commonly employed to describe physical assets like property, vehicles, or buildings, amortization instead covers intangibles such as product development, copyrights, or patents. Where liabilities are concerned, amortization relates to income in the future that will be paid out over a given amount of time. Depreciation is instead a lost income over a time period.

Several different kinds of amortization are presently in use. This varies with the accounting method that is practiced. Business amortization deals with borrowed funds and loans and the paying of particular amounts in different time frames. When used as amortization analysis, this is the means of cost execution analysis for a given group of operations. Where tax law is concerned, amortization pertains to the interest amount that is paid over a given span of time relevant to payments and tax rates. Amortization can also be employed with regards to zoning rules and regulations, since it conveys a property owner's time for relocating as a result of zoning guidelines and pre-existing use. Another variation on amortization is utilized with negative amortization. This pertains specifically to increasing loan amounts that result from total interest due not being paid up at the appropriate time.

Amortization can also be employed over a widely ranging time frame. It could cover only a year or extend to as many as forty years. This depends on the kind of loan or asset utilized. Some examples include building loans that span over as many as forty years and car loans that commonly span over merely four to five years. Asset examples would be patent right expenses that commonly are spread out over seventeen years.

Annual Percentage Rate (APR)

The annual percentage rate, or APR, is the actual interest rate that a loan charges each year. This single percentage number is truthfully used to represent the literal annual expense of using money over the life span of a given loan. Annual percentage rate not only covers interest charged, but can also be comprised of extra costs or fees that are attached to a given loan transaction.

Credit cards and loans commonly offer differing explanations for transaction fees, the structure of their interest rates, and any late fees that are assessed. The annual percentage rate provides an easy to understand formula for expressing to borrowers the real and actual percentage number of fees and interest so that they can measure these up against the rates that other possible lenders will charge them.

Annual percentage rate can include many different elements besides interest. With a nominal APR, it simply involves the rate of a given payment period multiplied out to the exact numbers of payment periods existing in a year. The effective APR is often referred to as the mathematically true rate of interest for a given year. Effective APR's are commonly the fees charged plus the rate of compound interest.

On a home mortgage, effective annual percentage rates could factor in Private Mortgage Insurance, discount points, and even processing costs. Some hidden fees do not make their ways into an effective APR number. Because of this, you should always read the fine print surrounding an APR and the costs associated with a mortgage or loan. As an example of how an effective APR can be deceptive with mortgages, the one time fees that are charged in the front of a mortgage are commonly assumed to be divided over a loan's long repayment period. If you only utilize the loan for a short time frame, then the APR number will be thrown off by this. An effective APR on a mortgage might look lower than it actually is when the loan will be paid off significantly earlier than the term of the loan.

The government created the concept of annual percentage rate to stop loan companies and credit cards issuers from deceiving consumers with fancy expressions of interest charges and fees. The law requires that all loan issuers and credit card companies have to demonstrate this annual percentage rate to all customers. This is so the consumers will obtain a fair comprehension of the true rates that are associated with their particular transactions. While credit card companies are in fact permitted to promote their monthly basis of interest rates, they still have to clearly show the actual annual percentage rate to their customers in advance of a contract or agreement being signed by the consumer.

Annual percentage rate is sometimes confused with annual percentage yield. This can be vastly different from the APR. Annual percentage yield includes calculations of compounded interest in its numbers.

Arbitrage

Arbitrage refers to the practice of taking advantage of the price imbalances sometimes arising in two or even more markets. People who work in foreign money exchange run their whole businesses on this model. As an example, they look for tourists who require a rapid exchange of their cash for the local currency. Tourists agree to accept this local money for a lower amount than the actual market rate, and the money changer gets to keep the spread created by the higher rate that he charges them for the local currency. This spread that the different rates create becomes his profit.

Many different scenarios allow for investors or businessmen to become involved in the arbitrage practice. Sometimes, one market is not aware of the existence of the second market, or it simply can not access it. Arbitrageurs, persons who avail themselves of arbitrage, are also able to benefit from the different liquidities present in various markets.

Arbitrage is typically employed to discuss opportunities with investments and money rather than price imbalances for goods. Because of arbitrageurs operating in various markets whenever they spot opportunities, the prices found in the higher market will commonly drop while the prices in the lower market will usually rise so that they meet somewhere around the middle of the price difference. The phrase efficiency of the market then deals with the rate of speed at which these differing prices converge towards each other.

There are people who make arbitrage their livelihood. Working in arbitrage offers the possibilities of lucrative gains and profits. It does not come free of risk though. The greatest danger is that the prices may change rapidly between the varying markets. As an example, the spreads could rapidly fluctuate in only the tiny amount of time that is necessary for the two transactions to take place. In instances where these prices are moving quickly, arbitrageurs may not only find that they missed the chance to realize the profit between the differences in the prices, but that in fact they lost money on the deal.

Examples of arbitrage in the financial markets abound. Convertible arbitrage is working with convertible bonds to realize arbitrage. The bond can be converted into stock of the issuer of the bond. Sometimes, the amounts of shares that the bond will convert to are worth more than the price of the bond. In this case, an arbitrageur will be able to make a profit by purchasing the bond, converting it into the stock shares, and then selling the stock on the exchange to realize the difference.

Relative value arbitrage is using options to acquire the underlying shares of stock. It might be that the option is less expensive relative to the shares of stock that it will purchase. If a stock trades at $200, and the option that permits you to buy a share of the stock for $120 is trading at only $50, then you could buy the option, exercise it for the shares, and sell it for $200. You would only have spent $170 per share on the purchase, and then realize a $30 per share profit.

Appraisal

Appraisals are professionally done estimates of a property's real value. These are conducted by appraisers. Many things can have an appraisal done on them, including smaller items like artwork or jewelry, as well as larger things like businesses, commercial buildings, or homes.

Appraisals are commonly required before many different transactions can be performed. In advance of getting a house, piece of jewelry, or an artwork insured, appraisals must be performed. Homes and offices have to be appraised for insurance, loans, and tax purposes. Appraisals ensure that these loans and insurance policies are comparable to the property's tangible market value.

Several different types of appraisals can be performed. Real property appraisal involves properly estimating Real Estate value. Personal property appraisal involves determining the worth of valuable individual objects like expensive china, jewelry, pottery, artwork, heirlooms, and antiques. Mass appraisals merge real property and personal property appraisals into a single appraisal. Business value appraisals consider all of the valuable tangible and intangible assets that a business owns, including logos, services, equipment, property, inventory, other assets and goodwill.

Perhaps the most commonly used type of appraisal is a home appraisal. Home appraisals prove to be professionally done surveys of a house to come up with an opinion or estimate of the home's value on the market. These kinds of appraisals are usually performed for banks that are considering the approval of a loan for a person purchasing a home. Such home appraisals turn out to be detailed reports. These cover many things including the home's neighborhood, the house's condition, how rapidly area houses sell, and what comparable houses actually sell for at the time.

Such a home appraisal could similarly be done for a replacement value for insurance purposes or as a sales comparison in marketing a home, as well. Cost and replacement appraisals determine what the actual cost to completely replace your home would be if something destroyed the house. This type of appraisal is most often employed for new houses. Sales comparison appraisals more often examine various additional properties within your house's neighborhood to determine at what price they are presently selling. The appraiser will then determine how such houses compare and contrast against your particular home.

Home appraisals commonly cost in the range of from $300 to $500 when people decide to order one done themselves. Such appraisals are not often accepted by banks. They will want to have their own contracted appraiser make the estimate in order to get a more independent number that they trust.

Home appraisers are always licensed by the state in which they operate. The highest of ethical standards are demanded of them. Their sole purpose is to act as an independent third party who will give their truthful opinion of a home's market value. Appraisers are not supposed to be associated with any party that is involved in the selling of a home.

Assets

Assets are any thing that can be owned by a company or an individual person. These are able to be sold for cash. Commonly, assets produce income or give value to the owner.

In the world of financial accounting, assets prove to be economic resources. They can be physical objects or intangible concepts that can be utilized and owned to create value. Assets are deemed to have real and positive value for their owners. Assets must also be convertible into cash, which itself is furthermore considered to be an asset.

There are several different types of assets as measured by accountants and accounting processes. These might be current assets, longer term assets, intangible assets, or deferred assets. Current assets include cash and other items that are readily and easily able to be sold to raise cash. Longer term assets are those that are held and useful for great periods of time, including such physical items as factory plants, real estate, and equipment. Intangible assets are non physical rights or concepts, like patents, trademarks, goodwill, and copyrights. Finally, deferred assets are those that involve monies spent now for the costs in the future of things like rent, insurance, or interest.

Though tangible, physical assets are not hard to conceptualize, intangible assets are often confusing for people to understand. Even though these are not physical items that may be touched, they still have value that can be controlled and sold to raise cash. Intangible assets include rights and resources which provide a company with a form of marketplace advantage. These can cover many different elements beyond those listed above, such as computer programs, stocks, bonds, and even accounts receivable.

On balance sheets, tangible assets are commonly divided into further categories. These include fixed assets and current assets. Fixed assets are objects that are immobile or not easily transported, such as buildings, office locations, and equipment. Current assets are comprised of inventory that a business holds. Balance sheets of companies keep track of a firm's assets and their value as expressed in monetary terms. These assets are both the cash and other items that the business or person owns.

Assets should never be confused with liabilities. Assets create positive cash flow that represents value or money coming into a business, organization, or individual's accounts. Liabilities are obligations that have to be paid and that create negative cash flow, or take money out of a business, individual, or organization's accounts. As an example of the difference between the two, assets would be houses that are rented out that bring in more rent every month than the expenses, interest, and upkeep of the houses. Liabilities would be homes that have payments that must be paid every month and do not provide any income stream to effectively offset this.

Assumable Loan

An assumable loan is one that permits a home buyer to take over, or assume, a home seller's contract on their mortgage. This is not permitted by every mortgage lender in the place of a typical home purchase. Loans that do not have Due On Sale clauses, such as the majority of VA and FHA types of mortgages, can usually be assumed and are considered to be assumable loans.

Assumable home loans work in the following manner. A current home owner will simply transfer over his or her mortgage contract and obligations to a purchaser who is qualified to take over. In the past decades of the 1970's and 1980's, these types of mortgage note assumptions proved to be quite popular. Back then, they could be done without even having to obtain the mortgage lender's authorization. These days, the only types of mortgages that may be assumable loans without needing a lender's actual permission are those that are made by the FHA or VA.

Assumable loans provide opportunities for both buyers and sellers. It is often the case that a home buyer will not be able to secure a better rate for a new mortgage than that provided by an already existing mortgage. This could result from the negative credit history of the buyer in question or the conditions existing in the market place at the time. As existing interest rates rise, the appeal of non-existent lower rates on mortgages commonly pushes prospective home buyers to look out for assumable loans. Such a home buyer who secures an assumable loan then has the responsibility for the mortgage that the home seller previously carried.

The existing rates of the mortgage carry over for the buyer as if the person had made the original contract themselves. This assumable loan process also saves the buyer a number of the settlement costs that are incurred in making a new mortgage. This can be a substantial cost savings benefit.

Sellers similarly benefit from assumable loans. It is not uncommon for sellers to wish to be involved in the savings that buyers realize in the process of transferring over an assumable loan. Because of this, the two parties commonly share in the savings.

As an example, when the sale price of the home in question is greater than the amount owed on the mortgage itself, then the buyer will often have to put down a significant down payment, which goes straight to the home seller in this case. Otherwise, the buyer might have to get another mortgage to come up with the difference in amounts. A seller's principal benefit in participating in such an assumable loan transfer lies in having a good chance of getting a better price for the home.

Bad Debt

Bad debts are those accounts receivable that simply can not be collected. Once businesses make the determination that they are not likely to be able to collect on such sums, then they actually write these off as complete losses for the company. A debt is not typically deemed to be un-collectable until every effort within reason has been made to collect on the debt that is owed. This status is not typically reached on a debt until the person or firm owing the debt has filed for bankruptcy. Another reason for a debt to be declared a bad debt would be when the costs of continuing to collect on the debt are greater than is the amount of the debt in question.

Such bad debts commonly show up on a company income statement as an expense. This actually reduces the company's net income. At this point, bad debts have been completely written off via crediting the account of the debtor. This cancels out any remaining balance on the debtor's account. Such bad debts prove to be money that has been totally lost by a firm. Because of this, these kinds of bad debts are referred to as expenses for a business.

Companies attempt to estimate their expenses in the form of bad debts using records from similar past time frames. They look to figure out how many bad debts will show up in the current time frame based on what happened before so that they can attempt to estimate their actual earnings. The majority of corporations come up with an allowance for bad debts, as they understand that a percentage of their debtors will never repay them completely. Banks and credit card companies are especially concerned with bad debt allowances, since much of their entire business model revolves around the issuing of credit and repayment of debts from businesses and individuals.

The real difficulty with bad debts lies in determining if and when they are actually dead. When a debtor disappears, the collateral is destroyed, a lawsuit statute of limitations expires, bankruptcy is discharged, or significant pattern of a debtor abandoning debts is present, then a debt is finally determined to be bad debt. These can be subjective measurements in some cases.

Income tax laws contain a different definition for bad debts. These debts can be deducted against regular income on a 1040 C Form. These personal debts are also able to be deducted against short term types of capital gains. Debts that are owed for services which have been rendered to a person or business are not considered taxing purpose bad debts. This is because no income is present for such unpaid services that can be taxed.

Where individuals are concerned, bad debt can refer to credit card debt or any other form of high interest debt. These kinds of debts take away money from the individual in interest payments every month, creating a negative cash flow. Good debt for an individual would be debt that is used to properly leverage investments. Such leveraged investments that create positive cash flow prove to be the most desirable forms of debt.

Bailout

Bailouts prove to be the action of handing money or other capital to a company, individual, or nation that will likely go down without help. This is done in an effort to keep the entity from financial insolvency, bankruptcy, or total failure. Sometimes bankruptcies are pursued to permit an organization to fail without panic, so that fear and systemic failure does not become endemic, taking down other similar entities along the way.

Various different groups might qualify for urgent bailouts. Countries like Greece have been prime examples in the year 2010. Companies such as major banks and insurance outfits have been deemed too big to fail in the several years preceding 2010, during the height of the financial crisis and resulting Great Recession. Other industries have qualified as well, including car manufacturers, airlines, and vital transportation industries.

A good example of companies that receive preferential bailout treatment lies in the transportation industry. The Untied States government believes that transportation proves to be the underlying core of the nation's economic versatility, necessary to support the country's geopolitical power.

Because of this, the Federal Government works to safeguard the largest companies involved in transportation from failing with low interest rate loans and subsidies, which are a form of bailout. Oil companies, airlines, railroads, and trucking companies could all be considered to be a critical part of this industry. Such firms are considered to be too big and important to fail because their services prove to be nationally and constantly necessary to support the country's economy and thereby its eventual security.

Bailouts that are done in an emergency fashion typically prove to be full of controversy. In 2008 in the United States, intense and angry debates erupted regarding the failing banking and car manufacturing businesses. The camp standing against such bailouts looked at them as a means of passing the expensive bill for the failures over to the taxpayers.

Leaders of this group savagely denounced any monetary bailouts of the big three car makers and large banks, which they said all needed to be broken up as punishment for mismanagement. They criticized a new moral hazard that was being created by guaranteeing safety nets to other businesses. They similarly did not like the big central bureaucracy that arises from government agencies selecting the size and disposition of the bailouts. Finally, government bailouts of these groups were attacked as a form of corporate welfare that continues the cycle of more corporate irresponsibility.

The other camp argued that these bailouts were necessary evils, since the state of the American economy did not prove to be solid enough to suffer the failure of either the major banks or the car makers. With the car makers, fully three million jobs stood on the line. The banking industry had the argument of systemic failure of the financial system backing it up. No one on the side of the bailouts pretended to like having to engage in them, but they were said to be necessary nonetheless. In the end, such bailouts were issued to both major industries totaling in the trillions of dollars.

Balloon Loan

A balloon loan is a kind of loan that does not divide its payments up evenly throughout the life of the loan. These kinds of loans are not fully amortized over the loan's term. As a result of this, one time balloon payments are mandatory at the end of the loan's time frame in order to pay off the loan's remaining principal balance.

Balloon loans have their advantages. They are often appealing to you if you are a short term borrower. This is because balloon loans commonly come with an interest rate that is lower than the interest rate of a longer term loan. These lower interest rates provide a benefit of extremely low interest payments. This leads to not only lower payments throughout the loan, but also incredibly low outlays of capital in the life span of the loan. Because the majority of the loan repayment is put off until the loan payment period's conclusion, a borrower gains great flexibility in using the capital that is freed up for the term of the loan.

The downsides to these balloon loans only surface when the borrower lacks discipline or falls victim to higher interest rates later on. If a borrower does not possess focused and consistent discipline in getting ready for the large last payment, then the individual may run into trouble at the end of the loan. This is because substantial payments along the way are not being collected. Besides this, if a borrower will be forced to engage in refinancing towards the end, then the borrower may suffer from a higher interest rate on the balloon payment that is rolled forward.

Some balloon loans also include a higher interest rate reset feature later in the life of the loan. This further exposes a borrower to the risk of higher interest rates. This is common with five year types of balloon mortgages. When a reset of the interest rate feature is present at the conclusion of the five year period, then the interest rate will be adjusted to the current rates. The amortization schedule will then be recalculated dependent on a final term of the loan. Balloon options that do not include these reset options, and many that do reset, generally encourage the loan holder to sell the property in advance of the conclusion of the original term of the loan. Otherwise, many borrowers will simply choose to refinance the loan before this point arrives.

The reasons that you might choose to get a balloon loan are several. A person who does not plan to hold onto a house or property for a long period of time would benefit from such a loan arrangement. This individual would plan to resell the house in advance of the loan expiration. Another reason for taking a balloon loan is in a refinancing. Finally, if a person anticipates a significant cash settlement or lump sum award, then they might take on a balloon loan. Commercial property owners often like balloon loans for the purchase of commercial properties as well.

Balloon loans are sometimes called balloon notes or bullet loans.

Bankruptcy

Bankruptcy is a term that refers to the elimination or restructuring of a person or company's debt. Three principal different types of bankruptcy filing are available. These are the personal bankruptcy options of Chapter 7 and Chapter 13 filings, and the business bankruptcy restructuring option of Chapter 11.

Individuals avail themselves of Chapter 7 or Chapter 13 bankruptcy filings when their financial situations warrant significant help. With a Chapter 7 filing, all of an individual's debt is erased through discharge. This provides a new start for the debtor. Due to changes in laws made back in October 2005, not every person is able to obtain this type of total debt relief any longer. As a result of this new bankruptcy law, a means test came into being that prospective bankruptcy filers must successfully pass if they are to prove eligibility for this kind of bankruptcy relief.

The net effect of this new test is that consumers find it much more difficult to qualify for total debt elimination under Chapter 7. Besides the means test, the cost of bankruptcy attorneys has now risen dramatically by upwards of a hundred percent as a result of the new laws. Before these laws went into effect, Chapter 7 filings represented around seventy percent of all personal filings for bankruptcy. Chapter 7 offered the individual the advantage of simply walking away from debts that they might be capable of paying back with sufficient time and some interest rate help.

Chapter 13 Bankruptcy filings prove to be much like debt restructuring procedures. In these proceedings, a person's creditors are made to agree to the repayment of principal and zero interest on debts over a longer span of time. The individual gets to keep all of her or his assets in this form of filing. The most common motivation for Chapter 13 proves to be a desire to stop a foreclosure on a home. Individuals are able to achieve this by halting foreclosure proceedings and catch up on back mortgage payments. Once a court examines the debtor's budget, it will sign off on the plan for repayment proposed by the person. Depending on the level of an individual's income, he or she may have no choice but to file a Chapter 13 filling, as a result to the 2005 law changes.

Companies and corporations that are in financial distress may avail themselves of bankruptcy protection as well. Chapter 11 allows for such businesses to have protection from their creditors while they restructure their debt. Some individuals who have a higher income level will take advantage of this form of filing as well, since it does not place income restrictions on the entity filing. It has been instrumental in saving many large and well known companies over the years, including K-Mart, that actually emerged strong enough from the Chapter 11 bankruptcy to buy out higher end rival Sears afterward.

Barristers

Barristers are one of two types of lawyers used in many systems for different functions in the case law and courts arenas. The other designation of lawyer is a solicitor. Barristers' roles prove to be one of simply representing clients as their personal advocate in the courts of the appropriate jurisdiction.

Barristers' duties include actually speaking in court. Here, they present a case to a jury or a judge. They do not engage in preparation tasks such as advising a client, handling or accepting client instructions, reviewing or writing up legal documents, handling the daily administration of a case, or getting evidence ready for the court. These tasks are commonly handled by a solicitor when the two roles of attorneys are separated out. In this way, barristers function as the in court lawyer on behalf of the solicitor trial preparation lawyer.

Barristers enjoy unrestricted access and audience to the higher law courts. This stands in contrast to various other legal personnel, who are only allowed limited access to the courts after demonstrating appropriate qualifications. As such, barristers' occupation has much in common with the duties of lawyers who argue trials before civil law courts.

Barristers have little or nothing at all to do with actual clients. The solicitor of a client acts as intermediary between the two parties, even engaging the barrister to argue a case. Any client correspondence would be addressed directly to a solicitor, and not a barrister. Solicitors generally handle the barristers' fees and provide barristers with their instructions for actually arguing the case on behalf of the client.

Generally, barristers work as individual sole proprietors, as they are restricted from forming corporations or partnerships. Barristers are able to form chambers where they share office expenses and the use of clerks. There are chambers that have evolved into sophisticated and big operations that feel like corporations.

Barristers are useful for their highly specialized understanding of precedent and case laws. Generally practicing solicitors will often seek out a barrister's professional opinion when they encounter a rare or atypical section of law. Some countries permit barristers to be engaged by corporations, banks, or solicitor firms as legal advisers.

The long held traditional division between the roles of barristers and solicitors is gradually breaking down in numerous countries. In the British Isles for example, barristers long enjoyed their unique right to make appearances in the higher courts. Nowadays, solicitors are allowed to argue directly on behalf of clients in trial.

Solicitor firms are more commonly keeping the more difficult litigation tasks within their own companies anymore. Barristers are also allowed to deal with members of the public directly now, yet many still do not. This results from their narrow training pertaining to arguing before the courts that does not qualify them to offer legal advice to everyday individuals.

Barristers still argue cases on behalf of solicitors and their clients. These days, they no longer play a significant role in getting a trial ready. Barristers are mostly given briefs from solicitors that they will argue either one or several days in advance of a hearing.

Barter

Barter is a concept that pre-dates the invention of money. It proves to be the practice of trading goods, products, or services for other such products, services, and goods. Barter is a simpler way of transacting business, commonly without using money.

Although money systems have been in existence and well established for several thousand years, bartering for things as a practice is still alive and well nowadays. Systems of barter are used much of the time between one nation and another. Countries and companies occasionally engage in the practice as well. Barter is frequent in between businesses, and is sometimes also seen between a person and a business, or two different people. Within the U.S., bartering involves billions of dollars of services and goods that are exchanged back and forth in a single year. Per the International Reciprocal Trade Association that monitors bartering, over 400,000 businesses around the world bartered for more than $11 billion in just 2009.

Barter is sometimes referred to as counter-trade, in particular when it is used between two different countries. Bartering can be supremely convenient for countries that have an abundance of one or more resources or commodities but little cash on hand. Countries that produce huge quantities of wheat might exchange it directly with other countries for produce, oil, or textiles.

Where businesses are concerned, barter usually involves trading out services or products in consideration for advertising. Radio stations, television stations, and newspapers are common participants in barter, who may accept promotional goods for ads or on the air time. Other companies will exchange goods and services for stock in a company, or advice in consideration for services and goods.

Companies and individuals sometimes engage in barter as well. One company might give a consumer free merchandise in exchange for helpful sales leads. Individuals barter between each other for almost any item imaginable. Auction sites represent outlets for trading and bartering things. Interpersonal bartering is also carried out using online and print versions of classified ads. Today there are even barter clubs that help individuals learn more about and practice bartering.

In some countries like Spain, barter markets have arisen and spread. These swap meets forbid the use of money in any transactions. Participants simply bring along unwanted items and trade them with one or more parties for other items that they desire.

In times of national crises, bartering becomes more popular and commonplace. When currencies become victims of hyperinflation or devaluation, barter is resurrected. In these times and situations, barter can even supersede money as the principal medium of exchange.

Bear Market

Bear markets are periods in which stock markets drop for an extended amount of time. These pullbacks typically run to twenty percent or even greater amounts of the underlying stock values. Bear markets are the direct opposites of bull markets, when prices rise for extended amounts of time.

Bear markets and their accompanying drastic drops in stock share prices are commonly caused by declining corporate profits. They can also result from the correction of a too highly valued stock market, where stock prices prove to be overextended and decline to more historically fair values. Bear markets commonly begin when investors become frightened by lower earnings or too high values for their stocks and begin selling them. When many investors sell their holdings at a single time, the prices drop, sometimes substantially. Declining prices lead still other investors to fear that their money that they have invested in the stock market will be lost too. This motivates them to sell out through fear. In this way, the vicious cycle down progresses.

There have been many instances of bear markets in the United States since the country began over two hundred years ago. Perhaps the greatest example of an extended bear market is that found in the 1970's. During these years, stocks traded down and then sideways for more than a full decade. These kinds of encounters keep potential buyers out of the markets. This only fuels the fire of the bear market and keeps it going, since only a few buyers are purchasing stocks. In this way, the selling continues, as sellers consistently outnumber buyers in the stock exchanges.

For long term investors, bear markets present terrific opportunities. A person who is buying stocks with the plan to keep them for tens of years will find in a bear market the optimal sale price point and time to purchase stocks. Though many individual investors become frenzied and sell their stocks continuously during a bear market, this is exactly the wrong time to sell them.

Bear markets provide savvy investors with the chance to seek out solid companies and fundamentals that should still be strong ten to twenty years in the future. Good companies will still do well in the coming years, even if their share prices fall twenty or forty percent with the overall market. A company like Gillette that makes razors will still have a viable and dependable market going years down the road, even if the stock is unfairly punished by a bear market. Making money in a bear market requires investors to understand that a company's underlying core business has to be distinguished from its short term share price. In the near term, a company's fundamentals and stock prices do not always have much in common.

This means that a discounted price on a good company in a bear market is much like a periodic clearance sale at a person's favorite store. The time to buy the products heavily is while they are greatly discounted. The stock market is much the same. History has demonstrated on a number of different occasions that the stock prices of good companies will rebound to more realistic and fair valuations given some time.

Bi-Partisan

In the two party system found in the United States and other countries around the world, Bi-partisan signifies any resolution, act, or bill, as well as any action taken by a political governing body, where the two major political parties agree on the item or action in question. Compromises between two parties are referred to as bi-partisan when they bring together the wishes of the two parties in a final version of a proposal or piece of legislation. When bi-partisan support can not be attained in a two party governing system, the end result is commonly gridlock. At this point, political party members and their home constituencies get angry with one another.

Bi-partisan is similarly used to describe the efforts of two radically differing groups who hold opposing views that they reconcile for a time or on an issue. Conservatives and liberals are two examples of such groups. If they can come to agreement on a course of action on a matter of urgent national importance, this is an example of bi-partisan efforts, or bipartisanship.

In the United States, the word bi-partisan commonly is employed to detail a political action or government policy that involves working together or compromising on behalf of the Republicans and Democrats, the two important political parties. Many politicians and political candidates cling to the mantle of bi-partisan efforts and policies, in particular during an election. In reality, these bi-partisan ideals are seldom actually put into place once a politician is securely and firmly in power.

In the history of the United States, precious little evidence exists to showcase that the answers to large, complex, and critical problems are found using bi-partisan agendas. The weight of evidence actually suggests that bipartisanship has little to do with the resolution of such conflicts and disagreements. Historians call bi-partisanship an invented construct that seeks to array itself as a noble tradition in order to hide its lack of results. In fact, in times of crisis, bi-partisan solutions rarely effectively deal with the problem.

The opposite of bi-partisan is partisan. American history actually demonstrates partisan ideas to be the more successful ones. The United States' civil liberties, existence as an independent country, and idea of equality before the law, as well as many of the most beloved and successful programs of the government, all started out life as extremely partisan causes. The truth is that many aspects that are central to American life were partisan accomplishments that previously divided the nation, even to extremes.

Blue Chip Stocks

A blue chip stock proves to be the nickname given to a stock that belongs to a firmly established company. Blue chip stock companies commonly feature no major outstanding liabilities and incredibly stable earnings track records. These blue chips are believed to be in excellent financial condition, and are commonly referred to as safe investments.

Blue chip company stocks feature many similarities with one another. On the one hand, they are all solidly established as a leader or the leader within their respective fields. They all pay reliable dividends to their shareholders, even if business is not as strong as is typical for them. On the other hand, for literally decades now, investors have thought highly of blue chip stocks in general. Blue chip stocks feature proven track records of solid growth and incredibly high market capitalization. Some examples of blue chip stocks are Coca-Cola, Wal-Mart, McDonald's, Berkshire Hathaway, IBM, Gillette, and Exxon-Mobile.

Blue chip stocks are occasionally also known as bell weather issues. The name blue chip came from casinos. In casinos, blue chips stand for the highest value chips out of all the various chip colors available.

The origin of the phrase Blue Chip Stock dates back to 1923/1924. At this time, Oliver Gingold of the Dow Jones coined the phrase one day. Dow Jones company history says that Gingold used the phrase for the first time when he stood beside a stock ticker at the firm that eventually became Merrill Lynch. After watching a few stocks trading at $200 to $250 each share and higher, Gingold reportedly said to Lucien Hooper from Hutton and Company that he would get back to his office so that he could "write about these blue chip stocks." Oliver Gingold's coined phrase stuck. It has been utilized to talk about successful stocks from that point forward.

Originally, Blue chip stocks were those that were expensively priced. Today they are more likely the ones that are the highest quality stocks and their associated companies. The financial channels and newspapers will regularly display the performance of blue chip stocks next to the major stock market averages such as the NYSE and the Dow Jones Industrial Average. This is why these blue chip stocks are also known as bell weather issues.

Bonds

Bonds are also known as debt instruments, fixed income securities, and credit securities. A bond is actually an IOU contract where the terms of the bond, interest rate, and date of repayment are all particularly defined in a legal document. If you buy a bond at original issue, then you are literally loaning the issuer money that will be repaid to you at a certain time, along with periodic interest payments.

Bonds are all classified under one of three categories in the United States. The first of these are the highest rated, safest category of Federal Government debt and its associated agencies. Treasury bills and treasury bonds fall under this first category. The second types of bonds are bonds deemed to be safe that are issued by companies, states, and cities. These first two categories of bonds are referred to as investment grade. The third category of bonds involves riskier types of bonds that are offered by companies, states, and cities. Such below investment grade bonds are commonly referred to as simply junk bonds.

Bonds' values rise and fall in directly opposite correlation to the movement of interest rates. As interest rates fall, bonds rise. When interest rates are rising, bonds prices fall. These swings up and down in interest rates and bond prices are not important to you if you buy a bond and hold it until the pay back, or maturity, date. If you choose to sell a bond before maturity, the price that it realizes will be mostly dependent on what the interest rates prove to be like at the time.

Bonds' investment statuses are rated by the credit rating agencies. These are Standard & Poor's, Moody's, and Fitch Ratings. All bond debt issues are awarded easy to understand grades, such as A+ or B. In the last few years of the financial crisis, these credit rating agencies were reprimanded for having awarded some companies bonds' too high grades considering the risks that the companies undertook. This was especially the case with the bonds of banks, investment companies, and some insurance outfits.

Understanding the bond markets is a function of comprehending the yield curves. Yield curves turn out to be pictorial representations of a bond's interest rate and the date that it reaches maturity, rendered on a graph. Learning to understand and read these curves, and to figure out the spread between such curves, will allow you to make educated comparisons between various issues of bonds.

Some bonds are tax free. These are those bonds that are offered by states and cities. Such municipal bonds, also known as munis, help to raise funds that are utilized to pay for roads, schools, dams, and various other projects. Interest payments made on these municipal bonds are not subject to Federal taxes. This makes them attractive to some investors.

Book Value

The book value refers to the tangible asset value of any company. Tangible value here is used to refer to any assets that can be felt, seen, or touched, such as inventory, plants, equipment, cash, offices, or properties. Because of this tangible factor to book value, it is often referred to as Net Tangible Assets.

Finding a company's book value is not particularly hard if you have a company's balance sheet. To determine this number, all that you have to do is to look at the shareholder's equity. From this number, you simply subtract out all of the intangible items' values, such as goodwill. What remains is the book value of tangible assets that the company has.

Book value, or the net tangible assets, that companies possess proves to be extremely important. You ought to analyze a company's balance sheet directly from them, not from a third party website. This means that the book value figure may not be determined on the balance sheet. Coming up with the figure is just a matter of taking all of a company's assets and subtracting the intangible types of assets from the figure. You will then be looking at the company's true components, including properties, office buildings, phones, computers, chairs, etc.

In the past, this book value represented the ultimate measurement for value investors who were looking for bargains on stock prices of companies. This meant that higher assets, and thereby book values, proved to be the principal measurement for making value investing decisions. During the last twenty or so years, investors who seek out value have shifted away from the importance of the dollar values of assets to preferring companies that create higher earnings using a smaller base of assets.

As an example of why book value is less valuable than smaller asset bases with earnings creation, consider a company that possesses thirty million dollars in physical assets and earns $10 million per year. Look at another company that makes the same $10 million in earnings while having $50 million in asserts. Relationships between the asset base of a company and its earnings are well known and established.

This means that doubling the earnings of the company with $30 million would require investing another $30 million. This would leave the business with $60 million in assets and $20 million in earnings. Doubling the earnings of the company with $50 million in assets would similarly require adding another $50 million in assets. The business would then own a $100 million of assets and create the same $20 million in earnings per year.

The new company with $100 million in assets has the higher book value to be sure. But the smaller asset company only needed to retain $30 million in earnings in order to double its profits. The $20 million difference could be used for expansion of the business, paying dividends, or buying back shares. So while higher book values are still important, higher returns on assets are actually more significant and beneficial.

Bookkeeper

A bookkeeper is an individual who maintains a business' important financial records. These are typically kept in journals or ledgers format. This is where the word books derives from, which is used in the title of bookkeeper.

Although bookkeepers typically engage in basic levels of accounting tasks, they are still not labeled as fully qualified accountants. This is because bookkeepers are given substantially less amounts of training than are accountants. On top of this, bookkeepers do not have the requirements of legal certification applied to them. Bookkeepers could perform their duties as employees of a single business. They might also become a small sole proprietorship, working on the behalf of several small groups or individuals. In such a capacity, bookkeepers actually keep the books of a number of different clients at a time.

An individual who labors as a bookkeeper has important responsibilities. They must dutifully record each and every financial transaction in which a business engages. Bookkeepers make notes of every payment received or made, and for what each of these amounts represented. Monies that are both spent and received have to be carefully tracked. All entries placed into the ledger books have to be balanced at the end of the period, so that a company's expenses and income are accurately and precisely detailed in the accounting.

Bookkeepers are not expected to do all of the financial tasks of a business. When an accounting period that is either a quarter or a month is reached, they will often carry the books over to a qualified accountant. Such an accountant will handle the tasks of figuring up the taxes that need to be paid to the IRS. They also create official accounting reports. There are a number of larger or mid-sized firms that simply engage their own accounting staff and accountant rather than have a bookkeeper as well. This is generally considered to be more efficient financially. Smaller companies will tend to have their own bookkeeper on staff then engage an accountant on a basis of need. Such accountants are generally used for reporting taxes, as well as profits or losses.

Bookkeeping tasks, like with accounting, can become very complicated. This is especially true as companies expand. Capable bookkeepers are able to work flexibly, handling a constant barrage of data and even unexpected issues. A reliable bookkeeper will also have to possess people skills. This is because bookkeepers actually interact with other employees through the company to make certain that the company is able to keep track of every expense, ranging from ink and paper for the copy machine to hotel stays for business related to work.

Bookkeeping can occasionally involve a bookkeeper in activities that are against the law, like with creating incorrect records on the ledgers in order to make a company look to be in better financial health than it truly is. When this happens, it is casually referred to as cooking the books. No only is such activity in bookkeeping immoral, but it is highly illegal.

Boom

A boom is an economic expansion that happens when the economy of a country is growing at a rapid economic pace. Booms are more precisely commonly defined as periods in which the Gross Domestic Product expands at a faster rate pace than the long term economic growth trend rate.

Total demand of goods and merchandise proves to be high in boom periods. Businesses generally respond to this rising demand by boosting production and accompanying employment. Sometimes they will choose to increase their profit margins through raising their prices. Higher demands finally pressure limited resources. If sufficient extra capacity is not present to address the demand, then demand pull inflation can result.

Economic booms are characterized by numerous factors. Increasing, strong demands are mostly pushed by consumption in households. Ultimately, demand is furthermore boosted by exports, fixed investments, and government spending. Export growth results along with an expansion of world trade growth.

Along with greater demand comes higher wages and employment rates. Booms lead to increasingly tighter employment markets and better incomes for those working. This tightness in labor market conditions is most evident in lower unemployment rates. It is also seen in the labor force percentage that is working, the quantities of job openings that are not filled, and reports on labor shortfalls in particular careers and fields. The actual incomes of those people working in boom times increase rapidly as the demand for labor is high and numerous chances exist to increase earnings from higher productivity and more overtime shifts.

In booms, the tax revenues accruing to government rise rapidly as well. This results from rising employment and income levels. This has been called a fiscal dividend that comes from a sustained expansion. A budget surplus typically results that can be utilized to further public spending or to reduce the amount of outstanding government debt.

Booms further see the rising of company investments and profits. These in turn often result in greater amounts of capital investments. The amount and strength of the given demand has a great impact on how many investments are planned during the boom.

Productivity also rises during booms. These booms that happen in cycles are healthy for the productivity of labor. This is because in these times, businesses stretch their employees and resources to keep up with the additional demand by utilizing the companies' resources more effectively and intensely. Productivity rises as a direct result.

Booms commonly also increase a country's demand for goods and services that are imported. This is especially the case in countries that are huge importers in general, such as the United States and Great Britain. Rising imports lead to higher trade deficits, which have to be offset with cash or debt in payment.

Brokers

Brokers are professional intermediaries that work on behalf of both a seller and a buyer. When brokers function as agents on behalf of only a buyer or seller, they become representatives and principal parties in any deal. Brokers should not be confused with agents, who instead work on the behalf of a single principal. In the financial world, there are stock brokers, commodity brokers, and option brokers.

Stock brokers are highly regulated broker professionals that sell and buy stock shares and related securities. They work on the part of investors who purchase and sell such securities. Stock brokers transact through either Agency Only Firms or market makers in a given security. These types of brokers are commonly employees of brokerage firms, such as Morgan Stanley, Prudential, or UBS.

Stock brokers are essential in stock transactions, since these exchanges of stocks can only occur between two individuals who are actual members of the exchange in question. A regular investor can not simply enter a stock exchange like the NASDAQ and ask to buy or sell a stock. This is the role that brokers fulfill.

Within the stock broker realm, three different kinds of broker services exist. One of these is advisory dealing, in which a broker makes recommendations to the client of what types of shares to purchase and sell, yet allows the investor to enact the ultimate decision. A second type is an execution only broker, who will simply transact the customer's specific buying and selling instructions. Finally, discretionary dealing involves brokers who learn all about the customer's goals in investing then carry out trades for the customer based on his or her interests.

These same functions are carried out by other financial market brokers as well. Commodities brokers deal in commodities contracts for clients in commodities such as gold, silver, wheat, and oil. Commodities contracts are comprised of options, futures, and financial derivatives. These commodities brokers act as middle men to an investor to transact buy and sell orders on such commodities exchanges as the New York Mercantile Exchange, Commodities Mercantile Exchange, and New York Board of Trade.

Options brokers deal in options on stocks, commodities, or currencies, depending on what their area of specialty proves to be. They specialize in providing research, trading, and education on options to individual investor clients. Besides handling the main options that include straddles, option spreads, and covered calls, a number of options brokers facilitate trade in related fields that include ETF's, stocks, bonds, and mutual funds.

Brokers in the financial world are typically regulated by one oversight group or another. Stock brokers, for example, are licensed and overseen by the Securities Exchange Commission. They must pass an exam called the Series 7 in order to practice their trade as a stock broker. Commodities brokers, on the other hand, must obtain a Series 3 license from the Financial Industry Regulatory Authority. They are closely monitored by the Commodities Futures Trading Commission. Options brokers are monitored by the regulatory agency associated with the area of options that they trade.

Bubble

In economic terms, a bubble is high volume levels of trade at prices that are significantly out of line with actual intrinsic values. A simpler definition is the trading of assets that have over inflated values. Bubbles are also called market bubbles, speculative bubbles, balloons, financial bubbles, and speculation mania. Prices within bubbles can vary wildly. At times, they are no longer predictable using the traditional market determining forces of only supply and demand.

There are countless explanations offered for the reasons that bubbles occur even when there is no speculation, uncertainty, or limited rationality in the market. Some have theorized that bubbles could be caused in the end by prices coordinating against each other and by changing social scenarios. Bubbles are generally identified with certainty after they have burst, in the light of drastic drops in prices. This results from the difficulty of ascertaining real intrinsic values in actual trading markets. Bubbles burst, sometimes violently, in what is known as a crash or a bursting bubble.

Mainstream economics holds that you can not predict or call bubbles before they happen or while they are forming. It argues that you can not stop bubbles from developing, and that attempting to gently prick the bubbles leads to financial crises. This school of economic thought favors authorities waiting vigilantly for bubbles to burst by themselves, so that they can handle the aftermath of the bursting bubble with fiscal and monetary policy tools.

The Austrian school of economics argues that such economic bubbles are most always negative in their impacts on economies. This is because bubbles lead to misappropriation of economic resources to inefficient and wasteful uses. The Austrian business cycle theory is based on this argument concerning bubbles.

Examples of economic bubbles abound within the U.S. economy. In the 1970's, as the United States departed from the gold standard, American monetary expansion led to enormous bubbles in commodities. Such bubbles finally ended after the Federal Reserve tightened up massively on the excess money supply by increasing the interest rates to in excess of 14%. This led to the bursting of the commodities bubble that caused gold and oil to fall down to more historically normal levels.

Another example of price bubbles proved to be the rising housing and stock market bubbles created by the extended period of low interest rates that the Federal Reserve enacted from 2001 to 2004. These bubbles burst once the interest rates returned to more normal levels.

An enormous amount of dislocation occurred in the following years as this bubble burst rippled over to the financial system and the entire economy in 2007 and 2008. The Great Recession and financial collapse were created in the wake of this bursting bubble. This example demonstrates how the larger bubbles grow before they finally pop, the more dangerous and damaging they become when they finally do burst.

Bull Market

A bull market is one in which an entire financial market or a select grouping of securities sees rising prices over an extended period of time. It is also used to describe a scenario in which prices are expected to rise. While the phrase bull market is most frequently utilized to address the stock markets, it can similarly reference any items that trade, such as sustained rising prices in commodities, currencies, or bonds. The opposite of a bull market is a bear market.

The simplest definition of a bull market is one that is rising. Bull markets are those that witness an increase in prices of market shares that is sustained for a period of time. In bull markets, investors show great confidence that this rising trend will only continue to exist over a longer term. When bull markets are in effect, a nation's economy remains strong and employment levels prove to be higher.

Bull markets show the characteristics of high investor confidence, general enthusiasm about the future, and anticipation that strong and successful results will continue to occur. Forecasting with any certainty when such bull market trends will wane is challenging. Much of the problem lies in attempting to decipher speculation's role and the psychological impacts of investors that can often have a major influence on the markets in general.

Bull markets in stocks commonly develop as an economic slow down is waning. They begin in advance of an economy demonstrating a convincing recovery. As investors' confidence levels grow, they show this by their buying and investing in a belief that stock prices will gain in the future. Bull markets generally turn out to be positive and winning scenarios for most investors.

The phrase bull market is derived from the animal world, as is its opposite concept of bear markets. Bulls attack their prey by using their horns in an upward thrust, as when markets are moving up. Bears on the other hand swipe their victims down with their paws, as when markets are falling down. When the trend is rising, the market is a bull market. When it is falling instead, it is called a bear market.

Examples of bull markets abound in both the United States and developing countries. Throughout most of the 1980's and 1990's, the U.S. stock markets rose in a long running bull market. Prices rose by nearly ten fold in that time period. The Dot Com bubble put an end to this bull market at the turn of the century.

Around the world, there have also been numerous bull markets in foreign stock exchanges. In India, the Bombay Stock Exchange, known as SENSEX, experienced a dramatic bull market for five years from mid 2003 to the first of 2008. In this time frame, the index ran from 2,900 points on up to 21,000 points.

Call Option

A call option is a contract that grants a person the right, and yet not the requirement, to purchase a given security at a certain price by a certain cut off time. The securities that have call options associated with them are generally stocks, commodities, bonds, and certain other instruments. Call options are commonly abbreviated as simply calls.

In practice, call options are regulated financial contracts made between a buyer and a seller of the particular option. The purchaser of such a call is given the right to buy a set amount of the underlying instrument or commodity in question from the party selling the call option at a particular time, which is the expiration date, and at a particular price, which is called the strike price. The seller binds himself or herself to selling the underlying commodity or financial issue if the buyer wishes to obtain it. For this opportunity, the buyer pays a premium, or a fee.

Purchasers of call options are hoping that the underlying commodity or instrument's price will go up in the future. Sellers hope that such a price will not rise. Otherwise, a seller may be agreeable to give away a portion of the rise in price in exchange for the premium that is paid to them upfront. The seller still has the opportunity to make any profits that exist all the way up to the particular strike price.

For buyers, call options prove to be at their greatest profitability as the instrument that underlies them goes up in price. The goal of a buyer is for the underlying instrument's price to approach, or rise over, the actual strike price. The purchaser of the call feels that the chances are good that the underlying asset's price will increase by the expiration or exercise date of the option. The risk of this happening influences the value of the premium paid.

Profits made on call options can be substantial. They are only restricted by how high the price of the underlying commodity or instrument can go. Options become in the money as the underlying instrument price exceeds the specified strike price. When they reach the strike price, such options are said to be at the money.

For a call writer, or seller, who does not own the underlying commodity or instrument, selling a call entails an unlimited amount of risk potential. The call writer sells such a call in order to obtain a premium. Losses for such sellers can be enormous, and are only limited to how high the price of the underlying instrument can rise.

Call options may be bought on a wide variety of instruments besides stocks in a company. You can buy options on interest rate futures or commodities such as oil, gold, and silver. There are also two different sets of rules for exercising call options. European call options permit option holders to exercise an option on just its date of expiration, while American call options give the owner this ability to do so at any time in the option's life span.

Capital Gains

Capital gains refer to profits that arise when you sell a capital asset like real estate, stocks, and bonds. These proceeds must be above the purchase price to qualify as capital gains. A capital gain is also the resulting difference between a low buying price and a high selling price that leads to a financial gain for investors. The opposite of capital gains are capital losses, which result from selling such a capital asset at a price lower than for what you purchased it. Capital gains can pertain to investment income that is associated with tangible assets like financial investments of bonds and stocks and real estate. They may also result from the sale of intangible assets that include goodwill.

Capital gains are also one of the two principal types of investor income. The other is passive income. With capital gains' forms of income, large, one time amounts are realized on an asset or investment. There is no chance for the income to be continuous or periodic, as with passive income. In order to realize another capital gain, another asset must be purchased and acquired. As its value rises, it can also be sold to lock in another capital gain. Capital gain investments are generally larger amounts, though they only pay one time.

Capital gains have to be reported to the Internal Revenue Service, whether they belong to a business or an individual. These capital gains have to be designated as either short term gains or long term gains. This is decided by how long you hold the asset before choosing to sell it. When an asset with a gain is held longer than a year, the capital gain is long term. If it is held for a year or less time frame, such a capital gain proves to be short term.

When an individual or business' long term capital gains are greater than long term capital losses, net capital gains exist. This is true to the point that these gains are greater than net short term capital losses. Tax rates on these capital gains are lower than on other forms of income. Up to 2010's conclusion, the highest capital gains tax rates for the majority of investors proves to be fifteen percent. Those whose incomes are lower are taxed at a zero percent rate on their net capital gains.

When capital gains are negative, or are actually capital losses, the losses may be deducted form your tax return. This reduces other forms of income by as much as the yearly limit of $3,000. Additional capital losses can be carried over to future years when they exceed $3,000 in any given year, reducing income for tax purposes in the future. These capital gains and losses should be reported on the IRS' Schedule D for capital gains and losses.

Cash On Cash Return (CCR)

Cash on cash return, also known by its acronym CCR, is an investing term. It describes a ratio of the yearly cash flow before taxes against the total sum of cash invested. This cash on cash return is expressed as a percentage.

Cash on cash return is mostly utilized to analyze any income generating asset's actual cash flow situation. This percentage is commonly applied as a simple and quick test to decide if an asset under consideration is worthy of additional study and analysis. An investor who believed that cash flow is the greatest goal would be most interested in an analysis based on cash on cash return. Others employ it to discover if a particular property or asset turns out to be under priced. This would mean that equity in a property would exist immediately upon purchase.

Cash on cash return formulas do not figure in any deprecation or appreciation of an income producing asset. This means that the cash on cash return number may be skewed to the high side if some of the cash flow produced turns out to be a return on capital. This is because return on capital is not income.

Another limitation to cash on cash returns as a measurement lies in the fact that the calculation is more or less one of simple interest. This means that it does not take into consideration the compounding of interest. As a result of this, investments that provide a lower compound interest rate might be better over time than those that provide greater cash on cash returns, which is only a simple interest calculation.

A last downside to using cash on cash returns as a means of evaluating an investment centers around the fact that they are only pre tax cash flow evaluations. This means that your tax situation as a unique investor will not be considered in the formula. Varying tax situations can determine if an investment is a good match for you or not.

Consider an example of figuring up out a cash on cash return. You could buy an apartment complex for $1,200,000 using a down payment of $300,000. Every month, the resulting rental cash flow after expenses for this property is $5,000. This means that in a year, the income before tax would amount to $60,000, as $5,000 was multiplied by twelve months. This would make the cash on cash return the cash flow for the year before taxes of $60,000 over the entire amount of money invested in the asset of $300,000. This results in an actual twenty percent cash on cash return.

Cash Savings Account

A cash savings account is a place that you can park your cash and gain interest on it. Effective short term savings accounts are ones that permit you to meet your needs in four important areas. The access to the funds is critical.

Cash savings accounts should allow you to withdraw funds from the account whenever you need. This should be accomplished through convenient methods like ATM cards or online means. Funds in all types of cash savings accounts are insured by the FDIC, or Federal Deposit Insurance Corporation, to $100,000 for all people and $250,000 for retiree accounts.

Interest is another area of concern for cash savings accounts. This pertains to the rate that the bank or institution will give you for holding your money. Larger amounts generally attract superior rates.

Penalties should not have to be endured for withdrawing cash from cash savings accounts either. Certificates of Deposits and other instruments feature such penalties, but cash savings accounts should not. These terms of withdrawal should be clearly specified in any cash savings account.

Finally, service is an issue to be considered with cash savings accounts. You might wish to have customer service in a bank branch included. Otherwise, do it yourself online accounts can be established.

There are several types of cash savings accounts from which you can choose. One is a checking account that includes interest. This might be called a money market account. Such money market accounts include check writing privileges and check based access to funds. These can be held at banks or brokerage houses, which are gaining in popularity at banks' expense. Some privileges besides check writing include higher money market rates of interest and ATM card and machine access to funds. Downsides to these types of accounts include sometimes high minimum balances and possible fees.

Standard savings accounts are another option with cash savings accounts. These were once called passbook accounts. The interest rates provided by these accounts are lower than inflation, which proves to be their major downside. Their major advantage lies in the extremely low account minimums and fees charged to have them.

High yield bank accounts are a third type of cash savings accounts. Providing versatility of adding or withdrawing funds without penalties, they also offer the liquidity of not tying up your money for long periods of time. Nowadays, there are high yield bank accounts that provide interest rates that prove to be comparable to Certificates of Deposits, without showcasing these investments' restrictions on taking out money. The highest rates available on high yield bank accounts come from banks that are online only versions of the traditional lending institutions.

They accomplish this by not offering branches and in person customer service benefits. This means that unless such an online high yield account includes an ATM card, the only way to withdraw the funds is through electronic transfers to other brokerage, savings, or checking accounts, which can result in delays of as much as two to five full days. Without such an ATM card, it can be inconvenient to access cash stored in these accounts in a hurry or emergency situation. High yield accounts sometimes offer shorter term teaser interest rates, so individuals should investigate the product's prior six month history of interest rates to learn what their consistent rates turn out to be.

Cash Flow

Cash Flow is either an incoming revenue or outgoing expense stream that affects the value of any cash account over time. Inflows of cash, or positive cash flows, typically result from one of three possible activities, including operations, investing, or financing for businesses or individuals. Individuals are also able to realize positive cash flows from gifts or donations.

Negative cash flow is also called cash outflows. Outflows of cash happen because of either expenses or investments made. This is the case for both individuals' finances, as well as for those of businesses.

Where both individual finances and business corporate finances are concerned, positive cash flows are required to maintain solvency. Cash flows could be demonstrated because of a past transaction like selling a business product or a personal item or investment. They might also be projected into a future time for some consideration that a company or individual anticipates receiving and then possibly spending. No person or corporation can survive for long without cash flow.

Positive cash flow is essential for a variety of needs. Sufficient cash flow allows for money for you to pay your personal bills and creditors. It also allows a business to cover the costs of employee payroll, suppliers' bills, and creditors' payments in a timely fashion. When individuals and businesses lack sufficient cash on hand to maintain their budget or operations, then they are named insolvent. Lasting insolvency generally leads to personal or corporate bankruptcy.

For businesses, statements of cash flows are created by accountants. These demonstrate the quantity of cash that is created and utilized by a corporation in a certain time frame. Cash flows in this definition are calculated by totaling net income following taxes with non cash charges like depreciation. Cash flow is able to be assigned to either a business' entire operations or to one particular segment or project of the company. Cash flow is often considered to be an effective measurement of a business' ongoing financial strength.

Cash flows are also used by business and individuals to ascertain the value or return of a project or investment. The numbers of cash flows in to and out of such projects and investments are often utilized as inputs for indicators of performance like net present value and internal rate of return. A problem with a business' liquidity can also be determined by measuring the entire entity's cash flow.

Many individuals prefer investments that yield periodic positive cash flow over ones that pay only one time capital gains. High yielding dividend stocks, energy trusts, and real estate investment trusts are all examples of positive cash flow investments. Real estate properties can also be positive cash flow yielding investments when they provide greater amounts of rental income than their combined monthly mortgage payments, maintenance expenses, and property management upkeep costs and outflows total.

Cash Flow Quadrant

The cash flow quadrant is a diagram that shows four types of individuals involved in a business. These four people make up the entire business world. The four quadrants are E, S, B, and I.

The E quadrant stands for employees. Employees have the same core values in general. This is security. When any employee sits down with a manager or a president, they will always tell them the same thing. This is that they are looking for a secure and safe job that includes benefits.

The S in the cash flow quadrant represents a small business owner or a self employed person. They are generally solo actors or one person outfits. These types would rather operate on their own, as their motto is always to have something done right, you should do it yourself.

On the right side of the cash flow quadrant are the B's. B stands for Big Business people. Big businesses have five hundred or greater numbers of employees. They are completely different from the others in the quadrants, as they are constantly looking for the most intelligent and capable people, networks, and systems to aid them in running their large business. They do not want to micro manage the company themselves, rather they want good people to do it on their behalf.

The last quarter of the cash flow quadrants is the I, which stands for Investor. Investors are those individuals who make money work effectively and efficiently for themselves. The main difference between them and the B quadrants it that the investors have their money working hard while the Big Business people have other people working hard for them. Both groups of B's and I's represent the wealthy. The employees and the self employed are the people who work hard for the business people and investors on the right, or wealthy side of the quadrant.

The cash flow quadrant explains the differences between the rich and the working poor. It is useful to describe four types of income that a person can generate as well. The smartest people in the cash flow quadrant are the ones who manage to make the other people and their money work hard for their benefit. That is why they are the wealthy, while the hard working members of society on the left side are the ones who do all of the working on the wealthy people's behalf. Learning to become wealthy means effectively changing which square of the cash flow quadrant a person occupies.

Central Bank

Central banks are national monetary authorities or reserve banks that are given the unique privilege and responsibility of loaning a government its currency. Central banks have many of the same characteristics that traditional banks do, such as charging set rates of interest on loans that they make to borrowers like the government of the country that they represent, or alternatively to commercial banks in dire need and as a last resort.

Central banks are different from regular banks in a variety of interest ways. Chief among these is their monopoly of creating the nation's currency. They also have the power to loan such currency out to their government as fully legal tender. These banks are the only ones that will lend to commercial banks in difficult times of need, too.

The main role of a central bank is to issue and oversee a country's supply of money. Besides this, they also engage in a number of more vigorous activities including setting and monitoring the interest rates of subsidized loans and helping out the banking sector in periods of financial difficulties or even crisis. Some central banks additionally supervise the commercial banking sector and individual banks in order to make certain that they do not engage in corrupt behavior or rash decision making and practices.

Not all countries possess central banks that are independent of the other branches of government's meddling and interference. Most of the wealthy countries of the world do have this type of central bank in a system that stops politicians from intervening in monetary policy. The European Central Bank, Bank of England, and Federal Reserve System of the United States are all good examples of independent central banks. Central banks can be privately held or publicly owned. In the U.S., the Federal Reserve proves to be a unique combination of private and public components.

Central banks are involved in many important functions. These include carrying out monetary policy and fixing the nation's interest rates. They also control their country's whole money supply. They act as both banker for the government and for all of a country's banks in difficult times. Central banks similarly handle the nation's gold reserves and foreign exchange reserves.

They may adjust these by buying or selling more gold, or by balancing the amount and kinds of currencies that they hold at any time. Many central banks supervise their banking industries as well, though not all perform this function. Central banks also help to deal with and combat inflation and manage a country's currency exchange rate by modifying the nation's official interest rates and utilizing similar policies to ensure that the desired outcomes of low inflation and stable currency exchange rates are in fact achieved.

Closing Costs

Closing costs are the fees that are charged when you buy a house. Many other costs are associated with buying a house than only the down payment. These closing costs are fees like recording fees, title policies, courier charges, inspections, lender fees, and start up reserve fees to create an impound account. The most expensive component of these closing costs is the lender charged fees. Such closing costs are charged beyond the home's purchase price. Most closing costs are set and predetermined, meaning that they are not open to negotiation.

The total price of closing costs is fairly standard. Typically, a good guideline for closing costs is that they will run you somewhere between two and four percent of a house's purchase price. The range is as large as this spread because the origination fees and points for making the loan vary significantly from one lender to the next. These points and origination fees that are charged by the lender are always revealed to a buyer in the Good Faith Estimates that are provided to the buyers. For example, a home that is $400,000 will have closing costs that run from around $4,000 to $16,000. They could be even higher than this amount, on some occasions.

Some closing costs are of the non-recurring kind. Such fees are charged to a buyer of a house on only a single time. They include escrow or closing, title policies, courier fees, wire fees, notary charges, endorsements, attorney costs, city or county or state transfer taxes, recording, natural hazard disclosures, home protection plans, lender fees for the HUD-1 800 line, and home inspections.

Other closing costs are called prepaid closing costs, or recurring closing costs. Although these are paid for in a single lump sump up front, they cover those costs that continue to recur throughout the life of the home loan. There are comprised of property taxes, flood insurance when required, fire insurance premiums, prepaid interest, and private or mutual mortgage insurance premiums.

Closing costs are also impacted by the month of the year in which you close on the house in question. This is because future insurance and tax payments will be collected on a pro rated basis for the number of months of premiums for the year. Not all loans come with an escrow or impound account either. Yet loans that are for in excess of eighty percent of the purchase price of your house will mandate such an escrow account and impound be established.

Closing costs are some of the unfortunately high expenses associated with buying a house. They are only avoidable when a person takes over an assumable mortgage. In these cases, most closing costs, such as lender points and origination fees, are side stepped by a buyer.

Collaboration

Collaboration proves to be a process where two or more individuals or entities choose to work in concert on behalf of a common goal or endeavor. Intellectual enterprises and other activities that tend to be creative by their nature are often most effectively accomplished through collaboration, which involves learning together, mutually sharing knowledge, and building up consensus. Scientific collaboration is very common because of this.

Most forms of collaboration must have leadership. Such leadership does not have to be in the form of traditional command structures, but can instead be social leadership affected in a group of equals or alternatively that is decentralized. Reasons for practicing collaboration are fairly evident. Teams working together in collaboration have access to a greater number of resources, rewards, and recognition when they compete for limited resources.

Collaboration can be extremely structured. When it is set up like this, then inward looking communication and behavior are encouraged. Such forms of collaboration particularly attempt to boost teams' successes as they work on problem solving in collaboration. Charts, graphs, rubrics, and forms are all utilized in this type of collaboration in order to lay out personalities and personal characteristics without bias, so that the future and present projects' collaboration will be bettered.

In business and finance, collaboration can be as simple as a partnership or as complicated as a multinational corporation. Team members that work together in an organization using collaboration achieve superior communication both in the business supply chains and the entire outfit.

Such collaboration proves to be a means of putting together the various ideas and concepts of a wide variety of individuals in order to assemble a great range of knowledge and information. This proves to be invaluable to businesses and other organizations that require both general and specialist forms of knowledge from as many viable sources as possible.

Mass collaboration has become a reality as a result of fairly recent technological innovations. These include wireless Internet, high speed Internet, and various Internet based tools for collaboration, such as wikis, blogs, and others. Through these means, individuals from literally all over the planet can effectively share ideas and discourse back and forth via the Internet and even Internet based conferences, without being limited to certain geographical locations or challenges. Thanks to these forms of collaboration in both business and other forms, the possibilities of improving a project's results are practically endless.

Collateralized Debt Obligations

Collateralized Debt Obligations are one of the financial weapons of mass destruction that helped to derail the global financial system in the financial crisis of 2007-2010. They are literally securities that are supposed to be of investment grade. The backing of collateralized debt obligations proves to be pools of loans, bonds, and similar assets. These investments are rated by the main ratings agencies of Moody's, Standard and Poors, and Fitch rating companies.

The actual value of collateralized debt obligations comes from their asset backing. These asset backed securities' payments and values both derive from their portfolios of associated assets that are fixed income types of instruments. CDO's securities are divided into different classes of risk that are called tranches.

The senior most tranches are deemed to be the most secure forms of securities. Since principal and interest payments are given out according to the most senior securities first, the junior level tranches pay the higher coupon payments and interest rates to help reward investors who are willing to take on the greater levels of default risk that they assume.

The original CDO was only offered in 1987 by bankers for Imperial Savings Association that failed and became folded in to the Resolution Trust Corporation in 1990. This should have been a warning about collateralized debt obligations, but their popularity only grew apace during the following ten years. CDO's rapidly became the fastest expanding part of the synthetic asset backed securities market. There are several reasons for why this proved to be the case. The main one revolved around the returns of two to three percentage points greater than corporate bonds that possessed identical credit ratings.

CDO's also appealed to a larger number of investors and asset managers from investment trusts, unit trusts, and mutual funds, to insurance companies, investment banks, and private banks. Structured investment vehicles also made use of them to defray risk. CDO's popularity also had to do with the high profit margins that they made for their creators and sellers.

A number of different investors and economists have raised their voices against collateralized debt obligations, derivatives in general, and other asset backed securities. This includes both former IMF Head Economist Raghuram Rajan and legendary billionaire investor Warren Buffet. They have claimed that such instruments only increase and spread around the uncertainty and risk that surrounds these underlying assets' values to a larger and wider pool of owners instead of lessening the risk via diversification.

Though the majority of the investment world remained skeptical of their criticism, the credit crisis in 2007 and 2008 proved that these dissenters had merit to their views. It is now understood that the major credit rating agencies did not sufficiently take into account the massive risks that were associated with the CDO's and ABS's, such as a nationwide housing value collapse.

Because the value of collateralized debt obligations are forced to be valued according to mark to market accounting, where their values are immediately updated to the market value, they have declined dramatically in value on the banks' and others owners' balance sheets as their actual value on the market has plummeted.

Collectibles

Collectibles can be almost anything of real or notional value. People enjoy collecting everything ranging from coins and stamps to baseball cards and paintings. It is the thrill of obtaining things that are new and putting them alongside an existing collection that proves to be so addicting and rewarding for people. Collectibles can be obvious items of great value, such as expensive antiques or works of art, or common things like sand from different beaches around the world.

From a business and investment standpoint, collectibles offer more than simply the joy and thrill of collecting. They offer another means of building up wealth. Collectible coins, stamps, baseball cards, and paintings all have intrinsic value that can appreciate over time. This is especially the case if the collectible items in question prove to be limited in issue, or they become rare over time, or the demand for them increases with the years. Values can increase to dramatic levels even in the millions of dollars with some collectibles.

The benefits of having collectibles as a past time go beyond simply investment opportunities, as lucrative as these can be for you. With a collectible, you are able to own a piece of living history. Coins, stamps, and antiques are especially useful ways of achieving this objective of owning history. Such collectibles also make exciting and personally fulfilling hobbies that provide you with a reason to go to antique shops, garage sales, flea markets, and hobby shops. You may also hope to meet new people and build up friendships through collectibles. Finally, collectibles are often an attractive way to decorate the interior of your house in your own one of a kind style.

Finding collectibles once required you to go to physical locations to seek them out. These could be auction sites, hobby shops, coin and stamp stores, swap meets, yard sales, and flea markets. The Internet age has made a tremendous impact on the past time of collectibles, since now such collectibles can simply be found by going to online auction sites or specialty websites.

The past practice of walking past booths and through stalls proved to be an integral part of being a collector but a few years ago, but this is changing. Collectibles can still be found at flea markets and garage sales, though these require more tracking down now than they did prior to the Internet revolution. It is still possible to find collectibles at a physical location that you would never encounter online.

A danger to acquiring collectibles on the Internet is that you have no guarantee as to an item's authenticity. The only way to thoroughly examine it is after you have already bought and received the item. One way to get around this lies in requesting certificates of authenticity from a seller. So if you decide to purchase a collectible over the Internet, you should consult an expert in the area and have him examine the collectible item in person.

Commodities

Commodities turn out to be items that are taken from the earth, such as orange juice, cattle, wheat, oil, and gold. Companies buy commodities to turn them into usable products like bread, gasoline, and jewelry to sell to other businesses and consumers. Individual investors purchase and sell them for the purposes of speculation, in an attempt to make a profit. Commodities are traded through commodities brokers on one of several different commodities exchanges, such as COMEX, or the Commodities Mercantile Exchange, NYMEX, or the New York Mercantile Exchange, and NYBOT, or the New York Board of Trade, among others.

Commodities are traded with contracts using a great amount of leverage. This means that with a small amount of money, a great quantity of the commodity in question can be controlled and traded. For example, with only a few thousand dollars, you as an investor are able to control a contract of one thousand barrels of heating oil or one hundred ounces of gold.

As a result of this high leverage that you obtain, the amounts of money made or lost can be significant with only relatively small moves in the price of the underlying commodity. This leverage results from the fact that commodities are nearly always traded using margin accounts that lead to significant risks for the capital invested. For example, with gold contracts, each ten cent minimum price move represents a $10 per contract gain or loss.

Commodity trading strategies center around speculation on factors that will affect the production of a commodity. These could be related to weather, natural disasters, strikes, or other events. If you believed that severe hurricanes would damage a great portion of the Latin American coffee crop, then you would call your commodity broker and instruct them to buy as many coffee contracts as they had money in the account to cover.

If the hurricanes took place and coffee did see significant damage in the region, then the prices of coffee would rise dramatically as a result of the negative weather, causing the coffee harvest to be more valuable. Your coffee contracts would similarly rise in value, probably significantly.

A variety of commodities can be traded on the commodities exchanges. These include grains, metals, energy, livestock, and softs. Grains consistently prove to be among the most popular of commodities available to trade. Grain commodities are usually most active in the spring and summer. Grains include soybeans, corn, oats, wheat, and rough rice.

Metals commodities offer you the opportunity to take positions on precious metals such as gold and silver. Changes in the underlying prices of base metals may also be traded in this category. Metals include copper, silver, and gold.

Energy commodities that you can trade are those used for heating homes and fueling vehicles for the nation. With the energy complex you can trade on supply disruptions around the world or higher gas prices that you anticipate. Energy commodities available to you are crude oil, unleaded gas, heating oil, and natural gas.

Livestock includes animals that provide pork and beef. Because these are staple foods in most American diets, they provide among the more reliable pattern trends for trading. Pork bellies, lean hogs, and live cattle are all examples of tradable livestock commodities.

Softs are comprised of both food and fiber types of commodities. Many of these are deemed to be exotic since they are grown in other countries and parts of the earth. Among the soft markets that you can trade are sugar, coffee, cocoa, cotton, orange juice, and lumber.

Common Stock

Common stocks are shares in an underlying company that represent equity ownership in the corporation. They are also known as ordinary shares. These are securities in which individuals invest their capital. Common stock is the opposite of preferred stock.

While common stock and preferred stock both represent ownership in the company, there are many important differences between the two. Should a company go bankrupt, common stock holders are only given their money after preferred stock owners, bond owners, and creditors. Yet, common stock performs well, typically seeing greater levels of price appreciation than does preferred stock.

Common stock typically comes with voting rights, another feature that preferred stock does not have. These votes are used in electing the board of directors at the company's annual meeting, as well as in determining such things as company strategy, stock splits, policies, mergers and acquisitions, and the sale of the company. Preemptive rights in common stocks refer to owners with these rights being allowed to keep the same proportion of ownership in the company' stock, even if it issues additional stock.

Common stocks do not always pay dividends to share holders, as preferred stocks typically do. The dividends of common stocks are not preset or fixed. This means that the dividend returns are not completely predictable. Instead, they are based on a company's reinvestment policies, earnings results, and practices of the market in the valuing of the stock shares themselves.

Common shares have various other benefits. They are typically less expensive than are preferred stock shares. They are more heavily traded and readily available as well. The spreads between the buying and selling prices on them tend to be tighter as a result. Common stocks generally provide capital appreciation as the price of the shares rises over time, assuming that the company continues to do well and meet or exceed expectations. Dividends are often paid to common share holders when these things prove to be the case.

Common stocks can be purchased in any denominated amount. Round lots of common stocks are sold by even one hundred share amounts. This means that five hundred shares of common stock would be considered to be five lots of common stock.

Common stocks represent principally capital gains types of investments, as an investor is looking to buy them low and sell them at a higher price. This leads to a capital gain when the stock is sold at this greater level. The capital gain is the difference between the selling price and the purchasing price. Common stocks can also be cash flow types of investments when they pay a reliable stream of dividends every quarter. These income amounts are typically smaller than the one time amounts realized in capital gains, though they are obtained four times per year on a quarterly basis, or occasionally more often on a monthly basis.

Capital Stock

A business' capital stock is the up front capital that the founders of the firm invest in or put into the company. This capital stock also proves useful as security for a business' creditors. This is because capital stock may not be taken out of the business to disadvantage the creditors in question. Such stock is separate from a business' assets or property that can rise and fall in value and amount.

A company's capital stock is segregated into shares. The complete number of such shares have to be detailed when the business is founded. Based on the entire sum of money that is put into the company when it is started up, each share will possess a particular face value that must be declared.

This value is referred to as par value of the individual shares. These par values are the minimum sums of money that may be issued and sold in stock shares by the business. It is similarly the capital value representation in the business' own accounting. In some countries, these shares do not contain any par value period. In this case, the capital stock shares would be termed non par value stock. Such shares literally represent a portion of an ownership in the business in question. These businesses may then declare various classes of shares. All of these could have their own privileges, rules, and share values.

The owning of such capital stock shares is proven by the possession of a certificate of stock. These stock certificates prove to be legal documents that detail the numbers of shares each shareholder owns. Other particular data of the capital stock shares, including class of shares and par value, is similarly detailed on these certificates.

These owners of the firm in question may decide that they need more capital in order to invest in additional projects that the company has in mind. Besides this, they might decide that they want to cash out some of their own holdings in order to release a portion of capital for their own private needs. They can do this by selling all or some of their capital stock to many partial owners. The ownership of one such share gives the share owner an ownership stake in the company. This includes such privileges as a tiny portion of any profits that may be paid out as dividends, as well as a small part of any decision making powers.

These shares sold from the capital stock each represent a single vote. The owners could decide to offer various classes of shares that could then have differing rights of voting. By owning a majority of the shares, the owners can out vote all of the little shareholders combined. This permits the original owners to maintain effective control of their company even after issuing shares of their capital stock to investors.

Compounding of Money

The compounding of money has everything to do with compound interest. Compounding of money through such compounding interest can become among the most potent of weapons in your investing arsenal. Compound interest allows your money to grow at a faster rate as a result of the way that the interest is added to your money's balance. Various types of compound interest are available for compounding your money.

Compounding your money with compound interest works through taking the interest that your money has earned over a time frame and adding it back to the initial amount of money. Then when the next period is figured up, this total dollar value is calculated in the next portion of interest that you will earn. Simply put, every time frame's interest is placed directly back in to the entire sum of money on which the interest will be earned. Every time the interest is figured up, your money will earn a greater amount of interest like this.

A variety of different forms of compound interest exist. These always relate to the time frame over which the interest and money compounds. Such time frames of compounding of money are comprised of yearly, monthly, and daily compounding interest. With yearly compounding interest, the interest rate is figured up each year. In monthly compounding of interest, this rate is applied to the new principal balance each month. Daily compounding of interest involves an every day accounting of the interest and new principal.

Compounding of money involves several factors. These are periodic rates of compound interest, which are the rates actually applied to your balance, and compounding periods, which are the amount of the time frame before such interest is literally applied on to your total balance. As an example, if you invested $10,000 in a .1% daily periodic rate money market form of account, then on the second day, your balance would be $10,010. The next day, this rate would then be applied to the new balance of $10,010. Figuring out the actual annual effective rate entails you taking the whole year's interest and dividing it by the amount of the investment that you started with at the beginning of the year, or $10,000 in this case.

Compounding of money through such compound interest proves to be an extremely potent weapon. This is because the interest earned is immediately added on to the account balance to be counted as principal for the next time period. Each time frame the interest rate applies to the greater balance. Accounts grow faster through the compounding of money as the interest is not held back.

This compounding of money effect multiplies when you use it with accounts that are tax deferred, such as municipal bond funds and annuities. As no penalties of taxes are paid in a given year, your money increases quicker and quicker since greater amounts are constantly in the account to receive interest.

An example of how effective compounding of money using compound interest can be is illuminating. If you put $10,000 into a simple interest account that does not compound but receives twelve percent interest, then it will increase to $46,000 over thirty years. The same money that is compounded annually will rise to about $300,000, and to as much as $347,000 if the money is compounded quarterly. Money that is compounded over a daily time frame would naturally earn the greatest amount of interest and highest principal over a period of time.

Consumer Price Index (CPI)

The Consumer Price Index, also known by its acronym of CPI, actually measures changes that take place over time in the level of the pricing of various consumer goods and services that American households buy. The Bureau of Labor Statistics in the U.S. says that the Consumer Price Index is a measurement of the over time change in the prices that urban consumers actually pay for a certain grouping of consumer goods and services.

This consumer price index is not literal in the sense of what inflation really turns out to be. Instead, it is a statistical estimate that is built utilizing the costs of a basket of sample items that are supposed to be representative for the entire economy. These goods and services' prices are ascertained from time to time. In actual practice, both sub indices such as clothing, and even sub-sub indices, such as men's dress shirts, are calculated for varying sub-categories of services and goods. These are then taken and added together to create the total index. The different goods are assigned varying weights as shares of the total amount of the expenditures of consumers that the index covers.

Two essential pieces of information are necessary to build the consumer price index. These are the weighting data and the pricing data. Weighting data comes from estimates of differing kinds of expenditure shares as a percentage of the entire expenditure that the index covers.

Sample household expenditure surveys are sourced to figure what the weightings should be. Otherwise, the National Income and Product Accounts estimates of expenditures on consumption are utilized. Pricing data is gathered from a sampling of goods and services taken from a sample range of sales outlets in varying locations and at a sampling of times.

The consumer price index is figured up monthly in the United States. Some other countries determine their CPI's on a quarterly basis. The different components of the consumer price index include food, clothing, and housing, all of which are weighted averages of the sub-sub indices. The CPI index literally compares the prices of one month with the prices in the reference month.

Consumer Price Index is only one of a few different pricing indices that the majority of national statistical agencies calculate. Inflation is figured up using the yearly percentage changes in the underlying consume price index. Uses of this CPI can include adjusting real values of pensions, salaries, and wages for inflation's effects, as well as for monitoring costs, and showing alterations in actual values through deflating the monetary magnitudes. The CPI and US National Income and Product Accounts prove to be among the most carefully followed of economic indicators.

Cost of living index is another measurement that is generated based on the consumer price index. It demonstrates how much consumer expenditures need to adjust to compensate for changes in prices. This details how much consumers need to keep up a constant standard of living.

Contingency

Contingency in business relates to insurance products that generally are not included within the most commonly accepted types of insurance products such as property, casualty, marine, and financial services handled by the majority of insurance companies. The London Market began the industry of contingency insurance products. These forms of insurance cover cancellation, non appearance, prize indemnity, transmission failure, weather, political risk, reduction in yield, and various other forms of unusual and esoteric coverage. These types of insurance products protect business clients from losses every bit as much as do typical insurance coverage.

Cancellation coverage pays a business or individual client back all of the costs and income associated with conventions, concerts, and other special events that are forced to be canceled or postponed for reasons beyond a promoter's control. Reduced attendance, ticket refunds, and obligations of contract may also be covered by this category of contingency insurance.

Non appearance contingency insurance protects a business' income should their scheduled famous performer not appear at the event as promised. Included with this type of contingency coverage are dangers such as sickness, extortion, accident, family catastrophe, and even incarceration of the performer. The total dollar amount that is covered includes not only the fee paid to the performer but also the revenue generated indirectly from the event appearance, including parking, ticket sales, merchandising, and concessions.

Prize indemnity contingency proves to be the widest type of contingency insurance business. Such products permit clients to be capable of insuring give away products and cash prizes to customers via promotions. To qualify for this coverage, a prize winning has to result from a lucky event.

Transmission Failure contingency safeguards a business' advertising money spent, or other revenues that would be generated, if a television signal somehow became preempted or interrupted. This contingency insurance is set up to provide coverage for a specific time frame or television event. Interruption has to be something that the insured is unable to control, such as catastrophic or segmented coverage.

Contingency insurance for the weather is commonly utilized alongside event cancellation coverage. These policies pay an insured entity if poor weather happens at a certain time on a particular day. Included in these types of weather are snow, rain, wind, lightning, or tornado watches and warnings. It might also be utilized in a promotion where weather turned out to be a factor in a prize being won.

Political risk contingency coverage pertains to an individual event that might lead to an event being canceled. Such coverage could pertain to delay, abandonment, or repatriation having to do with a covered event. Such coverage is available for limited time frames only.

Reduction in yield contingency is useful for casinos, amusement parks, and resorts. This policy actually pays if anticipated revenue from visitors or ticket sales does not reach the expected level because of a covered peril. If attendance is less than expected, the policy will pay to its limit.

Corporate Bonds

Corporate bonds are debt securities that a company issues and sells to investors. Such corporate bonds are generally backed by the company's ability to repay the loan. This money is anticipated to result from successful operations in the future time periods. With some corporate bonds, the physical assets of a company can be offered as bond collateral to ease investors' minds and any concerns about repayment.

Corporate bonds are also known as debt financing. These bonds provide a significant capital source for a great number of businesses. Other sources of capital for the companies include lines of credit, bank loans, and equity issues like stock shares. For a business to be capable of achieving coupon rates that are favorable to them by issuing their debt to members of the public, a corporation will have to provide a series of consistent earnings reports and to show considerable earnings potential. As a general rule, the better a corporation's quality of credit is believed to be, the simpler it is for them to offer debt at lower rates and float greater amounts of such debt.

Such corporate bonds are always issued in $1,000 face value blocks. Practically all of them come with a standardized structure for coupon payments. Some corporate bonds include what is known as a call provision. These provisions permit the corporation that issues them to recall the bonds early if interest rates change significantly. Every call provision will be specific to the given bond.

These types of corporate bonds are deemed to be of greater risk than are government issued bonds. Because of this perceived additional risk, the interest rates almost always turn out to be higher with corporate bonds. This is true for companies whose credit is rated as among the best.

Regarding tax issues of corporate bonds, these are pretty straight forward. The majority of corporate bonds prove to be taxable, assuming that their terms are for longer than a single year. To avoid taxes until the end, some bonds come with zero coupons and redemption values that are high, meaning that taxes are deferred as capital gains until the end of the bond term. Such corporate debts that come due in under a year are generally referred to as commercial paper.

Corporate bonds are commonly listed on the major exchanges and ECN's like MarketAxess and Bonds.com. Even though these bonds are carried on the major exchanges, their trading does not mostly take place on them. Instead, the overwhelming majority of such bonds trading occurs in over the counter and dealer based markets.

Among the various types of corporate bonds are secured debt, unsecured debt, senior debt, and subordinated debt. Secured debts have assets underlying them. Senior debts provide the strongest claims on the corporation's assets if the venture defaults on its debt obligations. The higher up an investor's bond is in the firm's capital structure, the greater their claim will ultimately be in such an unfortunate scenario as default or bankruptcy.

Cost Segregation

Cost segregation proves to be a procedure of identifying assets of personal property that commonly become lost or bunched together in the real property asset. Cost segregation involves reclassifying costs of assets to a depreciable life that is the shortest one possible. This allows owners of real estate to optimize their tax deductions in the depreciation category, which lessens the amount of present income tax due. Any investor who is buying a building, renovating a building, or getting into a construction project can qualify for significant Federal and state tax advantages using cost segregation.

Particular assets that pertain to these types of projects may be eligible for such accelerated depreciation. This translates to you being capable of realizing bigger tax deductions now in a shorter time frame. Advantages in bigger tax deductions now include a less expensive capital cost and greater positive cash flow over the principal several years after a purchase has been made or a project completed. Cost segregation studies help you to find such chances to claim more accelerated tax purpose depreciation. These cost segregation studies show always be performed by well qualified Certified Public Accountants.

Cost segregation is able to reduce the time frame for depreciation significantly via s simple strategy. These studies go through all of the costs involved in a property that are currently being tax depreciated over the usual thirty-nine year time frame. Many of these might be reclassified to far shorter time periods of depreciation, including fifteen years, ten years, seven years, or even only five years. The shorter the time frame of depreciation, the greater the tax deductions will be in this far shorter period of time. Greater amounts of depreciation are realized immediately when this is done properly. In this way, not only are tax savings in the present and coming years maximized, but cash flow is similarly increased.

Cost segregation studies make sense for anyone who is purchasing an already existing building. They are efficient for investors who are putting up a new facility. They similarly help those who are engaging in leasehold improvements to a present building. Finally, they give tremendous advantages to businesses or individuals who are renovating, improving, or expanding a building that already exists. Even older buildings can be cost segregated for better tax deprecation purposes.

Cost segregation should not be confused with simple deprecation analysis. A great deal more is involved than simply taking line items off of construction invoices to classify them. The procedure actually involves a team of professionals who are familiar with tax laws and accounting rules, along with construction and engineering concepts. A CPA will be the center of such a team, since he or she will have to make various building components tangible to quantify them in a way that they can be estimated as costs that work with IRS rules. This team would also feature an engineer, contractor, and possibly architect much of the time.

Between them, these professionals will examine in depth electrical and mechanical plans, working drawings, and even blueprints to break segregate out the electrical, mechanical, and structural parts of the building from other components that are associated with the personal property. Even engineering and architect fees as they pertain to various parts of the project are included as soft costs.

Counter Offer

Counter offers are those made by home sellers after buyers have turned in an official offer to buy the house. Usually, such counter offers spell out the terms with which the seller will accept the buyer's official initial offer. Many different specifics can be addressed with a counter offer.

Some of these things include the consideration of a higher offering price, presenting a larger earnest money deposit, and modifying time frames for contingencies. Others counter offer elements might revolve around altering service providers, excluding any personal property from the home selling contract, or changing the possession date or closing date. A seller might also refuse to cover the costs of certain fees or reports.

Not only can sellers counter a buyer's original offer, but buyers can similarly submit counter offers back to the seller on their counter offer. This is labeled a counter-counter offer. No limit to the actual numbers of counter offers which can be handed back and forth exists.

Counter offers are easily rejected. A number of purchase contracts for houses have places at the bottom of the contract for a seller to put his or her initials if the offer is being rejected. Many offers have time frames, or expiration dates, when the offer will be rejected if the seller has not responded. Sellers can simply write the word rejected over a contract's face, then date and initial it to reject a counter offer.

In some states, sellers are allowed to come back with various counter offers at once. For example, in California, sellers are allowed to counter more than one offer at a time and every counter offer is permitted to be different. Should one of these buyers choose to affirm the counter offer of the seller in this scenario, the seller is not required to agree to the acceptance of the buyer. This can become confusing, so talking with real estate attorneys can be a good idea in these complicated cases.

Counter offers can similarly be accepted without difficulty by the buyer. All that a buyer needs to do to take the counter is to accept the offer and send it back to the entity to which it goes. Like with anything, timing is critical. Counter offers expire much as purchase offers do. This means that a seller could always elect to take an alternative offer while a buyer contemplates whether or not to sign off on the counter offer.

Even though many agents become discouraged at the mention of a counter offer being on the table, this should not be the case. Houses can be secured with new offers submitted even while a counter offer is out. In such a scenario, sellers commonly go ahead and take the second buyer offer. They then withdraw their counter offer from the first buyer. This is permissible and proper in every state.

CPA (Certified Public Accountant)

CPA's, or certified public accountants, are accountants who have taken and successfully completed a series of demanding exams that are given by the American Institute of Certified Public Accountants. Many states also have their own state level exams that have to be passed along with the national one. CPA'a are accountants in every sense of the word, but not every accountant is qualified as a CPA. Because of the difficulties in becoming a CPA, there are many accountants who either never attempt or never succeed in successfully passing the Certified Public Accountant exam. This does not mean such an accountant is not qualified to practice accounting tasks, only that he or she will not be allowed to do tasks that require specific CPA credentials.

Such Certified Public Accountants do a number of varying tasks and jobs. Many will provide advice and simple income tax preparing for various clients who might be comprised of corporations, small companies, or individuals. Besides this, Certified Public Accountants practice many other tasks that include auditing, keeping the records of businesses, and consulting for business entities.

Keeping a CPA license is not accomplished through automatic renewal. Certified Public Accountants are required to engage in a full one hundred and twenty hours of courses on continuing education in every three year period. This is so that they will be on top of any and all changes going on in the field of their chosen profession.

The opportunities for Certified Public Accountants are many and varied. The FBI seeks to hire them routinely, preferring applicant candidates with either such a CPA background or alternatively an attorney background. Numerous state and Federal government agencies offer CPA's opportunities by providing CPA positions. Businesses ranging from small companies to large corporations also seek them out. With these firms, CPA's can occupy positions ranging from controllers, to CFO or Chief Financial Officers, to CEO's or Chief Executive Officers.

Among the most significant parts that CPA's can play proves to be one of a consultant. As a consultant, Certified Public Accountants can be looking into possible means of saving small businesses or even enormous corporations money on expenses or putting together specific financial plans that permit a corporation or business to appear more appealing to investors or possible buyers. Certified Public Accountants are sworn to a particular code of ethical conduct. They are required to provide their clients with honest and reliable advice that is also ethical.

Certified Public Accountants who do not stay within the bounds of their ethical code can lead to the total financial failure of a firm. This turned out to be the case in recent years at Enron, the energy trading and producing giant. Not only were Enron corporate executives charged for illegal accounting activities, but also a number of CPA's from nationally renowned accounting firm Arthur Anderson were charged with unethical practices of accounting.

Credit Default Swaps

A credit default swap, or CDS, is a contract exchange that transfers between two parties the exposure of credit to fixed income products. Two parties are involved in this exchange. The purchaser of a credit default swap obtains protection for credit. The seller of this credit default swap actually guarantees the product's credit worthiness. In this process, the default risk moves from the owner of the fixed income security over to the party that sells the swap.

In these CDS transfers, the purchaser of the protection gives a series of fees or payments to the seller. This is also known as the spread of the Credit Default Swap. The party selling the protection gets paid off in exchange for this, assuming that a loan or bond type of credit instrument suffers from a negative credit event.

In the most basic forms, Credit Default Swaps prove to be two party contracts arranged between sellers and buyers of credit protection. These Credit Default Swaps will address a reference obligor or reference entity. These are typically governments or companies. The party being referenced is not involved in the contract as a party or even necessarily aware of its existence. The purchaser of such protection then pays pre defined quarterly premiums, or the spread, to the party who is selling the protection.

Should the entity that is referenced then default, the seller of the protection pays the face value of the instrument to the buyer of the protection against a physical transfer of the bond. Such settlements can also be accomplished by auction or in cash. Defaults in Credit Default Swaps are called credit events. These defaults might include a bankruptcy, restructuring of the referenced entity, or a failure to make payment.

Credit Default Swaps are much like insurance on credit. The difference between them and such insurance lies in the fact that a CDS is not regulated like life insurance or casualty insurance is. Besides this, investors are capable of purchasing or selling this type of protection without having any such debt of the entity that is referenced. Resulting naked credit default swaps permit investors to engage in speculation on issues of debt and credit worthiness of entities that are referenced. These naked

Credit Default Swaps actually make up the majority of the CDS market.

The majority of Credit Default Swaps prove to be in the ten to twenty million dollar range. They typically have maturities ranging from one to ten years. The Credit Default Swap market is mostly unregulated and turns out to be the largest financial market on earth.

These CDS products were actually created in the early part of the 1990's. The market for them grew dramatically beginning in 2003. By the conclusion of 2007, the total amount of them in existence proved to be an astonishing $62.2 trillion dollars. This amount declined to $38.6 trillion in the wake of the financial crisis at the conclusion of 2008. Since then, it has been growing alarmingly again. Critics of Credit Default Swaps have consistently referred to them as financial weapons of mass destruction, capable of blowing up the financial system and world economies in the process.

Credit Report

A credit report is an individual or business' credit history. This includes their record of borrowing and repaying money in the past. It similarly covers data pertaining to any late payments made or bankruptcies that have been declared. In some countries, credit reports are also referred to as credit reputations.

When an American like you completes a credit application for a bank, a credit card company, or a retail store, this information is directly sent on to one of the three main credit bureaus. These are Experian, Trans Union, and Equifax. These credit bureaus then match up your name, identification, address, and phone number on the application for such credit with the data that they keep in their bureau's files. Because of this match up process, it is essential that lenders, creditors, and other parties always provide exactly correct information to the credit bureaus.

Such information in these files at the three major credit bureaus is then utilized by lenders like credit card companies in order to decide if you are deserving of having credit issued to you by the creditor. Another way of putting this is that they decide how likely that you will be to pay back these debts. Such willingness to pay back a debt is usually indicated by the timeliness of prior payments to other lenders. Such lenders will prefer to see the debt obligations of individual consumers, such as yourself, paid on time every month.

The second element considered in a lender offering loans or credit to individuals like you is based on your actual income. Higher incomes generally lead to greater amounts of credit being accessible. Still, lenders look at both willingness, as shown in the credit report and prior payment history, along with ability, as shown by income, in deciding whether or not to extend you credit.

Credit reports have become even more significant in light of risk based pricing. Practically all lenders of the financial services industry rely on credit reports to determine what the annual percentage rate and grace period of repayment of a loan or offer of credit will be. Other obligations of the contract are similarly based on this credit report.

In the past, a great deal of discussion has gone on considering the information contained in the credit reports. Scientific studies done on the issue have determined that for the most part, this credit report information is extremely accurate. Such credit bureaus also have their own authorized studies of fifty-two million credit reports that show that the information contained therein is right a vast majority of the time.

Congress has heard testimony from the Consumer Data Industry Association that in fewer than two percent of credit report issue cases have there been data which had to be erased because it was wrong. In the few cases where these did exist, more than seventy percent of such disputes are handled in fourteen days or less. More than ninety-five percent of consumers with disputes report being satisfied with the resolution.

Currency Standards

Currency standards are the typical means for fixing a currency at a set rate nowadays. A Currency Standard means that the value of a currency is pegged to a stronger, more internationally recognized currency, like the Euro or the Dollar. These Currency Standards are similarly known as reserve currency standards.

Within the world reserve currency system, single national currencies actually assume the important standard, or role, that gold always carried for hundreds of years in the gold standard. Another way of putting this is that a nation would fix the rate of its proprietary currency to so many units against another country's currency. As an example, Great Britain might choose to fix its British Pound Sterling currency to the

Euro at a real exchange rate of one pound equals one point twenty-five Euros. In order to keep this fixed rate of exchange, Britain's central bank, the Bank of England, would have to always be prepared to offer Euros for Pounds, or Pounds for Euros, upon demand for this set rate of exchange. The principal way that the Bank of England would affect this would be to keep Euros in its reserves against a day when a greater demand existed for Euros to be exchanged for Pounds on the world FOREX markets.

These currency standards stand in contrast to the gold standard. Under the long held, incredibly stable period of the gold standard, central banks instead held gold to back up and exchange against their own currency. Using the reserve currency standard, the same central banks instead keep a stockpile of the chosen reserve currency on hand. In whichever case, the reserve currency will be the one to which a given nation fixes its own currency.

The majority of nations that decide to fix their exchange rates will peg to one of two types of currencies. You might see them choose one of the main currencies utilized in international transactions for settlement. Alternatively, they could elect to fix their currencies to that of one of their major trading partners, which would also make sense for settlement purposes.

Because of this, you see many countries around the world peg their national exchange rate to the United States dollar, since it still proves to be the currency that is most widely held and traded around the world. As another fixing choice, the Euro is increasingly utilized for pegs. Fourteen different African countries which had all been French colonies in the past had set up the CFA, or colonies of French Africa, Franc zone. When they did this, they fixed their new CFA Franc to the French Franc.

After the French abandoned their Franc in favor of the newer continent wide Euro in 1999, the CFA Franc became pegged to the Euro. Another example is the Common Monetary Area of South Africa. Participating in this are Namibia, Swaziland, and Lesotho. These nations fix their currency against the South African Rand, the powerhouse currency of the South African continent, and their biggest trading partner by far.

Cyclical Manipulation

Cyclical manipulation refers to government interference in the natural economic cycles. This can lead to extreme booms and busts over the long run as governments attempt to prop up booms and forestall busts. Cyclical manipulation is mostly accomplished through the altering of government set interest rates. This is accomplished on a regular basis by the Federal Reserve Board in the United States.

Economic cycles as a concept are occasionally referred to as Business Cycles. This idea is one that explores the alterations in economic activity that change over time. Elements contemplated in explaining economic cycles are comprised of GDP growth, employment rates, and household incomes.

Within economic cycles, two main types emerge. These are booms and busts. Booms are commonly seen when a strong economy is operating. Busts, or recessions, are tied to economic growth that proves to be below trend. In the U.S., the NBER, or National Bureau of Economic Research, turns out to be the ultimate trusted source that gives out dates of troughs and peaks which actually make up economic cycles.

The NBER is part of this cyclical manipulation in the United States. The first step of the manipulation is the way in which they refer to booms and busts. They euphemize them as expansion or contraction. When a few portions of the economic data are getting better, then this is expansion, and when these same indicators are declining, it is called contraction. Such definitions focus entirely on the data movement, versus the historical norms.

Cyclical manipulation is accomplished principally through the changing of interest rates by the Federal Reserve. When the cycle is one of boom, or expansion, they attempt to cool the economy down to prevent inflation. They do this by raising the interest rates to slow down lending and spending. Unfortunately, as economic activity then slows, this leads to an economy that can then fall into bust, or contraction.

At this point, the Federal Reserve begins cutting the interest rates, sometimes massively, in an effort to stimulate the economy once more. As the interest rates fall, businesses and consumers borrow and spend larger sums of money. This gets the economy going once again. The irony of this cyclical manipulation lies in the fact that the very effort of the government to keep the cycles from becoming extreme leads to changes in the cycles that the Fed wishes to prevent altogether.

Economic Cycles Theory believes that even though these highs and lows average together to create an average trend economic rate of growth, this trending growth rate remains stable over time. The government through the Fed attempts to manipulate these cycles to keep the growth rate along these trend lines consistently. There has been no effort made in the Economic Cycles Theory to explain the economic activity levels in long running time frames of decline, but only in growth. This policy of only focusing on growth is yet another demonstration of the cyclical manipulation.

Debasing the Currency

Debasing the currency refers to the all too common historical process of lowering a currency's actual value. In the past, this phrase commonly came to be associated with commodity money made principally from either silver or gold. Should the sum total of silver, gold, nickel, or copper be reduced, then the physical money is called debased. Even venerable institutions like the Roman Empire, with a thousand year history of growth and stability, have stooped to such debasing of the currency.

Reasons that a government chooses to debase the currency in this way center around the financial benefits that the government is able to reap. These are done at the citizenry's expense though. Governments that lowered the quantity of gold and silver in their coinage found that they could quietly mint more coins from a given fixed quantity of metal on hand.

The downside to this for the general population centers on the inflation that this in turn causes. Such inflation is yet another benefit for the currency debasing government that then finds that it can pay off government debt or repudiate government bonds easier. The populace's purchasing power is significantly reduced as a result of this, along with their then lowered standard of living.

Debasing a currency lowers the value of the currency in question. Given enough time and abuse by the governing authorities, this debasing can even lead to a collapse in the existing currency that causes a newer currency or coinage to be created and launched for the nation or state.

In present day times, debasing the currency is accomplished in more subtle means. Since currencies these days are made of only paper, involving no metal, debasing the currency simply involves printing additional paper dollars. With the advent of electronic banking, even this printing press operation is no longer required. The government simply creates money on a computer screen, literally conjuring it out of thin air.

They are able to accomplish this in one of two ways. One way that they do this is via the Federal Reserve, which buys treasury securities by simply crediting the receivers' bank accounts with electronically created money. The Federal Reserve then has tangible assets in Treasury bills that is it able to trade or sell when it wishes.

Another way that this creation of money that debases the currency is able to be performed is through the Fractional Reserve Banking System. Since the Federal Reserve only requires banks to keep a ten percent reserve ratio of deposits on hand, these banks when they are credited funds from the Federal Reserve are able to loan this new money out in multiples that are equivalent to the leverage created by this ten percent only reserve ratio. In both of these ways, the Federal Reserve is able to create more money quietly and at will. This is how modern day debasing of the currency is effectively accomplished.

Debit Card

Debit cards are plastic cards that function like a check and are easily utilized like a credit card. Debit cards are commonly one of two types, either branded Visa or Master Card. When you use such a debit card to pay for a purchase, then this amount is deducted immediately from your checking account. Both convenience and security features are included in the use of a debit card.

Debit cards provide tremendous convenience in their ease of use. No longer do you have to make sure that you are carrying enough money on you, or to take the time to write out a physical check while the long line waits impatiently behind you. Besides this ease of use, debit cards are accepted at literally millions of places around the country and the world.

Nowadays, they can be used for almost any purchase, such as lunches or dinners at restaurants, monthly bill payments, merchandise in retail stores, groceries, prescriptions, gas, online purchases, over the phone orders, and even fast food.

Debit cards' spending is easy to keep track of as well. The majority of such transactions are both deducted and posted to a checking account in twenty-four hours or less. This allows for you to conveniently monitor your constantly updated transaction record and balance either over the phone or the bank or card issuer's website. Besides this, debit cards also offer statements, much like credit cards, that outline all purchases made, with details on the name of the merchant, date, location, and amount of transaction.

Debit cards offer another benefit in their security provisions. These cards include free fraud monitoring that helps to find and stop activity that is suspicious with your debit card. They also come with policies of zero liability that protect you from charges that you did not make or authorize. Fraudulently taken out funds are guaranteed to be returned to your account. The vast majority of debit cards also come with the security feature of three digit security codes that allow you to confirm your identity for both phone and Internet orders and purchases.

Debit cards allow two ways for completing in person transactions. One of these is through swiping the card and then signing the receipt issued by the merchant representative. The other is via using a pad with your PIN, or personal identification code, after the card is swiped.

A final benefit that you gain from a debit card is that most of them provide rewards that are earned simply by utilizing them. These are earned in one of two ways. With Visa Debit cards, you are able to receive discounts from some merchants who provide these special price breaks for the holders of Visa cards.

Other debit cards provide extras rewards programs. These rewards programs pay you back with some type of reward for every purchase that you make. These can be cash rebates or more commonly awards that are earned through the collection of such points.

Debit Service

Debt service refers to the cash that is necessary to be paid over a certain period of time in order to repay both principal and interest on a given debt. For individuals, monthly mortgage payments, or credit card bill payments, prove to be good examples of personal debt service. For businesses, payments on lines of credit, business loans, or coupon payments of bonds represent samples of corporate debt service.

Where businesses or personal debt service is concerned, this is used to calculate the DSCR, or debt service coverage ratio. This ratio is that of the cash that is on hand for servicing the debt's principal, interest, and lease payments. This measurement is a much utilized benchmark that helps to determine a company or an individual's capability of generating sufficient money to cover the payments on their debt. With a higher debt service coverage ratio, loans are easier to get for both companies and people.

The commercial banking industry also employs this phrase. Here, it can refer to the minimally acceptable ratio that a given lender will accept. This might turn out to be a condition of making the entity such a loan in the end. When this type of a condition is part of the loan covenant, then violating the debt service coverage ratio can sometimes be considered an action of default.

Debt service coverage ratios are similarly used in the world of corporate finance. Here, they describe the sum of available cash flow that is usable for covering yearly principal and interest payments on any and all debts. This includes payments for sinking funds.

Commercial real estate finance similarly utilizes debt service and debt service coverage ratios as the main means of discovering if a given property is capable of maintaining its level of debt using only its own cash flow. In the past ten or so years, banks would look for a minimum debt service coverage ratio of minimally 1.2. Banks that proved to be more aggressive were willing to work with lower ratios.

This practice led to greater risk in the system that helped to bring on the financial meltdown and resulting crisis that stretched from 2007 to 2010. When an entity has more than a ratio of one debt service coverage ratio, it is theoretically capable of covering its debt requirements with cash flow. Similarly, if this ratio is less than one, then the statistics claim that an insufficient amount of cash flow exists to meet the required loan payments.

Deferred Maintenance

Deferred maintenance proves to be the action of putting off maintenance procedures that are needed and routine on both personal property, such as machinery, or real estate property, such as infrastructure. This is done to save on expenses, to reassign money that is available in the budget, or to achieve the available levels of budget funding.

The downside to this avoidance or delay of generally needed repairs is that it causes the deterioration of assets, and finally their total impairment, if continued for an extended period of time. Usually over time, the practice of constantly deferring your maintenance will end up with greater costs in the future, the eventual failure of assets, and from time to time with safety and health concerns resulting.

Maintenance is one of the budgetary items that is forced to battle along side other needs' and programs' funding. Since the money is simply not always available for the category of maintenance's use, it is often short changed. Other times, the money is available until it is directed by management to higher priority assignments and requirements later.

Maintenance that is deferred is most usually not reported to the necessary parties right away. Many times, it is never even reported at all. Such deferred maintenance that goes on over a lack of funds appropriated to the cause will finally lead to a greater number of incidences of inefficient service for the public, possible safety dangers, operations that are inefficient and ineffective, and greater costs overall at a future point in time.

Examples of personal deferred maintenance and business deferred maintenance cases abound. Deferred maintenance in a home would include delaying the car's recommended one year inspection or tune up, or not having those repairs done that the mechanic recommended. As a result of this, the car will likely not operate as effectively or efficiently. It could also suffer mechanical or electrical failures or even become involved in an unnecessary crash over safety issues.

This term of deferred maintenance is more commonly used with large corporations or governments though. A large corporation slashing its budget might result in the company's plants and equipment not undergoing their annual cleaning and refurbishing.

The firm might get away with this for a year or even two. In time though, problems will begin to show up in machinery break down, equipment misses and failure, and possible shut downs of the plant, if this practice of ignoring critical plant maintenance is put off much or for too long.

Deficit

Deficits are shortfalls in government revenues that result from them spending more money than they bring in from revenues. The deficit of a government is measurable by including or excluding the interest it pays for its debt. Primary deficit is simply the difference in all taxes and revenues less the present level of government outlays. Conversely, total deficits, usually simply referred to as the deficit, prove to be all spending along with payments on the interest of the debt less the revenues coming in from taxes.

Such fiscal deficits also expand and contract as a result of changing trends in economics. As an example, higher amounts of economic activity in a nation give greater revenues in taxes to the Federal Government. At the same time, economic downturns generally cause a government to increase its levels of expenditures in order to boost spending on unemployment benefits and other types of social insurance programs.

The amount of public debt is also impacted significantly by the amounts of social benefits funded, alterations in the tax code or tax rates, methods of enforcing tax policies, and various additional decisions made with government policies. In other countries that have tremendous energy natural resources such as oil and natural gas, including Saudi Arabia, Russia, Norway, and other nations who are a part of the OPEC, or Organization of Petroleum Exporting Countries, these incomes form the energy sources have an enormous impact on the national finances.

Another impact on the real tangible value of a government deficit, or debt, comes from the amounts of inflation in a country. Over time, inflation lowers the real currency value of such debt. The downsides to inflation result in a government having to pay greater interest rate levels on its debts. This causes public coffers borrowing to become more expensive.

Government deficits are comprised of two main parts. These are cyclical deficits and structural deficits. Cyclical deficits result from any and all extra borrowing that a government has to engage in during the low point of a business cycle. This comes from higher unemployment levels. As unemployment rises, tax receipts fall and expenditures on things like social security inversely rise. The implied definition of cyclical deficits is that they will be completely repaid in the next cyclical peak. This is because a surplus in revenues will exist as taxes rises and spending is lower.

Structural deficits instead represent deficits that are constant regardless of the economic cycle. This results from the overall government expenditure levels being unsustainable in light of the current tax rates. The overall budget deficit is then figured by adding the structural deficit to the cyclical surplus or deficit that exists. Although this is the mainstream distinction between the types of deficits, there are economists who say that the differences between the structural and cyclical deficits are impossible to determine. They contend that cyclical deficits simply can not be measured properly.

Deficit Spending

Deficit spending is a generally unsustainable scenario where a greater number of resources are employed to secure purchases than are brought in to the organization through revenue generating means. When this is the case, the business or government outfit actually operates in a budget deficit. This simply means that not enough financial resources are being created by the organization in order to effectively fund the operating budget. As this occurs, the additional expenses are paid for by utilizing deferred payment plans that permit the organization to buy now and pay later, or alternatively with credit accounts.

Even though such deficit spending can occur with consumers and businesses, it is generally discussed pertaining to governments and their operations. These days, governments are mostly incapable of running their operations without resorting to deficit spending. As the taxes that are collected generally are insufficient to cover all of the costs that are proposed by the annual budget, the shortfall is commonly covered by buying things with money that has been borrowed. In such a way, these governments run their activities in a deficit spending scenario.

Not every government runs its affairs from a negative budget scenario all of the time. There are periods where governments can look forward to the revenues that come in from taxes and any investments surpassing the money that is required to cover the costs of budgetary items. In these moments, governments have the opposite of deficit spending situations. They are running on budget surpluses. Surpluses are used for a variety of different needs, such as infrastructure improvements, repayment of debt from past deficit spending, or savings for future budget deficits.

Without a doubt, deficit spending proves to be all too common for governments. This does not make it a wise economic policy to pursue continuously over extended time frames. The reason for this is that deficit spending commonly requires borrowing funds that must be paid back with interest that accrues over time. In such a way, enormous amounts of government debt can be built up in short time frames.

Because of this, a number of responsible governments attempt to intelligently manage their deficit spending in such a way that they only engage in it to keep up critical operations and services that the citizens need for their well being. Other less important programs they try to cut back on whenever possible.

Companies may sometimes operate on a deficit spending basis. If they do this for long periods of time, then they are often unable to turn the failing trend around. The end result of this behavior leads to bankruptcy or being purchased by other, more fiscally responsible businesses. Consumers that engage in deficit spending for longer periods than only temporary time frames similarly discover that the scenario ends up in financial destruction. Outstanding assets may then be liquidated to satisfy the debts that result.

Defined Contribution Plans

Defined contribution plans turn out to be a specific type of retirement plan. In these, an employer's yearly dollar amount contribution to the plan is spelled out clearly. Accounts are established on an individual basis for all employees participating. The amounts that are credited to such accounts include both the preset employer contributions, as well as any contributions coming from an employee. On top of this, earnings on investments are also accrued in defined contribution plan accounts.

With defined contribution plans, solely the contributions from employers are pledged to the accounts. Future benefits are not assured. In such plans, the benefits in the future go up and down based on the results of earnings on investments held in the plans.

Savings and thrift plans prove to be the most generally seen type of defined contribution plans. With this kind of a plan, employees put in to the account a pre arranged percentage of their typically pre taxed earnings. The monies go to the employee's individual account. Part of the contributions, or all of them in some cases, are then matched up by the employee's employer.

Once these pre set contributions are credited to the individual employees' accounts from both employees and employers, these contributions are subsequently invested. They might be invested in to the stock market, for example. The resulting investment returns are finally appointed to the account on an individual basis. This is the case whether the returns prove to be positive or negative.

When retirement time arrives for an employee, the participant's account then pays out benefits for retirement. This can occur through the account buying an annuity that will then assure a regular stream of income. In recent years, these defined contribution plans have expanded to be found in nearly all countries. For numerous nations, these are currently the main type of plan for the private sector retirement schemes. This growth in defined contribution plans has occurred at the expense of defined benefit plans, also known as pension plans, as employers seek to avoid the considerable expenses in funding and maintaining pension plans.

Money that is put into these defined contribution plans may come from employer contributions or salary deferral of an employee. These plans over time have evolved to become fairly easily portable from one job and company to the next as an employee changes companies. This did not always turn out to be the case.

One unique feature of defined contribution plans revolve around the rewards and risks of investments undertaken. Every employee is responsible for his or her own account's performance, rather than the employer or sponsor of the plan. Besides this, employees are not made to buy annuities with the retirement savings. This means that they could theoretically live beyond their retirement assets, and they take on the risk of this possibility. In Great Britain, the law requires that the majority of the retirement funds be employed in buying an annuity so that this does not happen.

Deflation

Deflation is simply the prices of goods and services going down in a given time frame. Deflation is the opposite of inflation, which is the rising cost of goods and services over a period of time. This does not make deflation a good thing in the long run.

Another way of defining deflation is the increasing value of money versus various economic goods over a span of time. With inflation, money is becoming less valuable versus goods over time. Deflation happens as a result of the interaction of four factors. On the one hand, the supply of money in circulation might decline. At the same time, supplies of available goods might increase. The need for goods could drop as well. Finally, the demand for money could go up. If any of these four things happen either separately or in concert, deflation is commonly the result.

The easiest way for deflation to occur is as the supply of goods available on the market goes up at a more rapid pace than does the supply of money. The combination of these elements explains how some goods' costs go up while the costs of others go down at the same time. Despite this, deflation can pose certain problems.

The majority of economists today concur that deflation proves to be both a symptom of economic problems as well as a malaise in and of itself. Some buy into the concepts of good and bad deflation. Good deflation happens as companies are consistently capable of manufacturing goods for cheaper and lower prices because of gains in productivity and other ways of reducing costs. This type of deflation permits a strong and growing GDP growth, with lower unemployment, and rising profits.

Bad deflation is more challenging to grasp. Bad deflation rises as a result of the central bank, or the Federal Reserve, choosing to revalue the country's currency. Or, you could say that the supply of money declining results in this negative form of deflation.

The actual problem that deflation causes is that it creates uncertainty for businesses and their relationships. As a rule, business thrives on confidence and falters on the unknown. Borrowers have to make loan payments that turn out to be greater and greater amounts of purchasing power in deflationary time periods. All the while, the value of the asset that you purchased with the loan is declining. In these circumstances, many borrowers elect to default on the loan and its payments.

A declining spiral similarly exists in deflationary periods. Since businesses begin to enjoy fewer profits, they decide to reduce their employment roles. Individuals do not spend as much money as a result. Businesses then realize smaller profits and again cut back. This degenerates into a vicious cycle down before long, as it becomes self reinforcing. Consumers learn that larger ticket items such as houses and cars will actually cost less in the future and then delay their purchases.

Though deflation has been discussed as a potential problem for the U.S. economy with the economic downturn, the reality is far different. At the same time, from 2006 to 2009, the Federal Reserve massively increased the money supply by more than three hundred percent. This argues not for deflation in the United States' future, but for inflation instead.

Depression

Depressions in economics are loosely defined as major declines in a country's GDP, or gross domestic product. The gross domestic product is made up of four major components. These include money that consumers spend, government spending for goods and labor, investment affected by government agencies and individual companies, and the net sum of the country's exported products. All of these elements are combined to come up with the country's annual gross domestic product. Another simpler way of stating the GDP is in the counting of everything spent on services, goods, research, investments, and labor in the nation.

Depressions are then commonly said to happen as the country's GDP drops by minimally ten percent in only a year. There is not any consensus on the precise amount of decline in terms of percentage that must occur. Following the notorious stock market crash in 1929, the Great Depression that happened in the United States and throughout Europe demonstrated a sharp decline in GDP not only the first year but also over the following years.

In the months that came after this market crash, the U.S. GDP fell by in excess of thirty percent. After that it rose for a while, though not nearly to the pre-crash levels seen earlier in the U.S. This demonstrates the difficulty in simply defining depressions simply by looking at GDP declines and increases.

The Great Depression is mostly held to have continued until the very end of the 1930's decade. Real recovery nationally then did not begin until the outbreak of World War II in 1939. The reason that this is the case is that additional factors besides simply GDP declines have to be considered in evaluating what is and is not truly a depression.

The Great Depression had many negative characteristics besides simply falling GDP's. With plummeting industrial output, major numbers of jobs disappeared. As significantly smaller amounts of money came into workers hands, a great deal less could be spent on consumer goods or business investments. Without this money circulating back to businesses, firms were unable to hire workers back. The numbers of people dependent on help from the public assistance funds were greater. Job recovery did not materialize as hoped.

From time to time the Gross Domestic Product did rise in the 1930's. It never returned to the normalcy seen before the beginning of the Great Depression until the United States became fully involved in the Second World War. Demands for military equipment and weapons for the war did many things to help the American economy. Young men found employment in the army, industry suddenly had rising demand for military products, and job openings were more than the able bodied people available to fill them. At this point, women began entering jobs in industry in the place of men for the first time.

Nowadays, some respected economists worry that a depression like one not seen since the thirties could again be gripping the nation. This is because unemployment from the Great Recession remains stubbornly high, goods and services' prices are rising at a faster pace than payrolls in the majority of industries, and requirements for public assistance are higher than they have been since the end of the Second World War. The biggest fear today is that many of the jobs that are disappearing, such as technology and manufacturing, will never return, as they are migrating overseas to countries where workers are paid significantly less.

Derivative

In the financial world, derivatives are agreements between two different parties that contain values that are dependent on the price movements of an asset, as anticipated in the future, to which they are linked.

This asset, which might be a currency, stock price, or other element is referred to as the underlying. Derivatives are also alternative investments and financial instruments, of which they are numerous kinds. The most common forms of derivatives are futures, swaps, and options.

Investors use derivatives for many different activities. These include for gaining leverage on an investment so that when a small movement occurs in the value of the underlying, they can realize a great gain in the derivative value.

They may also be employed for speculation to profit from, assuming that the underlying asset value goes in the direction that they anticipate. Businesses might similarly hedge their risks in an underlying through opening a derivative contract that moves conversely to their position in the underlying, canceling all or part of the risk in the process. Investors similarly are capable of gaining exposure to an underlying that does not have a tradable instrument associated with it, like with a weather derivative.

Investors can also utilize derivatives to give themselves the ability to create options in which the derivative value is associated with a particular event or condition being met.

Derivatives principally remain a means of offering hedging insurance, allowing one party to lessen their risk exposure while the other reduces a different kind of risk exposure. Derivatives examples of transferring risk are helpful to consider. Millers and wheat farmers might create a derivative by signing a futures contract. This could specify a certain dollar value of money in exchange for a particular quantity of wheat to be exchanged at a future time. In this case, the two parties have actually diminished their risk for the future. The miller is not exposed to possible shortages of wheat, while the farmer is saved from the possible variances in price.

Risk is not completely eliminated in this example since the derivative contract will not cover events that the contract does not mention in particular, like weather conditions. There is similarly a danger that one of the parties will default on their part of the contract. To mitigate these problems, clearing houses insure many futures contracts, although not every such derivative is insured for the risk of counter party default.

Another way of looking at derivatives in this example is that while they reduce one form of risk, they actually present another one. The miller and farmer both pick up another risk by signing off on this contract. For the farmer, the danger lies in the fact that although he is saved from declines in the price of wheat, he is also exposed to the possibility that wheat prices will rise above the set amount in the contract, costing him extra income that he might have obtained. The miller also picks up a risk that the cost of wheat will drop below the amount that he has locked in with this contract.

Discount Points

Discount points are also sometimes known as simply points. They represent a type of interest that is paid in advance. A single discount point is equivalent to one percent of the total loan amount. Through charging borrowers points, lenders boost their loan's yield to a total that is higher than the expressed interest rate.

Borrowers are able to give a bank or lender payment as a way of lowering the loan's interest rates. The up front sum of money gives them a lower monthly payment. With every point that a borrower buys, their loan's rate commonly falls by .125 percent. A buyer paying for points is not without risk. At some time within the life of the loan, the cost of the money given to lower the rate of interest will equal out to the money that you saved in being able to make lower amount loan payments because of the loan's better interest rate.

Should you refinance the loan or sell the house in advance of attaining this break even point, then you will actually take a loss on the transaction. On the other hand, if you hold on to the property and accompanying mortgage for a greater amount of time than the break even, then you will actually save money on the purchase.

It goes without saying that the longer amount of time that you hold the property mortgage and financing with the bought discount points, the better this money used for the points actually rewards you. At the same time, a person who plans on purchasing the property and then selling it or refinancing it quickly will only lose money by not simply paying the higher rate of interest on the loan in lieu of buying points.

Discount points can also be bought to help you qualify for loans. If the loan qualification basis is grounded in your monthly loan payment against your monthly income, then you may only be capable of getting approval by buying the discount points to lower the rate of interest which will result in the lower monthly payment that your approval requires.

Discount points should not be confused with broker fees or origination fees. Discount points only serve to lower the interest rates. Origination fees are those that the lender charges for creating and closing the loan. They could sometimes be a different name for lowering the interest rate as well.

Borrowers who will stay in the house for a longer period of time should definitely consider buying points. Lower interest rates will pay off in savings over time. Any changes in the fees and costs for the loan will be shown to you in the last good faith estimate that the lender provides.

Sometimes when you buy points, you may be able to get a no closing cost loan. This usually happens when the bank is getting a premium interest rate. As their fee is made off of a higher starting interest rate on the note, it can be utilized to cover the closing costs.

Discount Rate

The term discount rate actually has several meanings. Where interest rates and banks are concerned, the discount rate proves to be the actual interest rate that central banks charge their member depositing institutions. When these banks choose to borrow funds from the central bank or the Federal Reserve as their lender of last resort, then this is the rate that they will be required to pay them as interest.

Besides this, the discount rate can refer to the annual effective discount rate in investments. This rate turns out to be the yearly interest divided up by the capital that includes the interest. The rate provides a lower value than does the interest rate. The value following a year delay would be the nominal value in this case. The upfront value is this nominal value less a discount. This annual effective discount rate is commonly utilized for financial instruments that are like Treasury Bills.

For businesses, the discount rate is important as they are making critical decisions regarding their profits and what to do with them. When it is time to contemplate whether to purchase new equipment pieces or to instead return the profits to the share holders, this discount rate is helpful. If all else is equal, then the company will only elect to purchase the equipment if it returns a greater profit to the share holders at a future point.

The share holder discount rate would then be the dollar total that share holders expect to receive in the future so that they would rather have the company purchase the equipment now instead of return the profits to them now. Share price data is utilized to figure up the discount rate for estimating share holders' preferences. This is called the capital asset pricing model. Businesses commonly use this discount rate when they make choices regarding buying equipment by using the net present value in the decision making process.

This discount rate proves to be the weighted average cost of capital. It shows the cash flow risk. The discount rate can also be used by companies to show two different things. It demonstrates the time value that money has, or the risk free rate. Investors generally prefer cash now than cash that they must wait for, meaning that businesses have to compensate them by making them wait for it. The discount rate also establishes a risk premium. This proves to be the additional return that investors want as payment for the possibility that they might not ever see this money if the cash flow is not there in the future.

Disposable Income

Disposable income proves to be the remaining income after an individual has met all of his or her income tax obligations. It is utilized as a means of ascertaining the health of an entire society, as well as a person's general economic condition. Disposable income also turns out to be among the main measurements for determining personal wealth.

Although they are sometimes used interchangeably, disposable income should not be confused with discretionary income. Discretionary income is simply any income that remains following paying the taxes and other customary living expenses. This means that the value for disposable income is a greater amount than discretionary income proves to be in practically every case. Still disposable income does not really deal with the day to day costs of living that people encounter in their normal lives.

For you as an American, disposable income typically proves to be anywhere from ten to fifteen percent of the personal income of an individual. All of the rest of the money goes into one of a number of different taxes. Naturally, this would be individually determined as a result of the amount of income that you have, the withholding allowances that you enjoy, and the state in which you reside. Similarly, for other countries, disposable income can be figured more or less by examining the typical tax rates.

Disposable income commonly decreases in difficult economic times, such as recessions and depressions. This does not happen because of an increase in taxes. Instead, it is more a factor of the likelihood of it falling in challenging economic times as companies cut back on employee payrolls. Because of this, lower disposable income will mean that people have more difficult times in fulfilling their present obligations. This will make them far less likely to take on new financial responsibilities.

When people do not make enough money to be taxed, then their disposable income may actually prove to be about the same as their total income is. This is similarly the case in nations that do not charge their citizens personal income taxes. In such cases, gross income and disposable income are identical.

Besides being used for spending on needs and expenses, disposable income can also be saved and invested. Through wisely purchasing cash flow investments with disposable income, the resulting disposable income in the future can actually be consistently higher as regular investment income comes in to the person's account. Disposable income used for capital gains investments will commonly lead to one time gains on sales, which will only temporarily increase disposable income for one time.

Distressed Assets

Distressed assets are assets that a company or individual has been forced to place for sale at a significant discount to the acquired or actual value. This usually happens as the owner has no choice but to sell the asset to raise cash. Several different reasons might exist for why this is the case. These include excessive debt levels, bankruptcy, and regulatory requirements. Even debt can be put on sale at an amount that is lower than its face value. When this happens, it is known as distressed debt.

Although there are various types of distressed assets offered for sale, among the most common in the wake of 2007-2010's financial crisis and Great Recession are non performing loans on houses or foreclosures on mortgaged properties. Investors of all sizes are able to take advantage of such distressed assets in property by availing themselves of a homeowner's lack of ability to meet the mandatory mortgage payments or of his or her critical requirements for cash. In situations like this, such homeowners will consent much of the time to selling the property for a substantial discount in order to achieve a fast sale.

In the past, banks dealt with such distressed asset mortgages almost entirely themselves. As a result of the American banks still repairing their heavily damaged balance sheets from the countless write offs and over leveraging that they engaged in over the past five to ten years, they can not keep up any longer with the enormous number of foreclosures on their books. This leaves them with little choice but to have to sell some of their mortgage property asserts at massive discounts to actual value in order to be able to create quick cash flow.

The end result is that distressed assets can present a potentially profitable investment opportunity for you. The still ongoing crisis in global liquidity and credit has banks selling mortgages to individual, as well as to large, investors at significant discounts. Such discounts to perceived value would never occur in the days of normalized conditions in the mortgage and credit market place.

This means that investors are currently able to purchase distressed home assets with discounts amounting to as much as 72.5%. With as little as $100,000, smaller investors are able to get involved with this efficient and potentially lucrative investment strategy. Professional management teams are available to help small investors realize appropriate exit strategies whose goal is to generate an impressive 20% return on investment per year.

Purchasing distressed assets such as homes in mortgage payment trouble can offer ethical options and benefits as well. Investors are able to restructure the debt and payments of the home owner in such a way that distressed home owners are able to afford the new payments. This lets the troubled home owners stay in their houses so long as the investor owns the mortgage and the home owner is able to work with the newly arranged payment schedule.

Distressed assets of companies include many different types of assets. These might be commercial office buildings, commercial jets, and even factories and equipment sold at substantial discounts to real value. Many times, other corporations are able to acquire these distressed assets for their own uses at fantastic prices.

Diversifying

Diversifying refers to the means of effectively lowering your investing risk by putting your money into a wide range of various assets. A truly well diversified portfolio offers the benefits of lower amounts of risk than those that are simply invested into one or two asset classes or kinds of investments.

Everyone should engage in some amount of diversification, even if the individual proves to be one who is tolerant of risk. Those individuals who really fear the present day economic uncertainties and very real amounts of risk in the market place will perform better forms of diversification into more asset groups.

Mainstream diversification is always recommended by financial experts because of the common example of not placing all of your investment eggs into just a single basket. If you do have all eggs in the one basket and then drop the basket along the way, then they can all break. The idea is that by placing each egg into its own individual basket, the odds of breaking all of the eggs declines significantly, even if one or several of them do get broken themselves.

Portfolios that have not engaged in diversifying might have only one or two corporations' stocks in them. This proves to be a dangerous investment strategy, since no matter how good a company looks on paper, its stock could decline to as low as zero literally over night. The past few years of the financial collapse have taught many investors the extremely painful lesson that even once blue chip financial companies' stock can decline to practically nothing as they spectacularly collapse.

Any financial expert will confidently state that portfolios made up of a dozen or two dozen varying stocks will have far less chance of plummeting. This becomes even more the case when you pick out stocks from a variety of types, industries, and market capitalization sizes of corporations. Better diversifying in stocks would include some companies that are based in other countries. Diversifying does not simply stop with stocks. It steers investors into bonds, mutual funds, and money market funds as well. Though all of these different investments diversify you, they still leave you mostly exposed to the one currency of the U.S. dollar.

More thorough diversifying will put at least a portion of your investments into assets whose values are not solely expressed in terms of only the American currency. This would include commodities, such as gold, silver, oil, and platinum in particular. Foreign currencies, such as the Euro, Pound, or Swiss Franc are another fantastic means of diversifying, and they can be acquired on the world FOREX exchange in currency accounts.

Real estate, including commercial properties, residential properties, vacation homes, or even real estate investment funds, offers another way to diversify away from U.S. dollar based financial investments such as stocks, bonds, mutual funds, and money market accounts. The strongest diversifying advice is to have at least three to seven complete-ly different investment class vehicles, preferably one or more of which is not denominated in only U.S. dollars.

Dividend

Dividends represent portions of a company's earnings that are returned to the investors in the company's stock. These are typically paid out in cash that is either deposited into the investors' brokerage accounts or can be reinvested directly into the company's stock. As an example of a dividend, every share of Phillip Morris pays around 4.5% dividends on the stock price each year.

Investing in dividend paying stocks is a particular passive income in-vestment strategy that is also a cash flow investment. This passive, or cash flow, income means that you collect income just from holding these stock investments. This kind of strategy entails building up a group of blue chip company stocks that pay large dividend yields which add money to your account usually four times per year, on a quarterly basis. Investors in dividends tremendously enjoy watching these rou-tine deposits in cash arrive in either their bank account, brokerage ac-count, or the mail.

Dividend investors who understand this type of investment are looking for a number of different elements in the stocks that they buy. Such dividend stocks should include a high dividend yield. To qualify as high yields, most value investors prefer to see ones that pay more than do the interest rate yields on U.S. Treasuries. Dividend yields can be easily determined. All that you have to do is to take the amount of the divi-dend and divide it by the price of the stock. So a stock that offers a $2 dividend and costs $40 is paying a five percent dividend yield.

Dividend paying stocks should also feature high dividend coverage. This coverage simply refers to the safety of a dividend, or how likely it is to be reduced or even eliminated. Companies that earn their profits from a large array of businesses are more likely to be able to continue paying their dividends than are companies that make all of their money off of a single business that could be threatened.

A more tangible way of expressing the coverage lies in how many times the dividend total dollar amount is covered by the corporation's total earnings. A company with fifty million dollars in profits that pays twenty million in dividends has its dividend covered by two and a half times. Should their profits drop by ten percent or more, they will have no trouble still paying the same dividend amount to shareholders. The dividend payout ratio is another way of measuring this. On the above example it would be forty percent. Dividend investors prefer to see no more than sixty percent of profits given out as dividends, as this could signify that the company lacks future opportunities for growth and expansion.

Qualified dividends are a third element that dividend investors are looking for in their dividend paying stocks. This simply means that stocks that are kept for less than a year do not benefit from lower tax rates on dividends. Since the government is attempting to convince you to become a longer term investor, you should take advantage of these lower tax rates by only buying stocks with qualified dividends that you have held for a full year and more.

Dividend Yield

Dividend yield refers to the payout of dividend price ratio on a given company's stock. It is simply determined by taking the yearly dividend payment total and dividing it by the cost for each share. This dividend yield is commonly given out as a percentage. The reciprocal of dividend yield proves to be the price to dividend ratio.

Dividend yields vary depending on whether a stock is a preferred stock or a common stock. With preferred shares, these dividend yields are outlined specifically in the stock's prospectus. A company will generally call such a preferred class of stock by the name first given to it, which included the yield based on this initial price. This might be a five percent preferred share. Since the pricing of preferred stock shares go up and down with the dictates of the market, the current yield will vary with the changes in price.

Preferred share holders have a variety of yields that they can figure up. These depend on the eventual disposition of their preferred share security. Besides the current yield formula of amount of dividend per price of preferred share, there are present value yields and a yield to maturity. These other yields only apply to those investors who purchase preferred stock shares after they have been issued or who choose to hold them until the reach the stated maturity date.

Preferred share dividends are almost always higher than the dividend yields on common stock shares.

Common stock shares have a dividend yield that differs entirely. With such common shares, the dividend amount is not guaranteed, and could vary from one quarter to the next. These dividends that are given to you, the common stock holder, are determined by the company's management. As such, they depend on the earnings of the company for the given quarter.

With common stocks, you can not be assured that dividends will be paid in the future that match dividends paid previously, or that these dividends will be paid period. Since it proves to be so challenging to correctly predict future dividends, the figures used in determining dividend yields are the present dividend yields. This means that the present dividend yield is always determined by dividing the most current full year's dividend by the present share price.

Dividend yields can have a major impact on how much money a stock makes for its owners over time. Dr. Jeremy Siegel is a well respected professor of investments who has determined conclusively with his research that ninety-nine percent of all after inflation gains that investors realize with stocks come from only dividends that are reinvested. Reinvestment of dividends means that the dividend yield amounts are simply taken and used to purchase more shares of the stock, instead of paying them out as cash to the share holder's account. This allows for investors to compound the number of shares that they own in a company over time.

Dividends (Mutual Funds)

Where mutual funds are concerned, dividends are quite different than they turn out to be for stocks. Mutual fund dividends are actually required distributions of both income as well as capital gains that are realized that have to be paid out to investors in mutual funds.

Mutual funds often bring in varying types of income. The challenge lies in the fact that all of these incomes come with varying tax treatments. In the majority of cases, such differences in taxes are passed through to the investors in the mutual fund. As an example, should a mutual fund own a stock for longer than a single year and then sell it to realize a capital gain, then a portion of the investors' mutual fund dividends would be classified as a long term capital gain. This would permit you to realize the advantages of such types of income's lower tax rates.

There are varying types of dividends paid out by mutual funds. One of these is ordinary dividends. These cover every type of taxable income besides the long term capital gains. This does not mean that they are always treated as ordinary tax rate income, since some of these dividends will be qualified dividends that receive preferential tax rate treatment.

Some of the distributions that come from your mutual fund could be long term capital gains. These do get the better form of tax treatment. Shorter term capital gains in these funds are generally distributed along with the regular dividends.

Some mutual funds buy into state or local government debts or municipal bonds. This results in a portion of your mutual fund distributions being treated as interest that is tax exempt. These interest payments might still impact social security benefits though, so it is wise to consult a tax professional concerning them.

Should your mutual fund be investing money into the Federal Government's debt obligations, then these distributions can often be treated as interest paid by the federal government. Such income is not given favorable Federal income tax treatment. It does become exempt from state income types of taxation.

From time to time, mutual funds will issue payments that are not income at all. This is a non dividend distribution. All that it represents is a portion of the money that was invested by you in the first place being returned to you. These distributions usually do not even have to be reported. They must be used in determining the amount of loss or gain incurred when you sell the mutual fund shares, though.

A final mutual fund dividend paid out is a capital gain allocation. These are highly unusual, since the overwhelming majority of mutual funds do capital gain distributions instead. While it is highly uncommon to see such a capital gain allocation, if you do get one, then you will have to use the special Form 2439 that your mutual fund sends to you in dealing with the particular tax rules.

DJIA (Dow Jones Industrial Average)

The Dow Jones Industrial Average, commonly referred to by its acronym DJIA, is also many times called the Dow 30, the Dow Jones, the Dow, or even just the Industrial Average. It proves to be the second oldest stock market index in the Untied States after the Dow Jones Transportation Average. The Dow Jones Industrial Average came into being when Charles Dow, the co founder of Dow Jones and Company worked with a business colleague Edward Jones, a statistician, to come up with an index that monitors the industrial sector. This index demonstrates the daily stock market trading session progress of thirty of the largest companies that are publicly traded within the U.S.

Ironically, most of the present day thirty companies listed in this index no longer have much or even anything to do with the historical definition of heavy industry. The components in the average are weighted by price and scaled in order to adjust for the impacts of stock splits and varying other forms of adjustments. This means that the total value that you see in the daily representation of the Dow Jones does not prove to be the true average of the different company stock prices.

Instead, it is the total of such company prices that are added up and then divided by a special divisor. This divisor is a number that is adjusted any time one of the company stocks underlying it pays a dividend or engages in a stock split. In this way, the index presents a constant value that is not altered by the external factors of the component stocks.

The Dow Jones Industrial Average remains one of the most heavily followed and carefully watched indices in the American stock market, along with peers the S&P 500 Index, the NASDAQ composite, and the Russell 2000 Index. The founder Dow intended for the index to monitor the American industrial sector's actual performance. Even so, the index is constantly affected by much more than simply the economic and corporate reports issued. It responds to both foreign and domestic incidents and political episodes like terrorism and war, as well as any natural disasters that might cause economic damage.

The Dow Jones Industrial Average's thirty components simultaneously trade on either the New York Stock Exchange Euronext or the NASDAQ OMX, which are the two largest American stock market outfits. Derivatives based on Dow components trade via the Chicago Board Options Exchange, as well as with the Chicago Mercantile Exchange Group. The latter is the largest futures exchange outfit on earth, and it presently owns fully ninety percent of the Dow Jones founded indexing business, along with this Industrial Average.

Investors who are interested in gaining the ability to track the progress of the Dow Jones Industrial average have several choices. There are index funds that buy the components of the index so that you do not have to own all thirty companies yourself. You might also invest in the Dow 30 by purchasing shares of the Exchange Traded Fund known as the Diamonds ETF. This trades under the AMEX exchange via the symbol DIA. Finally, you could by options and futures contracts based on the performance of the Dow Jones Average on the Chicago Board of Trade.

Down Payment

A down payment is an upfront amount that is given as a portion of the price on a purchase of large ticket items such as houses or cars. These are given in cash or by check when the contract is signed. The balance of the sum due is then given as a loan.

Down payments are principally intended to make sure that the bank or other type of lending institution is capable of recovering the remaining balance that is owed on a loan should the borrower choose to default. In transactions of real estate, the underlying asset becomes collateral that secures the associated loan against potential default.

Should the borrower not repay the loan as agreed, then the bank or institutional lender is allowed to sell this collateral asset and keep enough of the money received to pay off the rest of the loan along with the interest and fees included. In these cases, down payments decrease the exposure risk of the lender to an amount that is smaller than the collateral's value. This increases the chance of the bank getting the entire principal loaned out back should the borrower default.

The amount of such a down payment therefore impacts the lender's exposure to the loan and protects against anything that might lessen the collateral's value. This includes profits that are lost from the point of the final payment to the final collateral sale. The making of this down payment assures a lender that the borrower has capital available for long term investments, further proof that the finances of the borrower are able to afford the item in the first place. Should a borrower not successfully pay down the full loan amount, then he or she will lose the entire down payment.

Down payments on houses bought in the United States typically range anywhere from 3.5% to 20% of the full purchase amount. The Federal Housing Administration helps first time borrowers to pay merely 3.5% as a down payment. In the excesses of the years leading up to the financial collapse of 2007, many banks were making loans with no down payments. On car purchases, these amounts of down payments might be in the range of from 3% to 13%.

Due Diligence

The phrase due diligence is utilized to discuss a wide variety of legal obligations, assignments, investigations, and reports. These all are practiced in business, manufacturing and law. The most commonly used version of the phrase has to do with businesses.

In business, the concept of due diligence pertains to the process gone through by venture capitalists in advance of pouring funding into a start up company. Also involved with this are investigations that continue later into the ways that the monies are being spent. Large companies similarly engage in such due diligence before making the decision to buy out a smaller company.

Venture capitalists practice a particular brand of due diligence that involves researching the present and past players and structures of the firm that is looking for venture funding. Venture capitalists are careful about putting money into firms that do not feature principals who showcase either a track record that is well proven or at least impressive credentials.

Such a due diligence investigation could be stricter or more relaxed based on the prevailing amount of caution held by the investment community at any given time. With most venture capitalist firms, there will be more than a dozen investigators employed who spend their time investigating particular information on the personal histories of the corporation's personnel. This task has become far easier than ever before thanks to the rise of the Internet and all of the subsequent access to information that is now available. Looking into an individual's experience and associations is now far quicker and more convenient.

Due diligence is also used for background checks. When venture capitalist decision makers make up their mind concerning the prospective firm, they will order these done. Most of the time, such venture capitalist partners will want to give funds to individuals that they either feel confident can be trusted, or to whom they have disbursed funds before with other ventures.

Despite the practice of due diligence, it does not guarantee that the investment will not fail. Companies that are comprised of successful proven people with tremendous educational backgrounds and practical experience still fail all of the time because of competition that no one foresaw coming, difficult conditions in the market, or even technical difficulties with products.

Due diligence involves a different understanding from one company to the next firm. Within the business of manufacturing, some environmental protections have to be taken. These are checked out in the due diligence report having to do with environmental site assessments. Such a report contains specifications in a checklist, as well as available sections for commentary.

Due diligence is also used by law firms concerning care that should be taken by companies or individuals in a particular scenario. An example of this might be a company making certain that their product was thoroughly checked out in advance of selling it and then finding out that it might be poisonous or harmful in strangling incidents. Should they not do this due diligence, then they may be charged with criminal negligence.

Earned Income

Earned income comes from involvement in a business or a trade. It is comprised of salary, wages, commissions, tips, and bonuses. Earned income proves to be the opposite of unearned income.

Any money given to you for work that you have done is termed earned income. As an example of money that is not considered to be earned income, if your employer advanced you money against your upcoming pay check, this would be unearned income. This is because you have not yet performed the work that earns the income.

Earned income is generated in one of two different ways. You might work for a person or company that pays you for the work. Alternatively, you could work as a self employed person in a business that is yours.

For taxing purposes, earned income is a broader category. It involves not only salary, wages, and tips, or alternatively self employment net earnings, in the calculations of the IRS. They also include benefits from union strikes and benefits for long term disability that are earned before a person achieves the minimum retirement age as unearned income. Combat pay for military personnel is not usually considered to be taxable earned income either.

There are various forms of income that are considered to be unearned income, or not earned. These include investment returns, such as dividends, interest, and capital gains. Social security and unemployment benefits are also unearned income. Finally, pensions, child support, and alimony are all not considered to be earned income.

Earned income is not only used by the IRS to determine an individual's tax liability for the current year. It is also employed to determine eligibility for the Earned Income Tax Credit, more commonly referred to by its acronym the EITC. This Earned Income Tax Credit proves to be a credit against taxes for individuals who work and receive low wages for their earned income.

Tax credits such as this one commonly translate to additional numbers of earned income dollars staying in the person's pocket, or a lower tax liability for the year than would otherwise be anticipated. Not only does this decrease the amount of tax that might be owed, but it could lead to a tax refund if the adjusted gross income results in negative income tax being due.

Earnings Per Share

Earnings per share refer to the given total of earnings that a company has for every share of the firm's stock that is outstanding. There are several formulas for calculating earnings per share. These depend on which segment of earnings are being considered. The FASB, or Financial Accounting Standards Board, makes corporations report such earnings per share on their income statement for all of the major components of such statements including discontinued operations, continuing operations, extraordinary items, and net income.

To figure up the basic net earnings per share formula, you only have to divide the profit for the year by the average number of common shares of stock. With discontinued operations, it is only a matter of taking the discontinued operations income and dividing it by the average number of common stock shares outstanding. Continuing operations earnings per share equal the continuing operations income over the average number of common shares. Extraordinary items works with the income from extraordinary items and divides it by the weighted average number of common shares.

Besides the basic earnings per share numbers, there are three different types of earnings per share. Last year's earning per share are the Trailing EPS. These are the only completely known earnings for a company. The Current earnings per share are the ones for this year. These are partially projections in the end until the last quarterly numbers are released. Finally, Forward earnings per share are earnings numbers for the future. These are entirely based on predictions.

Earnings per share calculations do not take into account preferred dividends on categories besides net income and continued operations. Such continuing operations and even net income earnings per share calculations turn out to be more complex as preferred share dividends are taken off of the top of net income before the earnings per share is actually calculated. Since preferred stock shares have the right to income payments ahead of common stock payments, any money that is given out as preferred dividends is cash which can not be considered to be potentially available for giving out to every share of the commonly held stock.

Preferred dividends for the present year are generally the only ones that are taken off of such income. There is a prevalent exception to this. If preferred shares prove to be cumulative then this means that dividends for the entire year are taken off, regardless of if they have been declared yet or not. Dividends that the company is behind on paying are not contemplated when the earnings per share is calculated.

Earnings per share as a financial measuring stick for a company are extremely important. In theory, this forms the underlying basis for the value of the stock in question. Another critical measurement of stock price is price to earnings value, also known as the PE ratio. This PE ratio is determined by taking the earnings per share and dividing them into the price of the stock. Earnings per share are useful in measuring up one corporation against another one, if they are involved in the same business segment or industry. They do not tell you if the stock is a good buy or not. They also do not reveal what the overall market thinks about the company. This is where the PE ratio is more useful.

Egalitarianism

Egalitarianism refers to a philosophy that believes in some type of equality. The main idea behind it is that all individuals should be regarded and dealt with as equals, at least pertaining to political, religious, social, economic, or cultural equality. The tenets of egalitarianism hold that every human being has an equal moral value or basic worth. It can be used as a political philosophy that claims that everyone ought to be treated as an equal, provided with the identical economic, political, civil, and social rights. It could alternatively be a social philosophy that pushes for the decentralizing of power and the breaking down of economic barriers between different people. Some individuals believe that this egalitarianism is the natural form of society.

Egalitarianism deals with the studies pertaining to social inequality. Unequal societies lead to many of the world's great social problems. Among these are infant mortality, homicide, teenage pregnancy, obesity, incarceration rates, and depression. A comprehensive type of study that was performed on the major economies of the world showed that a strong connection exists between all of these challenges in society and issues of social inequality.

Egalitarianism exists in numerous different forms. The most typical basis for it arises from political, religious, or philosophical backgrounds. Political precedents of egalitarianism date back to the Age of Enlightenment in the 1700's. At this time, modern government founders referenced egalitarian principals of morality that they lived by, such as the American concept of certain inalienable rights endowed to them by their Creator. These were laid into the modern framework of countries like the United States and France.

Religious egalitarianism is heavily rooted in Christianity. This Christian egalitarian world view states that the Bible is the basis for the common equality of men and women, as well as every economic, racial, ethnic, and age group. This comes from Jesus Christ's example and teachings, as well as other lessons taught throughout the Bible.

In philosophy, egalitarian ideas grew in substance and practice over the last two hundred years. Various sub-philosophies have arisen from this general philosophy, including communism, socialism, progressivism, and anarchism. Each of these concepts favored political, economic, and legal versions of egalitarianism.

Some of these egalitarian philosophies have gained significant and wide standing support with both the general population as well as the intellectuals in numerous countries. This does not mean that such ideas are actually put into universal effect though. On the other hand, democracy does involve many ideas of egalitarianism, at least in the political sphere. Representative democracy proves to be the ultimate realization of such political egalitarianism. Critics of this idea say that even though votes are given out on a one vote per one person basis, the actual power still rests with the ruling class and not the common people.

Emerging Markets

Emerging markets prove to be those countries of the world that possess business and development activities that stand in the midst of fast paced industrialization and growth. Today, twenty-eight different emerging markets are considered to exist around the globe. By far and away the largest of these are China and India. The largest regional emerging market today is the ASEAN-China Free Trade Area that began operating on the first of January in 2010.

The concept of emerging markets dates back to the 1970's, when the term used to refer to these particular markets was LEDC's, or less economically developed countries. The comparison alluded to their levels of economic development as compared to the U.S., Western Europe, and Japan. Such emerging markets were supposed to offer higher risk levels for investors as well as the opportunity to make greater profits.

As this term had a slightly negative connotation, the phrase emerging markets replaced it. Some have claimed that this newer term is deceptive, since no one can be assured that a given country will actually migrate from less developed to a more substantially developed one. This has generally proven to be the case, but there are exceptions. Argentina has occasionally digressed from more to less developed.

Numerous examples of these types of emerging market economies exist, since twenty-eight different ones are labeled. These include countries that are grouped in more advanced emerging economies, such as Brazil, Mexico, Taiwan, South Africa, Poland, and Hungary. The secondary emerging economies are as follows: China, India, Chile, Colombia, Egypt, the Czech Republic, Indonesia, Morocco, Malaysia, Peru, Pakistan, Russia, the Philippines, Turkey, Thailand, and the United Arab Emirates. This list is compiled and occasionally updated by the FTSE group based in London, Great Britain.

In the last few years, several competing terms have arisen to challenge the emerging markets phrase. One of these is that of rapidly developing economies that refers to emerging markets like Chile, Malaysia, and the United Arab Emirates. All of these nations are experiencing torrid paces of growth.

The biggest of the emerging markets have earned their own acronyms in the past several years as well. Chief among these are BRIC, signifying Brazil, Russia, India, and China. BRICS includes the above four nations along with South Africa. BRICM is the original four BRIC nations and Mexico. BRICET signifies the first four BRIC members plus Turkey and Eastern Europe. BRICK includes the original four nations of the BRICK along with South Korea. Finally, CIVETS is comprised of Columbia, Indonesia, Vietnam, Egypt, Turkey, and also South Africa. Although none of these countries are particularly aligned by policy or ideology, they are currently gaining a more important role within the overall world economy, as well as in international politics.

For an investor who wishes to invest in these economies, there are several different investment vehicles available to them. Among these are both Exchange Traded Funds and Mutual Funds. One of these is the iShares sponsored MSCI Emerging Markets Index ETF with a symbol of EEM. Another is the iShares run MSCI EAFE Index ETF that has a symbol of EFA. Though these funds' prices can be up spectacularly in good years, they can also experience precipitous declines in periods of instability, such as during the worldwide financial crisis of 2007-2010.

Employees

Employees are individuals who work in the service of a business endeavor or trade. They do this by contributing their expertise, abilities, and labor to another individual's small business, a corporation, for the government, or in their own self employed business. Employees are also a critical component of the factors of production that include land, capital, and labor. In this capacity, they contribute the labor to a business enterprise.

In particular, an employee proves to be an individual who is engaged by some employer in order to perform a specific job or task. Within the majority of advanced nations and their economies, this word pertains to a specifically spelled out relationship that is established between companies and individual persons. This relationship is markedly different from that of a client or customer.

Attaining the status of employee generally results from undergoing a job interview with a certain business or corporation. Assuming that the person in question matches up well with the organization and their position, then she or he is made a formal employment offer for a given initial salary and place in the company. Such a person then attains all of the privileges, responsibilities, and rights as other employees. These commonly include vacation days and medical insurance benefits. Human Resource departments typically manage the actual relationships between such employees and major companies. This department works with new employees' coming on board and integrating into the organization, as well as handling the set up of their new benefits to which they are entitled. HR departments also commonly resolve any problems or grievances that employees experience.

Employees may group themselves into labor unions that can come to represent the positions and demands of the majority of an organization's work force. These labor unions are then capable of bargaining as a whole on behalf of the employees with a company's management. They do this to make demands for the members concerning payroll, benefits, and working conditions.

Employers are quick to point out that these offers of employment never assure employment for any future specified amount of time. Either the employer or the employee is capable of ending this particular relationship whenever it suits them. This capability is known as at will employment. Many professions expect a two week notice when an individual employee quits his or her job. This is a customary courtesy that the law does not require. It may be necessary in order to obtain a satisfactory job reference for future employment opportunities.

Entrepreneurs

Entrepreneurs are individuals who have new business ventures, enterprises, and concepts. They take on substantial responsibility for both risks inherent in these as well as their end results. As such, entrepreneurs prove to be unique people for many reasons.

For one, entrepreneurs have trouble working for other people, even though they do work on behalf of clients. They will put all of their assets and money at risk because they have a driving passion to watch their endeavor expand. As a result of this, they occasionally have a couple of failures to their credit along the way. These individuals enjoy putting in the extra time and effort in the procedures of strategizing, modifying, amending, and adjusting their businesses. They are not afraid of long hours and constantly working when everyone else has given up and gone home for the day.

Entrepreneurs must have vision and foresight. They are required to see their enterprise not only as it is now, but also as it will look in a year from now, and two years, three years, and even five years to ten years in the future. This involves understanding what the process of the business will tangibly look like, not necessarily the employees who change from time to time. This is essential for any entrepreneurs to be successful in reaching their end goals.

Entrepreneurs are loners in a very real sense. They stand by themselves with their vision that only they can see so clearly. They are also alone in having the drive and passion to see their endeavor through. They understand that no one else in the business will care about it like they do, since no one else possesses the dream.

Very few people are entrepreneurs. It takes a hardy individual to be one. This is evident when you consider that the number of new businesses that go down in only the first year is fully seventy-five percent, mostly a result of insufficient commitment from the founder. Ninety percent of such businesses have folded by the conclusion of the second year for a variety of reasons including funding difficulties, family problems from working all of the time, and challenges in dealing with employees. Entrepreneurs are capable of overcoming these types of problems using their determination and energy.

Entrepreneurs are also those who invest money and have the risk of losing it. Many times they will act as venture capitalists and pour money into firms that have not long been operating. When you purchase items cheaply and sell them dearly, this makes you an entrepreneur on a smaller scale too. In the end, entrepreneurs are those who are willing and able to utilize their money in order to make more money.

Similarly, entrepreneurs are born leaders. They know what they want, and understand what to do in order to achieve it. They dream big dreams, form important ideas, and come up with concepts and opportunities. These leaders who are willing to engage in financial risks are true entrepreneurs.

Equities

Equities are another name for stocks and similar types of investments. Stocks turn out to be financial instruments that represent ownership, or equity position, within a given corporation. As such, they give an owner a stake in a representative share of the company's profits and assets.

Such ownership in a given firm is determined by taking the total numbers of shares in the company's equities that the individual owns, and dividing it by the actual number of shares that exist. The majority of these equities similarly give voting rights that provide representative votes in some decisions that the company makes. Not every company issues equities; only corporations engage in the practice, while limited partnerships and sole proprietorships do not. Equities can be further divided into smaller categories based on the market capitalization, or size, of the company in question.

Because equities often yield greater returns over significant periods of time, they are typically characterized by higher amounts of risk than are bonds and money market funds. Because of these unique potential returns and associated risks, equities are generally considered to be their own class of assets that are utilized to a degree in putting together investment portfolios with proper diversification. Many different kinds of equities exist, including domestic equities, emerging market equities, developed market equities, and Real Estate Investment Trusts.

Domestic Equities prove to be those stocks for the publicly traded corporations that principally conduct their business in the same country in which the investor lives. When a person holds such equities, they receive their share of dividends that the corporation pays. Equities come with a higher degree of risk than do bonds, as bond holders have a greater claim on a corporation's assets should liquidation follow bankruptcy. Equity holders are commonly wiped out in such liquidation.

Emerging Market Equities are equities in corporations that are based in countries that are still developing their economies. Included in these are China, Brazil, and India. These nations feature economies that are commonly volatile and lack many protections for investors, like auditing and laws or monitoring of securities that are found in the industrialized countries.

Developed Market Equities are equities in firms that work primarily outside of an investor's home country but still in an industrialized country. For Americans, this mostly translates to European country companies, as well as those in places such as Japan, Australia, and New Zealand. Such companies and economies in these nations prove to be more stable than those in developing countries.

Real Estate Investment Trusts, also known as REIT's, are equity funds that invest in residential and commercial real estate. Because they receive lease and rent payments off of their investments, these typically pay greater percentage returns in dividends. These higher distributions mean that REIT's are much like a combination of fixed income and typical equity investments. This means that they commonly feature greater risk along with better anticipated returns than do the majority of fixed income investments.

Equity

Equity represents the homeowner's total dollar amount of ownership in their property. Determining equity is a simple calculation. It is found by taking the home's assumed fair market value and subtracting out the balances of liens and debts secured by the property along with the mortgage balance that is still unpaid. As a home owner pays down the mortgage, reducing the outstanding principal balance, the equity of a home owner goes up. It similarly increases as the property gains in value. To obtain one hundred percent equity in their property, home owners have to pay down both any outstanding debts that are secured by the property and the full mortgage.

Associated with the equity value of a home is the LTV, or loan to value ratio. This loan to value ratio proves to be a means of stating the property's value as against the total dollar amount of your actual loan. The loan to value ratio is simply figured up by taking the amount of your loan and dividing it by your property value. Alternatively, you could divide the amount of your loan by the purchase price or selling price, whichever of the two is the lower amount.

An example helps to illustrate the concept. If you were to purchase a $300,000 house, you might put down a $60,000 down payment using your money. The remaining $240,000 would be covered by taking out a mortgage. Dividing the $60,000 amount by the $300,000 home value yields equity of twenty percent. If you divide the $240,000 by the $300,000 home value, then you will get the loan to value ratio that amounts to eighty percent.

Should you determine later that you will sell this house, then the equity that you have will be concretely and accurately figured up for you. This will simply prove to be the fair market value of your house minus the loan that you still owe the bank on the house. Using the example from the paragraph above, consider what would happen if you lived in and made payments on your house for five years following the purchase.

In this time frame, your monthly mortgage payments lower the balance that remains on the loan to the tune of $10,000, diminishing it from

$240,000 to $230,000. Besides this, over those five years, your home value goes up. This allows you to realize a selling price of $330,000. Since the balance that you owed is still $230,000, then your equity is simply figured by taking the $330,000 selling price and subtracting the $230,000 from it. This leaves you with a final equity value of $100,000. Once all selling costs and realty commissions are figured up and taken out, you would be able to utilize the $100,000 equity in order to invest or to put down the down payment on the next house that you purchase.

Naturally, this home value can cut both ways. Should the value on the home drop from $300,00 to $250,000 in the time that you own it, then your remaining equity would be only $50,000, less than the original $60,000 that you put into it upfront.

ERISA

ERISA is the acronym for The Employment Retirement Income Security Act that was enacted in 1974. This ERISA legislation set up a basic level of standards for health, retirement, and various additional types of plans for welfare benefits. These include disability insurance, life insurance, and apprenticeship plans.

This Employment Retirement Income Security Act is both overseen and run by the EBSA, which turns out to be the acronym for Employee Benefits Security Administration. This EBSA operates as a division under the United States DOL, or Department of Labor. If you have any questions about the act, concerns that you are not being treated according to the law, or complaints regarding treatment as the ERISA laws relate to you, then you should contact your area ERISA office for help and clarification.

It is important to note that these protecting regulations mandated by ERISA only pertain to non government, private employers who choose to provide benefits plans and health insurance that is employer sponsored for their employees. ERISA does not force such employers to provide such these plans for employees. Rather, it only lays out regulations for the employee offered benefits that such employers make available. It is also significant that the rules and regulations set up by ERISA do not pertain to those benefits or insurance policies that are purchased by an individual privately.

ERISA does establish the requirements and standards for a number of different related elements. Reporting and accountability is required to be detailed and made available to the U.S. Federal government. The conduct for HMO's and other managed care, as well as for other people who have financial responsibility for the administration of the plan, is strictly regulated by the ERISA rules.

ERISA also pertains to safeguards and procedures. Written policies have to be set up to determine the way that claims have to be filed, along with the claims' appeals process in writing for any claims that are denied. ERISA further stipulates that these appeals should be decided in a reasonably timed and fair way. ERISA also proves to be a protection that insures that all plans are both offered, safeguarded, and funded in the ways that most appropriately favor the members and their best interests.

ERISA does not permit discrimination in the ways that benefits in the plan are gathered and collected for those members who are qualified. Finally, ERISA insists that a variety of disclosures be made to the participants in the plan. These include a plan summary that specifically lists out the provided benefits, the associated rules for obtaining such benefits, any limitations of the plans, and other matters including getting referrals before doctor and surgeon visits.

Escrow

Escrow is a concept that relates to a sum of money that is kept by an uninvolved third party for the two parties involved in a given transaction. In the U.S., this escrow is most commonly involved where real estate mortgages are concerned. Here is it utilized for the payment of insurance and property tax during the mortgage's life.

When you place your money into such an escrow account, an escrow agent who is a neutral third party holds it. This agent works on behalf of both the borrower and home lender. The escrow agent's job in the transaction is to act as the principal parties instruct him or her. As all transaction terms are fulfilled, the money is then released. These escrow accounts may be a part of transactions ranging from small purchases affected on online auction sites to building projects that total in the multiple millions of dollars.

Escrow is utilized in these property transactions when it is time for your mortgage to close. At this point, the borrower's lender will commonly insist that you establish an escrow account for paying for both home owner's insurance and property taxes. You are required to make a first deposit to the account. After this, you make payments into the account each month. Typically, these are simply a part of your monthly mortgage payments. When it is time for your insurance premiums and taxes to be paid, your escrow agent then releases the funds.

The concept behind this escrow is to give your lender peace of mind and protection that your insurance and taxes are both paid in a timely manner. Should you not pay your property taxes, the city might place a lien on this house, making it hard for the bank to sell it if they needed to. Similarly, if a fire burned down the house and the insurance premiums had not been paid, the bank would not have any underlying collateral for the mortgage anymore.

You the borrower also benefit from this escrow account. It allows you to stretch out your taxes and insurance costs over the course of the entire year's twelve payments. As an example, your annual property taxes might prove to be $3,000, with a yearly insurance cost of $600. This would mean that when spread out over twelve even payments, the escrow costs would amount to only $300 each month.

The nice thing about escrow accounts and payments is that they come with an included safeguard built in. Should you miss a single payment, then the responsible lender is still capable of paying the accounts in a timely manner. The U.S. Federal law actually stops these lenders from storing up in excess of two months' worth of payments in escrow. As insurance and tax amounts will vary a little from one year to the next, the lender will have to examine and make adjustments to your annual escrow payments.

ETF

ETF stands for Exchange Traded Funds. These ETF's prove to be stock market exchange traded investment funds that work very much like stocks. Exchange Traded Funds contain instruments like commodities, stocks, and bonds. They trade for around the identical net asset value as the assets that they contain throughout the course of a day. The majority of ETF's actually follow the value of an index like the Dow Jones Industrial or the S&P 500. Since their creation in 1993, ETF's have evolved into the most beloved kind of exchange traded instruments.

The first Exchange Traded Fund particular to countries proved to be a joint venture of MSCI, Funds Distributor, and BGI. This first product finally turned into the iShares name that is accepted and recognized all over earth today. In the first fifteen years, such ETF's were index funds that simply followed indexes. The United States Securities and Exchange Commission began allowing firms to establish actively managed ETF's back in 2008.

Exchange Traded Funds provide a number of terrific advantages for smaller investors. Among these are elements like simple and effective diversification, index funds tax practicality, and expense ratios that remain very low. While doing all of this, they also offer the appeal of familiarity for you who trade stocks. This includes such comfortable and helpful options as limit orders, options, and short selling the ETF's. Since it is so inexpensive to purchase, hold, and sell these ETF's, many investors in ETF shares choose to keep them over a longer time frame for purposes of diversification and asset allocation. Still other investors trade in and out of these instruments regularly in order to participate in their strategies for market timing investing.

Exchange Traded Funds boast of many advantages. On the one hand, they provide great flexibility in buying and selling. It is easy for you to sell and buy them at the actual market price any time during a trading day, in contrast to mutual funds that you can only acquire at a trading day's conclusion. Since they are companies that trade like stocks, you can buy them in margin accounts and sell them short, meaning that they can be used for hedging purposes too. ETF's also allow limit orders and stop loss orders, which are helpful for assuring entry prices and protecting profits or safeguarding from losses.

ETF's also provide lower costs for traders. This results from the majority of ETF's not being actively managed. Also, ETF's do not spend large amounts of money on distribution, marketing, and accounting costs. The majority of them do not have the fees associated with most mutual funds either.

ETF's are among the greatest vehicles for diversifying portfolios quickly and easily. As an example, with only one set of shares, you can "own" the entire S&P 500 index. ETF's will give you exposure to country specific indexes, international markets, commodities, and even bond indexes.

ETF's have two other advantages. They are both transparent and tax efficient. Transparent in this regard means that they are clear in their portfolio holdings and are priced all day long. They are tax efficient as they do not create many capital gains, since they are not in the business of buying and selling their underlying indexes. They also are not required to sell their holding in order to meet redemptions of investors.

Eviction

Eviction involves the forced removal of a rental tenant from a landlord's rental property. Other terms that convey the same or a similar meaning include repossession, summary possession, and ejection. Eviction proves to be the term most commonly utilized in landlord and tenant communications. Evictions can not simply happen without going through a legal process that could include an eviction lawsuit.

A notice must first be given to the tenant by the landlord. This is most often referred to as the notice to vacate or notice to quit. It has to be delivered to a tenant in advance of beginning official legal eviction procedures. In most cases, the tenant will then receive somewhere from three to ten days to address the issue causing eviction. These offenses likely are caused by either a failure to pay the rent in a timely manner or contractual breach of the lease for something like have a pet.

Should the tenant refuse to leave the property in question after the expiration of the notice to quit, then the landlord next provides the tenant with a complaint. These complaints mandate that the tenant in question will have to go to court. If the tenant refuses to appear at the court date or does not provide an answer to the complaint, then the landlord is able to seek a default judgment, in which he or she automatically wins the case. A tenant response should include his or her side of the story as well as defense that could include the tenant not being provided with repairs that the lease stipulates.

Following an appropriate answer, trial dates are determined. With the issues being dependent on time, these cases are commonly hurried through the system. Should a judge back up a tenant, then the tenant is allowed to stay, although he or she would have to pay back due rent. Should the landlord be victorious, then the tenant receives a little window to move out of the property before being forcefully evicted. This is commonly only a week, though with a stay of execution, the tenant could be given more time.

Some jurisdictions permit a tenant to have a right to redemption in the eviction process. This would allow a tenant to cancel a pending eviction and to stay in the rented property by catching up immediately on the back rent along with other appropriate fees. These rights become waived should the tenant constantly be late in paying the rent.

Finally, after a tenant has lost his or her eviction lawsuit, the tenant is commonly given a particular number of days in which to abandon the property. This has to be done before other repercussions occur. Sometimes the tenant will be told to leave immediately.

Landlords are given writs of possession by the court after the tenant has lost the lawsuit and still refused to leave. These writs of possession are then turned over to a law enforcement officer. Such an officer would then put up an official notice for a tenant to depart the property before the date on which the officer will return to forcibly remove the tenant. If the tenant is not gone when the officer returns, he is permitted to take the tenant and anyone else on the property and remove them. They will be allowed to take away their possessions or place them in storage before the property is given back to the landlord.

Exchange Rate

In finance and business, exchange rates are also known as Forex Rates, foreign exchange rates, or FX rates. These exchange rates are the rates that are valid between two currencies. They are stated in terms of one currency's value in the other currency. Such an exchange rate is also the foreign nation's currency value as stated in the currency of the home nation.

There are various distinctions within the category of exchange rates. Present day exchange rates are termed spot exchange rates. Exchange rates which are quoted to you and traded today but available for payment and delivery in the future on a particular date are called forward exchange rates.

It is instructive to look at some examples. If the GBP/USD rate is 1.60, then it means that the exchange rate of the British Pound garners $1.60 in US dollars. Alternatively, a USD/CHF rate of .97 would mean that only .97 of a Swiss Franc will buy one U.S. dollar.

Exchange rates are determined on the foreign exchange market. This is the largest single market on the whole planet, trading literally trillions of dollars in currency values every single day. It is estimated that this market exceeds three trillion dollars in U.S. valued currencies on a given trading day. This market trades six days a week, and is only closed from Friday at 5PM New York time until Sunday afternoon at 3PM New York Time.

Exchange rates can be freely trading on the world exchange markets. Some countries choose to instead peg the value of their currency to another proven, more responsible, and reliable currency, such as the Euro or the dollar. In these cases, the exchange rates are constant against those that they peg to, and only fluctuate against other currencies on the market at the same pace as the currency that they are pegged to does.

Exchange rates on FOREX can be pursued for hedging purposes or for investment opportunities. Businesses that have operations in two or more countries are often interested in locking in their exchange rate in order to protect themselves from possibly violent currency swings. By buying forward exchange rates, they can lock these in for any given day that suits their needs. Alternatively, they can take on FOREX spot positions in the currency totals that they anticipate needing, so that as the price rises and falls, it will be canceled out as they repatriate their foreign currency back into home currency.

Investors can participate in the exchange rate markets for investment opportunities. Besides buying these spot currency positions or forward positions, they can purchase options contracts on these pairs. The advantage and disadvantage to these markets is the leverage that they provide, which is commonly one hundred to one. This signifies that an individual investor is able to control one hundred thousand Euros against the dollar with only a thousand dollar account value. Major gains, as well as substantial losses, become possible with only small moves, since every ten cent price change in this case represents a hundred dollars literally gained or lost.

Export

The word export refers to a good or service that is sold and shipped out of a country. In business and economics terms, an export can be any kind of commodity or other good that is utilized in trade and transported out of one nation into another nation. These must be done in legal ways to qualify as exports. The opposite of the word export is the word import.

The word export is originally taken from the idea of shipping such services and goods out of the port of a given country. This made it an item that was sent literally "ex" port. This term came from the time when practically all international trade proved to be conducted via shipping.

Sellers of services and goods are known as exporters. These individuals are based in the exporting nation. The party who receives the goods or services in the overseas country is known as an importer. In the realm of international trade, exports means vending goods and services that are manufactured in the producing home nation to markets in other countries. Once these goods are received by the importer in the foreign country, they are offered to the consumers in the foreign country by distributors and domestic producers.

When a person or company wishes to become involved in exporting commercial amounts of goods, then they will have to become engaged with the customs entities in both the exporting home country and the importing receiving country. Smaller quantities of goods are exempt from such customs departments, particularly when they are of low individual value. This is why the rise of auction sites and other online retailers vending to international customers, such as e-Bay and Amazon, have managed to side step the customs departments in the majority of countries. This does not exempt small value export items from the legal rules and restrictions that are applied by the exporting nation.

A nation's exports can be many different things in practice. Resource rich countries like Australia or South Africa will commonly export big ticket natural resource items like gold, oil, natural gas, uranium, or diamonds. Agricultural countries such as the Philippines and Honduras export rice and bananas to other countries in the world. The main exports of industrial countries such as Germany and Japan are instead final manufactured product goods like cars and machinery.

Some items may not simply be exported to every nation. They are subjected to export control. Export control involves Federal laws and rules that forbid the exporting of some information and commodities without a license. This is done to protect certain trades or because of sensitive issues related to national security. Specifically, the government might be worried about the final destination country or group that will receive the goods, such as Iran or North Korea. They may fear what the actual use of the export will be, such as equipment for enriching uranium. Sometimes, exports have capabilities that will allow them to be used for possible military applications that the government wishes to control and supervise, like with missile technology.

Federal Reserve

The Federal Reserve, also known as the Fed, or the Federal Reserve Board, proves to be the United States' central banking system. This central bank came about in 1913 as a result of Congress passing the Federal Reserve Act. Congress created the organization because of a number of serious financial panics that culminated in the severe panic of 1907.

With time, the Federal Reserve's roles and areas of responsibility have grown as the organization has expanded. Economic events such as the Great Depression have only served to encourage this.

The Federal Reserve today counts among its duties many responsibilities. Among these are regulating and overseeing the country's banks, managing the country's monetary policy and supply, assuring the financial systems' continuance and stability, and offering a variety of financial services to depositing banks, foreign central banks, and the United States government.

The Federal Reserve's structure is made up of a number of different components. Among these are the Federal Reserve Board of Governors, all of whom are appointed by the President. The Federal Open Market Committee, also known by its acronym of FOMC, sets the monetary policy, like the interest rates, for the nation. There are also Federal Reserve Banks, which are twelve regional institutions that are found in the biggest area cities around America. They offer physical currency to member banks when demand proves to be unusually high. Several councils that advise it are a part of The Federal Reserve, as are technically the member banks throughout the country.

The FOMC component of the Federal Reserve is actually comprised of all of these seven Board of Governors members along with the presidents of the twelve regional banks. Only five of these presidents are voting members at a time. Together, they review the state of the U.S. national economy in order to determine what fiscal policies need to be pursued. When the economic growth is slowing, or a recession is occurring, they cut the national interest rates. When inflation is appearing or the economy is overheating, they raise these interest rates.

The Federal Reserve proves to be a unique entity among the major central banks. This is because it divides up the various responsibilities into some public and some private parts of the institution. The Federal Reserve furthermore serves to create the currency used for the country, the

U.S. dollar. The fact that it is both a public and private institution, with so many varied and vast powers, makes it one of a kind.

Because the U.S. dollar is still the reserve currency of the world, the Federal Reserve's powers are far greater than simply managing the U.S. economy. In actual practice, they also are the custodians and managers of the world's reserve currency. This gives them considerable power and influence throughout the entire world economy, since they are able to create not only dollars for the U.S. economy, but also for other central banks use in foreign countries. As a result of this, more than half of the physically printed U.S. dollars are found outside of the United States.

Federal Reserve Act of 1913

The Federal Reserve Act of 1913 created the Federal Reserve Bank. This proved to be the Act of Congress that set up the Federal Reserve System. This system became the Central Bank organization for the United States. As part of the act, the Federal Reserve acquired the powers to issue the nation's legal tender currency. President Woodrow Wilson actually signed this act, making it law in 1913.

The leadership of the country felt the need to create such a central bank for several reasons. The United States had operated without a central bank going back to the expiration of the Second Bank of the United States' charter. This meant that for about eighty years, the country had existed without any form of central bank.

In time, a number of financial panics had ensued without any central bank to intervene in them. The one that really galvanized congressional and public opinion for having a central bank proved to be the serious financial panic of 1907. As a result of these factors, a number of Americans decided that the nation required serious currency and banking reforms that could handle such panics by offering an available liquid assets' reserve. They also figured such an institution might be capable of managing a consistent expansion and contraction of credit and currency from time to time as appropriate.

The original Federal Reserve Act plan recommended an establishment of an unusual combined public and private entity system. They suggested that minimally eight and as many as twelve regional private Federal Reserve banks should be created. All of them were to have their own boards of directors, regional boundary lines, and branches. This new entity would be led by a Federal Reserve Board comprised of seven members and made up of public officials that the President appointed and the Senate would confirm. An advisory committee known as the Federal Advisory Committee would be created, along with a brand new U.S. currency that would alone be accepted nationally, the Federal Reserve Note. In the final version of the bill, twelve regional Federal Reserve Banks were actually created. The rest of the above provisions became law and subsequently a part of the newly created Federal Reserve System.

Another important decision that Congress settled on with the Federal Reserve Act revolved around the private banks throughout the U.S. Every nationally chartered bank had to join the Federal Reserve System as a part of this act. They were made to buy stock that could not be transferred in their own area's Federal Reserve Bank. It furthermore required that a set dollar total of reserves that did not pay interest had to be deposited to their own regional Federal Reserve Bank. Banks that are only state chartered have the choice, but not the obligation, of joining this system and being regulated by the Fed.

Finally, the act allowed the member banks to receive loans at a discounted rate from the discount windows of their own regional Federal Reserve Bank. They were promised a six percent yearly dividend on their Federal Reserve stock and provided with additional services. The act also gave the Federal Reserve Banks the authority to assume the role of U.S. government fiscal agents.

Federal Reserve Bank

Twelve different Federal Reserve Banks make up the Federal Reserve System that functions as the central bank for the U.S. Federal reserve banks are also utilized to sub-divide up the country into the twelve Federal Reserve Districts. Every Federal Reserve Bank bears the responsibility for individually regulating the various commercial banks that are found in such a bank's geographical district. Ensuring the continuation of the financial system and all of the member banks is among the primary responsibilities of the Federal Reserve System.

Each Federal Reserve Bank also issues its own stock shares that can only be acquired by participating member banks. The banks are required to obtain these shares by law. While the shares may not be traded, pledged as a loan security, or sold, they do pay dividends that run as high as six percent each year.

American banks are required by law to keep certain fractional reserves of their actual deposits. These are mostly held by the regional Federal Reserve Banks. Although in years past, the Federal Reserve did not pay member banks interest on these funds kept on reserve, as of 2008 Congress passed the EESA that permits them to pay the participating banks interest.

The twelve Federal Reserve Banks and districts are found geographically spread out around the nation. They include the Federal Reserve Banks of Boston, New York, Philadelphia, Cleveland, Richmond, Atlanta, Chicago, St. Louis, Minneapolis, Kansas City, Dallas, and San Francisco.

The largest and still most important of the individual Federal Reserve Banks proves to be the Federal Reserve Bank of New York. Not only does this bank have the greatest asset base of all the twelve branches, valued at over a trillion dollars and representing four times the asset base of the next largest Federal Reserve Bank, but it also boasts the biggest gold depository on earth, valued at in excess of $25 billion. The gold kept in the New York Federal Reserve Bank vaults belongs to other nations who store it there for safe keeping. Saudi Arabia and Kuwait both keep their significant holdings here.

Among the various states that have Federal Reserve Banks headquartered there, a few of them contain more than one branch within their state. California, Missouri, and Tennessee are the ones that make this claim. Tennessee actually contains two branches from two different districts within its state boundaries. The only state that has two Federal Reserve Banks headquartered within it is Missouri. For the largest geographical areas covered by the districts, San Francisco is the largest, Kansas City is second biggest, and Minneapolis is the third largest.

Fiat Dollars

Fiat dollars refer to dollars that do not possess any sort of intrinsic value. They are not backed up by gold or any other tangible asset, only by the full faith and trust in the United States government. Since the United States abandoned the venerable and stable gold standard back in 1971, the U.S. currency has been one of only fiat dollars.

Fiat actually refers to the Latin for "let it be done." Dollars that are fiat dollars are valued based on the decree of the government. They are not redeemable for anything else.

Until 1971, the dollar proved to be convertible into a certain set quantity of gold. This had been the case along with all other major currencies around the world for nearly two hundred years. Gold backed dollars and other currency proved to be extremely stable and constantly valued for huge spans of time stretching from forty to sixty years before some turbulence like the Civil War would impact their value for a few years. This resulted in part from governments only being able to print as many dollars and other currency as they had gold.

Since the U.S. currency became one of fiat dollars, its stability has vanished, along with its former constant value. One ounce of gold only represented $38.90 valued U.S. dollars at the end of 1970. Today the same ounce of gold equates to $1,350. Another way of putting this is that one 1970 gold backed dollar is equal to nearly $35 fiat dollars in 2010. You might also say that the Fiat dollar has declined by more than ninety-seven percent in the time span of almost forty years since it began its life as a Fiat dollar.

This says several important things about Fiat dollars. They are at the mercy of the international markets, since they are not backed up by any tangible value. They are also able to be printed or electronically multiplied in infinite quantities, since they are not restricted by a given fixed amount of gold. It also means that they are unstable in their values and can collapse fairly easily and quickly, since their real worth is only one of perceived value as determined by the confidence of buyers and sellers.

Fiat dollars are not the only currency that has been decoupled from real valued backing like gold. Euros, Japanese Yen, British Pounds, and practically all major currencies of the world are similarly only based on the faith and trust of their respective governments. The only currency among the major developed economies that might be considered to be non fiat is the Swiss Franc.

The Swiss constitution requires that the government holds a full quarter of the number of Swiss Francs in existence in gold in their vaults. This would give them a twenty-five percent gold backing to their currency. The truth is that since the Swiss value their gold reserves at $250 per ounce, and gold is trading consistently well over $1,200 per ounce to even $1,350 per ounce, at over five times the Swiss value of their gold, this means that they actually have their currency covered by in excess of one hundred percent of actual valued gold holdings, since five times their twenty-five percent gold reserve amounts to one hundred and twenty-five percent.

Fiat Money

Fiat Money proves to be money that has no real intrinsic, or actual, value. It instead derives its worth from governments accepting it as legal tender. The concept of fiat money on a large scale is a relatively new one. Throughout practically all of history, the majority of currencies around the world derived their value from silver or gold. Fiat money is instead entirely based on trust and faith in the issuing monetary authority.

The problem with fiat money lies in the ability of the governments to inflate its value away. They can do this by over printing it. Since fiat currencies are not restricted by a requirement of hard reserve assets, they can be created in any quantity that the issuing government desires. As the supply of fiat money continues to rise while the demand remains constant, its purchasing power will fall. When the supply of the fiat money is drastically increased, then hyperinflation will result. Fiat money that falls by hundreds of percent in value is deemed to be a victim of hyperinflation.

The other disadvantage to fiat money is that only peoples' trust in it ultimately gives it practical value. As fiat money suffers from inflation and finally hyperinflation, then the confidence in it becomes shaken. Fiat money that lacks the confidence of its citizens will finally collapse in value and then no longer be of any trading use for daily transactions. When fiat money fails, people either return to barter systems, or the government establishes a currency based on hard assets once again.

The history of money has proven on a number of occasions that governments debase currency to the point of fiat money when it suits them. They do this because it allows them to print as much as they need to pay for things. While this creates inflation for their citizens, it gives the money issuing government the ability to repay their debts with cheaper fiat money. Finally, as a society has had enough of the devalued money and currency instability, they force the government to return to asset backed money. This has happened before, and some monetary experts say that you are starting to see this happen again nowadays.

Financial Mentor

A financial mentor is a trusted guide or counselor that helps a person in the arena of business, personal finance and investments. Mentors can be many different people, but they typically have several characteristics in common. They are all loyal advisers who have the person's best interests at heart.

Mentoring is most widely used in business. Other settings that use it include medical fields and educational settings. Business experts will tell you that among the most useful, helpful, and valuable career assets that you can have in your business career is a helpful and experienced mentor.

Financial mentors are commonly older individuals who have more wisdom and experience to share with the individual than he or she already possesses. Though they do not have to be older in every single case, they must always have more experience than the person whom they are mentoring. These mentors both guide financial development and assist the person with their overall financial and business goals. They do not engage in this process with the expressed intent of making money or benefiting financially from the arrangement usually.

With financial mentors, you as the person being mentored have some preparation that you can do. You should listen carefully to the mentor and what he or she has to tell you. This is most easily accomplished by coming to the meeting with the financial mentor with some sort of recording means prepared. This might be a voice recorder, PDA, laptop, or even pen and paper. If a mentor made specific recommendations in the prior discussions, then you should have both noted and tried to apply them. Be ready to review any steps that you have taken specifically with the mentor.

You should also allow a mentor to be a part of your big picture goals and plans, and not only the particular details. The overall goals for you who are being mentored should be set together, in conjunction with the mentor. They should talk not only about present challenges and difficulties, but also concentrate on long term and short term goals together.

Good financial mentors will also do more than simply hold official meetings. They will take the time to get to know you. This does not have to be extensive amounts of time, but it should be quality time spent. This might involve a fifteen minute friendly chat over coffee or a quick bite to eat out some night. The key is not to take up too much of the financial mentor's time until you get to know him or her better. Then as the relationship broadens out into a friendship, more opportunities to get together will naturally arise.

Financial mentors can help out with many areas of your life. They can make helpful suggestions for getting out of debt. They can guide you with good concepts for practical and smart investing. They can share personal, actual experience for navigating through difficulties with a business that you own. They might suggest advice to assist you in your career development. Whatever help that you specifically request from a mentor, you should always remember to be appreciative and take the time to write thank you notes.

Financial Statement

Financial statements are official records of a business' or personal financial activity. With businesses, financial statements present any and all pertinent financial activity as usable information. They do this in a clear, organized, and simple to comprehend way.

Financial statements are commonly comprised of four different types of financial accounts that come with an analysis and discussion provided by the company's management. The Balance sheet is the first of these. It is known by several other names, including statement of financial condition, or statement of financial position. The balance sheet details will outline a corporation's ownership equity, liabilities, and assets on a particular date. This will give a good picture of the general strength and position of the company.

Financial statements similarly include income statements. These can also be called Profit and Loss statements too. They outline numerous important pieces of company information, such as corporate expenses, income, and profits made in a certain time period. This statement explains all of the relevant financial details to the business' operation. Sales and all associated expenses are included under this category. This section of the financial statement proves to be the nuts and bolts of the whole document. It provides a snap shot of the company's ability to generate sales and turn profits.

A statement of cash flow is also a part of a complete financial statement. As its name implies, this section will share all of the details regarding the company's activities pertaining to cash flow. The most important ones that will be outlined include operating cash flow, financing, and investing endeavors.

The last element of a financial statement includes the statement of retained earnings. This section of the document makes good on its name to detail any changes to a corporation's actual retained earnings for the period that is being reported. These four sections of a financial statement are all combined together to make the consolidated financial statement, once they are combined with the analysis and discussion of management.

With large multinational types of corporations, such financial statements are typically large and complicated, making them challenging to read and understand. To assist with readability, they may also come with a group of notes for the financial statement that also covers management's analysis and discussion. Such notes will go through all items listed on the four parts of the financial statement in more thorough detail. For many companies, these notes for financial statements have come to be deemed a critical component of good and complete financial statements.

Financial statements are used by several different groups of people who are looking at a company. Investors use them in order to determine if the company and its stocks or bonds make a sound investment with a chance of providing good returns on investments and profits in exchange for limited risks. Banks utilize these financial statements to decide if a company is a good credit risk for their loan dollars. Institutions and other groups that may be considering a cash infusion or buyout of the company use such financial statements to decide if the company is a viable investment or acquisition target.

Financing Terms

There are two different financing terms available for businesses. These are short term financing and long term financing. In today's economic environment following the financial collapse and Great Recession, many businesses require both types. The two types of financing involve more differences than only the time frames.

Short term financing is commonly utilized for the daily business operations' funding and needs. This is also known as working capital. The financing terms for these short term facilities commonly require the short term loans to be paid back in a year or less.

Long term financing is more often utilized for the upkeep or purchase of fixed asset types. This might include a building or machinery that a firm owns. The financing terms for long term loans are for periods of time that are greater than a year.

Among the short term financing means are bank loans, bank overdrafts, trade credit, and leasing. For individuals, bank overdrafts prove to be the most common means of short term finance, since their finance terms permit an individual to draw out a greater amount of money that the person has in the bank, up to a predetermined amount.

Trade credit is useful for small businesses who may require the ability to buy goods and services or supplies before they receive payments and incoming receipts. With such trade credit facilities, the finance terms are commonly from thirty to ninety days to pay the full balance.

Long term financing might also involve bank loans, as well as corporate bonds or mortgages. With corporate bonds, a company is borrowing money from investors and members of the public. The financing terms of these types of instruments commonly require periodic interest payments that are known as coupon payments. The principal is then repaid on the agreed upon day. Many corporate bonds also feature a recall option that allows a company to pay off its long term debts early. This might be of interest to such a firm if they feel that they can borrow the funds for less money elsewhere or with lower interest rates.

Mortgages are extremely long term financing options made available to individuals or consumers for the purchase of a house or commercial property. These financing terms commonly run to thirty years or longer. Mortgages involve complex calculations for figuring out payments that often involve property taxes, mortgage insurance, and loan repayments.

Financing terms can also relate to the specifics of a particular loan, mortgage, or credit facility. They would spell out the interest rate, due dates of payments, and number of payments anticipated. In many cases, they would also specify the amount of interest that would be paid over the course of the loan or credit facility, as well as the penalties for not making the payments on time.

Fixed Rate Mortgage

Fixed Rate Mortgages are products for mortgage loans that the FHA, or Federal Housing Administration, first created. In this type of mortgage, the interest rates in effect on the mortgage note stay at the same level during the entire life of the loan. This stands in stark contrast to loans where the interest rates are adjustable, or floating. There are also hybrid types of loans that involve fixed rates for a portion of the loan's life.

Fixed rate mortgages will have monthly payments that must be made to keep current on the mortgage. Besides the monthly payment there are property taxes and property insurance costs. These are typically set up in escrow accounts. With such escrow amounts, these are likely to change every so often. Still, the main share of the payments, which are associated with interest and principal on the mortgage, will stay the same.

Figuring up the monthly payments with fixed rate mortgages is relatively easy. You will have to acquire three pieces of data to do so. These are the interest rate with compounding of interest period, mortgage term, and amount of loan.

Fixed rate mortgages are also known by their nickname of plain vanilla mortgages. They have this moniker because of how simple they are for borrowers to understand. Such fixed rate mortgages do not entail the many risks and perils associated with adjustable rate mortgages that include pre set teasing rates or Adjustable Rate Mortgages. As such, Fixed rate mortgage default rates and foreclosure rates are commonly far lower than are these more experimental and risky mortgage products.

Several terms are commonly associated with Fixed Rate Mortgages. These include the fully indexed rate and the term. Fully indexed rates are the interest rate index plus the margin charged by the lender. Such a fully indexed rate proves to be the actual interest rate for the loan's entire life.

The term represents the amount of time that the fixed rate loan covers. This is not the same thing as the number of payments. Thirty year terms might have thirty payments if you were on an annual payment plan, or it might alternatively have 360 payments on a more usual monthly payment plan

The most popular and proven form of home loans and mortgage products within the United States are undoubtedly these fixed rate mortgages. Among the various mortgage terms that can be acquired, the most prevalent ones are either thirty year or fifteen year mortgages. Both shorter and longer time frames can be had with fixed rate mortgages.

These days, even forty and fifty year mortgages are presently offered. They are especially utilized in places with housing prices that are exceptionally high, as thirty year mortgage terms do not prove to be affordable for the average income family in such scenarios.

In contrast to fixed rate mortgages are various other types. These include graduated payment mortgages, balloon payment mortgages, and interest only mortgages. These unusual other types of mortgages commonly get borrowers into trouble, which is why they are not nearly so popular as are the fixed rate mortgages.

Fixer-Upper

Fixer-Upper is a term that is commonly associated with real estate property, such as houses, that need some significant repair and renovation work. Although these kinds of houses might be lived in despite their present condition, they usually want redesign, reconstruction, or redecoration of some form. Depending on how much repair or renovation work they require, fixer-upper's can be major projects that require significant investments of time and money.

Fixer-Upper's commonly result from houses that have not been taken care of or properly maintained. Because of this, they tend to possess market values that are lower than comparable houses found in the same locale. Fixer-Upper's can be discovered in the majority of communities, even in neighborhoods whose housing prices are not depressed.

Fixer-Upper's commonly prove to be very popular with buyers who act as investors in houses. They want to acquire the property cheaply so that they can repair it and increase its likely real estate value in order to acquire a nice profit on the investment. These projects as investments have gained greatly in popularity as a result of various do it yourself types of renovation shows that are all about home improvement. Many times in downturns in the real estate market, such as the one that has been ongoing since 2007, the interest in fixer-upper's declines.

There is a danger with Fixer-upper's for many buyers who think to improve and then flip them, or resell the house for profits. This is simply that they do not realize how much time and money will be required of them in repairing the house in question. Making a house salable will require addressing not only relatively simple cosmetic issues, but also potentially structural or service problems. When the plumbing or foundation is in need of major repairs or replacing, the work involved commonly turns out to be very expensive and needs professional contractors.

This is why determining if a Fixer-upper is a viable and worthy investment requires some experience and work. First, you will have to determine for how much the typical house in the neighborhood is selling. It is also wise to know what makes the most desirable houses in the neighborhood so in demand and how much they cost. Real estate agents can be helpful in this respect.

If you decide to pursue buying a Fixer-upper, then you should be watching for the truly cosmetic Fixer-upper's. These only require more basic improvements such as wallpaper, paint, new appliances, some landscape work, and possibly new window and floor coverings. Houses that look run down and require substantial structural repairs can be very dangerous and should be avoided. Houses that are priced too reasonably usually have a reason for this. Intelligent buyers should learn why this is the case before they commit their money.

The best strategy is to find the house that is the least wanted in the best neighborhood possible. The house and estimated repair cost must both be within your budget. Once at full fair market value, such a property should pay you back handsomely.

Foreclosure

Foreclosures represent houses or commercial properties that have been seized by a bank or other mortgage lender. These properties are then sold to recoup mortgage loan losses after an owner and borrower has not made the payments as promised in the mortgage agreement.

Foreclosure is also the legal procedure in which the lender gets a court order for the termination of the mortgagor's right of redemption. This is the case since most lenders have security interests in the house from the borrower. The borrower will secure the mortgage using the house as the collateral.

Borrowers fall into home foreclosure for several reasons, most of which could not be predicted in advance. Owner might have been let go from their job or forced to take a job transfer to another state. They might have suffered from medical problems that prevented them from working. They might have gone through a divorce and split up assets. They could have been overwhelmed by too many bills. Whatever the reason, they are no longer able to make their promised monthly mortgage payments.

Foreclosures represent potential opportunities for investors. They may be purchased directly with a seller in advance of a bank completing foreclosure proceedings. Many investors who concentrate on foreclosures prefer to deal with the owners directly. They have to be aware of many laws pertaining to foreclosures, which are different in every state. For example, while in some states home owners can stay in their properties for a full year after defaulting on payments, while in others, they have fewer than four months in advance of the trustee sale.

Practically all states also allow a redemption period for the delinquent homeowner. This simply means that a seller possesses an irrevocable ability to catch up on back payments and interest in order to retain ownership of the house. The owner will likely be required to pay any foreclosure costs experienced by the bank up to that point.

Another means of purchasing a foreclosure home is to buy it at the Trustee's Sale. When this means is pursued, it is better to bid on a house that allows you to look it over in advance of putting up an offer. This is helpful so that you can determine how many repairs will be needed to make it salable and even possibly habitable. It is also worth knowing if the occupants are still living in the house and will have to be forcefully evicted. The process of going through an eviction can be both expensive and time consuming.

Many Trustee Sales will have certain rules in common that have to be followed for a foreclosure house to be purchased. They may demand sealed bids. They could require you to demonstrate your proof of financial qualifications. They might similarly insist on you putting up a significant earnest money deposit. Many of them will state that the property is being purchased in its present condition, or as is.

FOREX Markets

FOREX markets are the world wide foreign exchange markets. They are called FX markets as well. FOREX markets are different from all of the other major financial markets in that they are over the counter and decentralized. They exist for the purpose of trading currencies. Unlike with other markets, the FOREX markets are also open twenty-four hours a day during the week and on Sunday, since the different financial centers around the globe serve as trading bases for a variety of buyers and sellers. This foreign exchange market is the place where supply and demand mostly decides the different currencies' values for nations around the world.

The main point and reason for the FOREX markets are to help out investment and trade internationally through permitting businesses to easily change one currency to the other one that they require. In practice, individuals or businesses actually buy one amount of foreign currency through paying for it with a given amount of a different currency.

As an example, Canadian businesses may import British goods by paying for them in British Pounds, even though their income and base currency are Canadian dollars. The foreign exchange markets allow for investors to speculate on the rising and falling values of various currencies as well. It also makes the infamous carry trade possible, where investors are able to borrow currencies with low yields or interest rates and use them to purchase higher interest rate yielding currencies. Critics have said that the FOREX markets also hurt some countries' competitiveness against other countries.

This market is extremely popular and unique for a variety of reasons. It possesses the greatest trading volume on earth, managing in the three to four trillion dollar range every single trading day. This gives it enormous liquidity. It is also geographically centered all over the world, from Wellington in New Zealand to London in Great Britain to New York in the United States. Traders love that the market runs fully twenty-four hours per day except for on the weekends, when it reopens Sunday afternoon.

Finally, an enormous degree of leverage, that can be as much as two hundred to one, allows for even people with small accounts to make potentially enormous gains. Because of all of these factors and its world wide trading base, the FOREX markets have been called the ones where perfect competition is most evident. This is the case even though central banks sometimes intervene directly in these markets to increase or decrease the value of their currency relative to a trading partners' or trading competitors' currency value.

Fractional Banking System

The fractional banking system is also known as the fractional reserve banking system. This system is the way that virtually all modern day banks around the world operate. In a fractional reserve banking system, banks actually only maintain a small amount of their deposited funds in reserve forms of cash and other easily liquid assets. The rest of the deposits they loan out, even though all of their deposits are allowed to be withdrawn at the customers' demand. Fractional banking happens any time that banks loan out money that they bring in from deposits.

Fractional banking systems are ones where banks constantly expand the money supply beyond the levels at which they exist. Because of this, total money supplies are commonly a multiple bigger than simply the currency created by the nation's central bank. The multiple is also known as the money multiplier. Its amount is determined by a reserve requirement that the financial overseers set.

This fractional reserve system is managed ultimately by central banks and these reserve requirements that they enforce. On the one hand, it sets a limit on the quantity of money that is created by the commercial banks. The other purpose of it is to make certain that banks keep enough readily available cash in order to keep up with typical withdrawal demands of customers. Even though this is the case, there can be problems. Should many depositors at once attempt to take out their money, then a run on the bank might occur. If this happens on a large national or regional scale, the possibility of a banking systemic crisis emerges.

Central banks attempt to reduce these problems. They keep a close eye on commercial banks through regulations and oversight. Besides that, they promise to help out banks that fall into difficulties by acting as their ultimate lender of last resort. Finally, central banks instill confidence in the fractional reserve banking system by guaranteeing the deposits of the customers of the commercial banks.

A significant amount of criticism has been leveled against this fractional reserve banking system. Mainstream critics have complained that because money is only created as individuals borrow from the banking system, the system itself forces people to take on debt in order for money to actually be created. They say that this debases the currency. The biggest problem that they have with the commercial banking system growing the money supply is that it is literally creating money from nothing.

Other critics associate fractional banking with fiat currencies, or money that is only valuable because the governments say that they are. They decry these as negative aspects of current money systems. They dislike that fractional banking systems and fiat money together do not place any limits on how much a money supply can ultimately grow. This can lead to bubbles in both capital markets and assets, such as real estate, stock markets, and commodities. All of these can be victims of speculation, which is made easier by the creation of money through debt in the fractional reserve system.

Futures

Futures prove to be financial derivatives that are also called forward contracts. Such a futures contract gives a seller the obligation to deliver an asset, such as a commodity, to the buyer at a pre set date. These contracts are heavily traded on major produced commodities like wheat, gold, oil, coffee, and sugar. They also exist for underlying financial instruments that include government bonds, stock market indexes, and foreign currencies.

The history of futures goes back to Ancient Greece where the first recorded example is detailed about an olive press arrangement that philosopher Thales entered into. Futures contracts become commonplace at trade fairs throughout Europe by the 1100's. Merchants did not feel secure traveling with significant amounts of goods, so they would only bring display samples along and then sell merchandise that they would deliver in greater quantities at future dates.

Futures contracts created an enormous bubble in the 1600's with the Dutch Tulip Mania that caused tulip bulbs to skyrocket to unthinkable levels. In this speculative bubble, the majority of money that was exchanged turned out to be for tulip futures and not the tulips themselves. The first futures exchange in the United States opened in 1868 as the Chicago Board of Trade, where copper, pork bellies, and wheat were traded in futures contracts.

In the early years of the 1970's, futures trading grew explosively in volume. Pricing models created by Myron Scholes and Fischer Black permitted the quick pricing of futures and options on them. Investors could easily speculate on commodities prices through these futures. As the demand for the futures skyrocketed, additional significant futures exchanges opened and expanded around the world, especially in Chicago, London, and New York.

Futures trading could not happen effectively without the exchanges. Futures contracts are spelled out in terms of the asset that underlies them, the date of delivery, the last day of contract trading, transaction currency, and size of ticks or minimum permissible price changes. Exchanges have developed into major and predictable markets through their standardizing of all of these various factors for many different kinds of futures contracts.

Trading futures contracts involves major leverage. This means that they carry tremendous opportunities as well as risks. Futures, with their ability to control enormous quantities of commodities and financials, have been the root causes for many collapses. Enron and Barings Bank were both brought down by financial futures. Perhaps the most famous futures meltdown involved the Long Term Capital Management group.

Even though this company had the inventors of the futures pricing models Scholes and Black working for them, the company lost money in the futures markets so quickly that the Federal Reserve Bank had to become involved and bail out the company to stop the whole financial system of the Untied States from collapsing.

GDP

GDP is the acronym for Gross Domestic Product. GDP stands for the entire value in dollars of all goods and services that have actually been produced within the nation in a particular period of time, commonly a year. A simpler way of putting GDP is how large the economy proves to be. The Gross Domestic Product turns out to be among the most closely watched and important measurements for how healthy the economy is. GDP is commonly given out as a comparison against a prior year or quarter. When the financial news reports that the Gross Domestic Product has increased by three percent year on year, it is referring to the economy having expanded by three percent during the last year.

Coming up with the actual measurement of Gross Domestic Product is complex. In simplest terms, it is figured up in one of two methods. The income approach works by totaling up the earnings of all individuals in the country over a year. The expenditure approach simply tallies up the money that everyone in the nation spends over the year. It stands to reason that through both means you should come to approximately a similar total.

With the income approach, economists take all of the employees' compensation in the nation. They add this to all of the profits that both non incorporated, as well as incorporated, companies have made throughout the country. Finally they add on all taxes paid minus subsidies given. This is known as the GDP(I) method of calculation. The expenditure based means proves to be the more typically utilized method. To figure up GDP this way, all government spending, net exports, consumption, and investment in the country have to be tallied up together.

You can not overstate the importance of GDP to an economy's growth and production. Almost every person within the nation is massively impacted by gross domestic product. If an economy is in good shape, then wages will rise and unemployment will prove to be low as businesses require greater quantities of labor in order to produce to keep up with the expanding economy. Major changes to Gross Domestic Product, revised to the downside or upside , have significant repercussions for the stock markets. The reasons for this are simple to grasp.

Economies that are contracting translate to smaller amounts of profits for corporations. This leads to lower prices for stocks. Investors also become nervous about decreasing growth in GDP, since it commonly means that the nation's economy is falling into recession or is already in a recession. Conversely, economies that are expanding signify that corporations' profits in general will be higher. Investors bid stock prices up on this news as they become increasingly confident in the future economic prospects. Because of these effects of Gross Domestic Product on peoples' lives, it could be said to be the most significant economic measurement for all of the people in the country in general.

Gold Roth IRA

Gold Roth IRA's are IRA's that are allowed to contain gold and other precious metals. Gold Roth IRA's make sense for many investors. This is because gold and other precious metals like silver and platinum have been considered to be the greatest form of long term storage for cash and valuables throughout history. This means that gold in particular could be considered to be the best asset for retirement. Although there are many other types of instruments used for retirement accounts and planning, including bonds, stocks, savings, and annuities, gold is the only one whose final value does not rest on an institution or individual's performance or success. This makes physical gold an ideal means for saving for retirement.

Gold Roth IRA's are specially created either through initially funding one or by rolling over a Roth IRA or traditional IRA to a gold backed Roth IRA. Rolling over an existing employee held 401K to a Gold Roth IRA can be difficult if the employee has not left the company. This is because employees are not usually allowed to do rollovers until they separate from their company.

IRA's that already exist can be transferred to Gold Roth IRA's. They can be moved from credit unions, banks, or stock broker firms to a trust company that is allowed to hold your Gold IRA holdings. In this type of transfer, you could choose to move securities held in the account along with cash, or cash by itself.

Gold Roth IRA's must be created by sending in cash to the administrator of the IRA. They will then purchase the gold, silver, or platinum physical holdings as you instruct them. The gold must then be kept by a gold IRA custodian on your behalf. These depositories provide safe places for the gold, as well as easy access to buy or sell it. The gold kept in a Gold Roth IRA may not be sent to your house or assumed in your personal possession. Instead, it has to be liquidated before the funds from it can be accessed. Gold that is requested as a distribution will be penalized at your personal tax rate plus a ten percent penalty.

Only certain forms of gold and precious metals are allowed to be purchased and held within a Gold Roth IRA. Gold bars have to demonstrate a twenty-four karat purity to be eligible. They can be one ounce, ten ounces, a kilogram, one hundred ounces, or four hundred ounces in size. Gold coins that are permitted are twenty-four karat bullion coins from the United States, Canada, Austria, and Australia. The most heavily minted gold coins of all time, the South Africa Krugerrand's, are not permitted, as they are only twenty-two karats.

Silver bars and coins that have .999 or higher purity are permitted to be held in a Gold Roth IRA account. This allows the Canadian Silver Maple Leaf, the U.S. Silver Eagle, and the Mexican Silver Libertad one ounce bullion coins. Silver bars that are one hundred ounces and one thousand ounces are also permitted.

Gold Standard

The gold standard represents a centuries' used system of money for backing up currencies with tangible, physical gold holdings in a central bank vault. Under the gold standard, the basic economic currency unit proved to be a pre set amount of gold by weight. Several different types of gold standards exist.

The Gold specie standard proves to be a system where the money unit itself is represented by gold coins that are in circulation. Alternatively, it could be represented by an exchange unit of value that is literally expressed in units against a specific gold coin that circulates, along with other coins that are minted from a metal with less value, such as silver or copper.

Conversely, the gold exchange standard usually has to do with silver and other valuable metal coins that are circulating. In this type of exchange system, the monetary authorities promise that a set exchange rate against the currency of another country practicing the gold standard will be maintained. This gives rise to a gold standard that is not literal but still de facto. The silver coins circulating then trade with a set external value in gold terms that stands independently of the actual silver value contained within the coins.

The most common gold standard that has been seen in the last few hundred years turns out to be the gold bullion standard. The gold bullion standard refers to a money system where no gold coins are actually circulating throughout the economy. Instead, the monetary authorities have consented to exchange a set amount of gold in exchange for their paper currency. This is done at a set price that is established for the paper currency that circulates.

The gold bullion standard existed in the world economy from the 1700's until 1971. During this span of almost three hundred years, the values of major world currencies proved to be exceptionally stable, as were the supplies of money in existence. This resulted from a restriction of the gold standard that only allowed such paper currency to be printed as greater amounts of gold existed in the respective nation's treasury and vaults. The positive of this proved to be that the world could count on currencies that did not fluctuate wildly in value or decline consistently over time. Governments disliked the gold standard as it kept them from increasing the money supply or spending more money than the country actually had. They found it too restrictive.

The gold standard in the world collapsed when President Nixon initiated what became known as the Nixon shock by unilaterally taking the country off of gold exchange and convertibility for dollars in 1971. The currency of both the U.S. and most countries of the world then became Fiat currencies, only backed up by the government decree. Since the gold standard was abandoned, the U.S. dollar has declined so severely that a single dollar in 1971 would today be worth $35 2010 dollars.

Good Debt

Good debt is debt that benefits a person or business to carry. Such good debts demonstrate both the creditworthiness and the responsibility of a borrower. They also create a good base to build on in the future. There are many examples of good debt, which stands in contrast to bad debt.

Good debts are typically those debts that are taken on to acquire an item or investment that only grows in value with time. Examples of this include things like real estate loans, schooling loans, home mortgages, business debt, and passive income investments. Each of these items could provide a significant and real advantage with time. Real estate could increase in value and be resold for profits.

Higher education commonly leads to greater amounts of earnings. Loans on homes are commonly wonderful for building credit and provide properties that serve as excellent collateral. Loans for businesses may result in profits earned from trade and sales. It is important to note that cars and other items are not included in these lists. This is simply because they lose value the moment that they are purchased and driven away.

Bad debts in contrast are those that result in higher interest rates and considerable deprecation of the items purchased with time. Goods that are for short time frame use and bought on credit are commonly considered to be bad debts. Since the item's life span will only decline with time, and the interest rates are typically high, no benefit is derived from purchasing these things with debt. A great number of such purchases rapidly decline in value, even after one use.

A significant benefit to good debts lies in the increase in cash flow that they commonly create. Properly structured good debts lead to tax advantages, to the ability to invest in still more assets that can produce cash, and to higher credit scores as well. Good debts that are paid on time furthermore build up a good financial base for the future. Good debts create cash flow, which stands in contrast to bad debts that do not.

Investments that produce passive income are among the best good debts. For example, purchasing an apartment building using debt will result in both income revenue and substantial tax deductions. This proves to be good debt, since although you are borrowing money, you are receiving passive income and gaining the ability to depreciate assets that can actually appreciate with time. On top of this, you are allowed to live there while you accrue all of these other benefits.

When considering a good debt, you should make certain that the income that the investment will provide is high enough to make the investment and the accompanying debt worth while. A number of experts offer advice on this. They suggest that not tying up in excess of twenty percent of your overall value in debt is a better practice. Higher debt levels than this can sound off warning bells with banks and other lenders.

Great Depression

The Great Depression represented the most serious economic contraction that affected the world in the twentieth century. It occurred the decade before the Second World War broke out, in the 1930's. The Great Depression began and ended in differing years in the various countries and economies of the world. In general it started around 1929 and held countries in its grip through the end of the 1930's and the early years of the 1940's.

The Great Depression turned out to be the deepest, hardest, longest, and most geographically encompassing depression that the world had seen. Nowadays, the Great Depression is still held up as the model for how badly the economy of the world can collapse. In the eighty years since the great depression began, economists have not named another economic contraction in the world or the United States as a depression.

The Great Depression began in the United States. It commenced with the stock market crash that began on September 4, 1929. The far steeper stock market decline of October 29, 1929 became known as Black Tuesday and eclipsed the worldwide newspaper headlines. This rapidly spread from the U.S. to nearly all countries around the globe.

Practically all nations of the world, whether rich or poor, felt the tragic and crushing impacts of the Great Depression. International trade plummeted by as much as one half to two thirds of its previous level. Along with this, profits, personal incomes, tax revenues, and prices plunged. In the United States, unemployment soared to twenty-five percent, but in other countries, this level reached even thirty-three percent.

Cities all over the globe suffered especially, particularly those that relied on heavy industry as their economic mainstay. In a great number of nations, construction came practically to a stop. Even farming suffered terribly with the prices of produce crashing by around sixty percent. The areas that depended on industries in the primary sector took the worst hit, including logging, mining, and cash cropping. Job losses in these industries turned out to be among the worst.

A few nations' economies began recovering in the middle of the 1930's. For most countries around the world, the terrible consequences of the Great Depression remained until the outbreak of the Second World War. The military output required by the conflict rapidly increased production and employment everywhere.

Numerous events and problems caused the Great Depression's original economic collapse of 1929. Structural weaknesses were present, only waiting for particular events to turn the crash into a worldwide depression. It is particularly interesting how the contraction ran from one country to the next like a wildfire in a forest. Regarding the structural weaknesses of the 1929 economic contraction, historians are quick to point out that enormous and widespread bank failures only became worse as the stock market crashed. Others hold up specific monetary policy like the Federal Reserve in the United States contracting America's money supply, and the British Empire choosing to go back to the pre-World War I parity of the Gold Standard with one pound equal to $4.86.

Great Recession

The Great Recession proved to be the worst American and world wide economic downturn since the 1930's era Great Depression. It began within the U.S. in December of 2007 and is said to have ended in June of 2009 officially. There is ongoing debate with some economists as to whether the full effects of the Great Recession have really ceased, or this is merely a lull in between bouts of a greater depression.

The Great Recession started in the U.S. but later spread to most industrialized countries around the globe. This world wide recession led to a severe drop in trade and a significant drop in economic activity. The financial crisis of 2007-2010 actually kicked off the Great Recession.

The financial crisis and resulting Great Recession ultimately stemmed from irresponsible lending policies practiced by banks on a widespread level and encouraged by the U.S. and British governments. Along with this, the increasingly common practice of securitizing real estate and mortgages led to the financial collapse. Mortgage backed securities from the United States were promoted and sold around the globe. They turned out to be far more speculative and risky than anyone had predicted or disclosed.

Besides this, a worldwide boom in credit encouraged a speculative asset bubble in stocks and real estate. As prices continued to rise, the risky lending only grew more prevalent. The crisis actually flared up as a result of severe losses on sub prime loans that started in 2007. These demonstrated that other loans were also at risk amid too high real estate prices. As the loan losses continued to rise, Lehman Brothers suddenly collapsed on September 15th of 2008.

An enormous panic ensued in the inter-banking loan markets. With stock and real estate prices sharply declining, historical and major commercial and investment banking institutions throughout both the U.S. and Europe showed how much they had over extended themselves with major leverage as their losses quickly mounted. The governments of their home countries had to step in with enormous amounts of public tax dollars in order to save many of them from imminent bankruptcy.

This resulting Great Recession has led to a substantial decline in international trade, dropping commodity prices, and high and mounting unemployment around the world. Although the National Bureau of Economic Research declared the Great Recession officially over at the end of 2009, other economic experts are not convinced. Nobel prize winning economist Paul Krugman has said that this Great Recession heralds the start of a second Great Depression. Others who are less pessimistic have claimed that true recovery in the United States will not emerge until the end of 2011.

A number of events have been blamed for causing the financial crisis and Great Recession. The environment that preceded the crisis included an unnatural rise in asset prices along with an accompanying boom in worldwide economic demand. These are believed to have resulted from

the multi-year period of too easily available credit, insufficient regulation, and poor oversight from the regulatory bodies who all too often
simply looked the other way when times were good.

Gross Income

Gross income can be several different things in the United States. In tax
law for business, gross income signifies all proceeds realized from
every source minus the cost of goods that have been sold. Gross income
is also used for individuals and pertains to all income earned from any
and every kind of source. As such, gross income is not simply cash that
has been realized, but it can also be income received in kind, as property, or as services. For a taxpayer, gross income is commonly believed to
be all of the monies and values received. Although most income is tallied into this figure, a few kinds of income are excluded deliberately.

For companies, individuals, trusts, estates, and others, gross income is
necessary for figuring up the mandatory income taxes within the United
States. Taxes are figured up using a taxable income number that starts
with gross income and then subtracts permissible tax deductions. Taxes
are then calculated based on the resulting taxable income.

Many different types of income are considered to be a part of the gross
income category. Wages are the earnings for work performed payable
as tips, salaries, and related income. Income made as a result of such
personal service is always tallied up in a person's gross income. Gross
profits made from selling an inventory of products are also considered
gross income. Gross profits result from sales prices of items minus the
cost of the goods actually sold.

All interest received is also considered to be a part of gross income.
Dividends, along with distributions of capital gains from companies or
mutual funds are similarly a part of gross income. Gains on property
that has been disposed of are also tallied into the gross income total
after the extra proceeds beyond the adjusted cost in the property is determined. Also included are royalties and rents from intangible and
tangible items.

A number of other non traditional types of income are also considered
to be a part of gross income. Pensions, income from life insurance, and
annuities income are counted. So are alimony, child support, and other
maintenance payments. Shares of partnership income that are dis-

tributed fall under this category. Even the proceeds from national and state tax refunds are considered to be gross income.

The Internal Revenue Service claims that such gross income includes all forms of income from any source of which they are derived. As such, gross income can result from any gains having to do with labor, capital, the two together, or profits having to do with the sale of anything or a capital asset. A notable exception to gross income includes gifts and inheritances. While these could be taxed under the category of estate taxes or gift taxes, they are not deemed by the IRS to be a part of gross income.

Hedge Account

A hedge account is an account established with a hedge fund. There are several reasons why a person or business would be interested in setting up a hedge account. These mostly center on the desire for investments that commonly produce higher profits or the wish to hedge, or protect, a business' operations from certain unpredictable and undesirable swings in market prices. Businesses can open up their own hedge accounts in various futures and commodities markets to protect themselves from these business impacting price movements in important related commodities.

A person who is interested in opening a hedge account will have to make application to a hedge fund. Hedge funds are typically restrictive in the types of funds that they will accept from an investor. The investor will have to prove certain income levels or asset base holdings that demonstrate that they are capable of bearing the substantial losses that could result from trades in a hedge account. They must also have liquid cash that they can tie up for long periods of time, since most hedge funds do not allow immediate on demand withdrawals.

Funds that are invested with them could be tied up for a year or longer, and minimum waiting periods apply. Because of all of these reasons, hedge funds are typically looking for people as investors who have in excess of a million dollars of liquid net worth.

Hedge accounts can also be accounts that businesses use to offset the changes in commodities' prices. A company's products may be heavily dependent on prices such as sugar and cocoa if they are a chocolate company, oil and other energy prices if they use energy intensive processes or are shipping companies, or even industrial metals such as copper if they produce wires or cables. Gold and silver mining companies, along with oil producers, routinely hedge their quantities of precious metals and energies that they expect to produce to protect against anticipated declining prices. By locking in the present price for these goods and commodities that they require or will produce later on in the year, they can insulate themselves from price swings that move against them.

This can mean the difference between having to raise prices and risk losing market share or selling goods at a much lower profit margin. Because of this, many major multinational companies around the world routinely protect themselves and their operations through the use of hedge accounts. Some of them even have individuals or departments that oversee these operations.

For a business to set up such a hedge account is not difficult. They only have to open a commodities account with one of the major commodities exchanges, such as the Chicago Mercantile Exchange, the Chicago Board of Trade, New York Mercantile Exchange, or the New York Board of Trade. These accounts can be used by companies for speculating on the price movements of underlying commodities as well, and not only for hedging their operations. In this case, care has to be taken, as the leverage provided by hedge accounts, such as commodities accounts, is enough to bring down a company overnight if they are irresponsible with the trades in the account.

Hedge Funds

Hedge funds are investment funds which are commonly only open to a specific group of investors. These investors pay a large performance fee each year, commonly a certain percent of their funds under management, to the manager of the hedge fund. Hedge funds are very minimally regulated and are therefore are able to participate in a wide array of investments and investment strategies.

Literally every single hedge fund pursues its own strategy of investing that will establish the kinds of investments that it seeks. Hedge funds commonly go for a wide range of investments in which they may buy or sell short shares and positions. Stocks, commodities, and bonds are some of these asset classes with which they work. As you would anticipate from the name, hedge funds typically try to offset some of the risks in their portfolios by employing a number of risk hedging strategies. These mostly revolve around the use of derivatives, or financial instruments with values that depend on anticipated price movements in the future of an asset to which they are linked, as well as short selling investments.

Most countries only allow certain types of wealthy and professional investors to open a hedge fund account. Regulators may not heavily oversee the activities of hedge funds, but they do govern who is allowed to participate. As a result, traditional investment funds' rules and regulations mostly do not apply to hedge funds.

Actual net asset values of hedge funds often tally into the many billions of dollars. The funds' gross assets held commonly prove to be massively higher as a result of their using leverage on their money invested. In particular niche markets like distressed debt, high yield ratings, and derivatives trading, hedge funds are the dominant players.

Investors get involved in hedge funds in search of higher than normal market returns. When times are good, many hedge funds yield even twenty percent annual investment returns. The nature of their hedging strategies is supposed to protect them from terrible losses, such as were seen in the financial crisis from 2007-2010.

The hedge fund industry is opaque and difficult to measure accurately. This is partially as a result of the significant expansion of the industry, as well as an inconsistent definition of what makes a hedge fund. Prior to the peak of hedge funds in the summer of 2008, it is believed that hedge funds might have overseen as much as two and a half trillion dollars. The credit crunch hit many hedge funds particularly hard, and their assets under management have declined sharply as a result of both losses, as well as requests for withdrawals by investors. In 2010, it is believed that hedge funds once again represent in excess of two trillion dollars in assets under management.

The largest hedge funds in the world are JP Morgan Chase, with over $53 billion under management; Bridgewater Associates, having more than $43 billion in assets under management; Paulson and Company, with more than $32 billion in assets; Brevan Howard that has greater than $27 billion in assets; and Soros Fund Management, which boasts around $27 billion in assets under management.

Hedging

In the world of finance, hedging is the act of putting together a hedge. Hedging involves building up a position in one market whose goal is try to counteract risk from changes in price in another market's position that is the opposite. The ultimate goal is to diminish or eliminate the business or person's possibilities of risk that they wish to avoid. A number of specific vehicles exist to help with hedging. These typically include forward contracts, swaps, insurance policies, options, derivatives, and products sold over the counter. Futures contracts prove to be the most popular version of hedging instruments.

In the 1800's, futures markets open to the public came into existence. These were set up to permit a standardized form of effective, viable, and open hedging of commodity prices in agriculture. In the intervening century, these have grown to include all manners of futures contracts that allow individuals and businesses to hedge precious metals, energy, changes in interest rates, and movements in foreign currencies.

There are countless examples of individuals who might be interested in hedging. Commercial farmers are common types of people who practice hedging. Prices for agricultural crops like wheat change all the time as the demand and supply for them fluctuates. Sometimes these price changes are significant in one direction or the other. With the present prices and crop predictions at harvest time, a commercial farmer might determine that planting wheat for the season is smart.

The problem that he encounters is that these predicted prices are simply forecasts. After the farmer plants his wheat crop, he has tied himself to it for the whole growing season. Should the real price of wheat soar in between the time that the farmer plants and harvests his crop then he might make a great amount of money that he did not count on, yet should the real price decline by the time the harvest is in then the farmer might be ruined completely.

To remove the risk from his wheat crop equation, the farmer can set up a hedge. He does this hedging by selling a certain quantity of futures contracts for wheat. These should be sold at an amount equal to the wheat crop size that he expects when he plants it. In such a way, the commercial farmer fixes his price of wheat at planting time. His hedging contract proves to be a pledge to furnish a particular quantity of wheat bushels to a certain place on a fixed date in time at a guaranteed price. Now the farmer is hedged against changes in the prices of wheat. He does not have to worry anymore about the wheat prices and whether they are falling or rising, since he has been promised a fixed price in his hedging wheat futures contract. The possibility of him being totally ruined by falling wheat prices is completely removed from the realm of possibility. At the same time, he has lost the opportunity of realizing extra money as a result of rising wheat prices when harvest time arrives. These are the upsides and the downsides to hedging; both the positives and the negatives of uncertainty are eliminated.

Hyperinflation

In the field of economics, hyperinflation proves to be inflation, or rising prices over time, that is extremely high and even beyond controlling. This state of the economy exists as the overall levels of pricing in a certain country are rising sharply and quickly at the same time as the actual values of these economic goods remain roughly the same price as measured in other more stable currencies. In other words, the nation's own currency is diminishing in value rapidly, commonly at rate that grows in pace.

The IASB, or International Accounting Standards Board, gives a precise definition of hyperinflation. They state that when the rate of inflation during three cumulative years nears one hundred percent total, or at least twenty-six percent each year compounded annually for three consecutive years, then hyperinflation has been reached. Other economists such as Cagan have declared hyperinflation to be when inflation is greater than fifty percent each month. Hyperinflation can witness the overall price levels go up by five to ten percent and higher even in single days for extended periods of time. This stands in sharp contrast to regular inflation which is commonly only reported over a quarterly or annual basis.

As greater and greater amounts of inflation are created in each printing of money instance, a truly vicious cycle takes effect. Such hyperinflation is clearly evident as the money supply grows at an uninterrupted rate. It is typically seen alongside the population's unwillingness to keep the hyper-inflationary currency for any longer than they have to in order to use it for any hard good that will prevent them from losing more actual purchasing power. Hyperinflation is typically a part of wars and their after effects, social or political upheavals, and currency meltdowns such as seen in Zimbabwe.

Hyperinflation is a phenomenon that is unique to fiat currencies that are not backed up by anything but a government's faith and trust. As the money supply is not limited by normal restraints like gold in a vault, it

is instead run by a paper money standard. The supply of it is completely dependent on the discretion of the government.

Hyperinflation commonly leads to intense and long lasting economic
depressions. This is not always the case though. In Brazil which suffered in the grips of hyperinflation for thirty years in the 1964 to 1994
period, the government managed to avoid economic collapse by valuing all non-monetary goods, services, and investments for the whole
economy in an involved index. The government supplied this daily
updated index that they measured with the daily Brazilian currency
against the United States dollar.

In contrast to Brazil, Zimbabwe did not bother to set up such an index
measured against the dollar. They did offer the day by day changes in
the U.S. dollar as a comparison for everyone in the country to see. This
voluntary comparison only served to worsen the problem and finally
destroyed the real value of non monetary items that did not get updated
as expressed against the Zimbabwe dollar. All monetary items in the
country finally lost every bit of value during the hyper-inflationary
meltdown.

Import

In simple terms, imports are goods that are utilized in one country that
were produced in another country. The term import refers to the idea of
bringing goods and services into a nation. It originally came from the
concept of bringing these things into a port via ships. A person who is
engaged in the practice of bringing these goods and services into the
other country is called an importer. Importers live and are based in the
country into which they bring these goods and services.

Export is the opposite of import. It refers to sending the goods made in
one country abroad to the importing country. Exporters are based overseas from the importer and importing country.

Imports are then any items, such as commodities or goods, or alternatively services that are brought to a country from a different country in
legitimate means. They are commonly used for trade purposes. Such
goods are then put on sale to people in the importing country. Foreign
manufacturers make such goods and services that are then offered to
the domestic consumers of the importing country. Imports for the country receiving them are the exports of a country that sends them.

International trade is actually based on such imports and exports. Importing any goods commonly means dealing with customs agencies in both exporting and importing nations. Imports can be subjected to trade agreements, tariffs, or quotas much of the time.

Imports can refer to more than simply services or goods that have been brought into the country. They can also be the resulting measured economic worth of any goods and services that are being imported. Such imports' values are measured over periods of time, such as monthly, quarterly, or yearly. The abbreviation of I represents the value of such imports in macroeconomics.

From an economic strength point of view, imports are considered to be somewhat negative. Exports are nearly always regarded as positive, since they represent produced items that are being sold to others for currency consideration. When a nation's imports are greater than their exports, this leads to a trade imbalance, or trade deficit. Such trade imbalances must be paid for with something eventually. Much of the time it ends up being debt instruments that are exported back to the countries from which the imports come. Countries like the United States and Great Britain are guilty of having significantly greater values of imports than exports. They commonly run large trade deficits.

Index Funds

Index funds are typically exchange traded funds or mutual funds. Their goal is to reproduce the actual movements of an underlying index for a particular financial market. They do this no matter what is happening in the overall stock markets.

There are several means of tracking such an index. One way of doing this is by purchasing and holding all of the index securities to the same proportion as they are represented in the index. Another way of accomplishing this is by doing a statistical sample of the market and then acquiring securities that are representative of it. A great number of the index funds are based on a computer model that accepts little to no input from people in its decision making of the securities bought and sold. This qualifies as a type of passive management when the index fund is run this way.

These index funds do not have active management. This allows them to benefit from possessing lesser fees and taxes in their accounts that are taxable. The low fees that are charged do come off of the investment returns that are otherwise mostly matching those of the index. Besides this, exactly matching an index is not possible since the sampling and mirroring models of this index will never be one hundred percent right. Such variances between an index performance and that of the fund are referred to as the tracking error, or more conversationally as a jitter.

A wide variety of index funds exist for you to choose from these days. They are offered by a number of different investment managers as well. Among the more typically seen indices are the FTSE 100, the S&P 500, and the Nikkei 225. Other indexes have been created that are so called research indexes for creating asset pricing models. Kenneth French and Eugene Fama created one known as the Three Factor Model. This Fama-French three factor model is actually utilized by Dimensional Fund Advisers to come up with their various index funds. Other, newer indexes have been created that are known as fundamentally based indexes. These find their basis in factors like earnings, dividends, sales, and book values of companies.

The underlying concept for developing index funds comes from the EMH, or efficient market hypothesis. This hypothesis claims that because stock analysts and fund managers are always searching for stocks that will do better than the whole market, this efficient competition among them translates to current information on a company's affairs being swiftly factored into the price of the stock. Because of this, it is generally accepted that knowing which stocks will do better than the over all market in advance is exceedingly hard. Developing a market index then makes sense as the inefficiencies and risks inherent in picking out individual stocks can be simply eliminated through purchasing the index fund itself.

Inflation

Inflation proves to be prices rising over time. It is specifically measured as the increase in a given basket of goods and services' prices. These goods and services are taken to represent the entire economy. Inflation is also the going up in cost of the average prices of goods and services as measured by the CPI, or consumer price index. The opposite of inflation is known as deflation. Deflation turns out to be the falling of an average level of prices. The point that separates the two from each other, both deflation and inflation, is price stability, or no change in the costs of goods and services.

Inflation has almost everything to do with the amount of money available. It is inextricably tied to the money supply. This gives rise to the popularly remarked observation that inflation is actually an excessive number of dollars chasing too small a quantity of goods. Comprehending the way that this works is easier when considering an example.

Pretend for a moment that the world possessed only two commodities: oranges that are gathered up from orange trees and paper money created by government. In seasons where rain is limited and the oranges are few as a result, the cost of oranges should go up. This is because the same number of printed dollars would be competing for a smaller number of oranges.

On the other hand, if a bumper crop of oranges are seen, then the cost of oranges should drop, since the sellers of oranges have no choice but to cut prices to sell off their large inventory of oranges. These two examples illustrate inflation in the former and deflation in the latter. The main difference between the real world and this example is that inflation measures changes in the price movement on average of many or all goods and services, and not simply one.

The quantity of money in an economy similarly impacts the amount of inflation present at any given time. Should the government in the example above choose to print enormous amounts of money, then there will be many dollars for a relatively constant number of oranges, as in the lack of rain scenario. So inflation is created by the number of dollars going up against the quantities of oranges that exist, or overall goods and services existing. Deflation, as the opposite of inflation, would be the numbers of dollars dropping compared to the quantity of oranges available.

Because of this, levels of inflation result from four different factors that often work together in combination. The demand for money could drop. The supply of money could expand. The available supply of various other goods might decline. Finally, the demand for other goods increases.

Even though these four factors do work in correlation, economists say that inflation is mostly a currency driven event. This means that in the vast majority of cases, it results from governments tampering with the money supply. Generally, they do this by over printing their own currency to have money to pay for spending, resulting in higher inflation.

Intellectual Property

Intellectual property, also known by its acronym of IP, is the concept having to do with creations from a person's mind. The ownerships of such property are recognized as rights that can be possessed, bought, and sold. As such, they have also given rise to relevant fields of law. As a result of this intellectual property rights and law, creators and owners of many intangible assets obtain exclusive rights to them. This includes literary, musical, and art works; inventions and discoveries; and also phrases, designs, symbols, and words. The most prevalent forms of intellectual property are then trademarks, copyrights, trade secrets, patents, and industrial design rights.

Intellectual property rights go back to the 1600 and 1700's in early modern Great Britain. The Statute of Monopolies from 1623 is viewed as the origin of patent law, while the Statute of Anne from 1710 is looked at as the basis for copyright laws. The phrase intellectual property arose in the 1800's. It finally became common in the U.S. in the late 1900's.

Intellectual property rights are believed to create economic growth and a flourishing free enterprise system. This is because such rights of exclusivity permit the creators and owners of these intellectual properties to realize financial benefit from their creation. It gives individuals and businesses motive to develop and invest in intellectual property. With patents, such businesses are willing to come out of pocket for the development and research costs because of this incentive.

Because of this, the creation and maintenance of these intellectual property laws are given the credit for major contributions made to great economic growth in the Western World like the United States and Great Britain. Many economists point out that around two thirds of big businesses' value lies in intangible assets. It is also said that industries that use intellectual property intensively create as much as seventy-two percent more added value for every employee than do those industries that do not use intellectual property intensively. This is to say that a great deal of economic growth is generated by intellectual property rights and associated industries.

Critics of intellectual property rights do exist. Those in the free culture movement hold up intellectual monopolies as examples of things that hold back progress, damage health, and concentrate ownership to the disadvantage of the common people. They argue that the public good is hurt by monopolies that constantly grow out of software patents, extensions of copyrights, and business method patents.

Besides this, some claim that intellectual property rights that are strictly enforced slow down the transfer of technological advances and scientific break through to poor countries. Still, developing nations are beneficiaries of developed nation technologies like vaccines, the Internet, mobile phones, and higher yielding crops. Critics claim that patent laws come down too hard in favor of the people who develop innovations versus those who employ them.

Interest Rate

Interest rates are the levels at which interest is charged a borrower for using money that they obtain in the form of a loan from a bank or other lender. These are also the rates that individuals and businesses are paid for depositing their funds with a bank. Interest rates are central to the running of capitalist economies. They are commonly written out as percentage rates for a given time frame, most commonly per year.

As an example, a small business might require capital to purchase new assets for the company. To acquire these, they borrow money form a bank. In exchange for making them this loan, the bank is paid interest at a pre set and agreed upon rate of interest for lending it to the company and putting off their own use of the monies. They receive this interest in monthly payments along with repayments of the principal.

Interest rates are also used by government agencies in pursuing monetary policies. Central banks set them to influence their nation's economic performance. They impact many elements of an economy such as unemployment, inflation, and investment levels.

There are several different interest rates to consider. The most commonly expressed one is the nominal interest rate. This nominal interest rate proves to be the amount of interest that is payable in money terms. If a family deposits $1,000 in a bank for a year, and is paid $50 in interest, then their balance by the conclusion of the year will be $1,050. This would translate to a nominal interest rate amounting to five percent per year.

The real interest rate is another type of rate used to determine how much purchasing power is received. It is the interest rate after the level of inflation is subtracted. Determining the real interest rate is a matter of calculating the nominal rate and removing the amount of inflation from it. In the example above, supposed the economy's inflation level is measured at five percent for the year. This would mean that the $1,050 in the account at year end only buys what it did as $1,000 at the beginning of the year. This translates to a real interest rate of zero.

Interest rates change for many reasons. They are altered for political gains of parties in power. By reducing the interest rate, an economy gains a short term boost. The help to the economy will often influence the outcome of elections. Unfortunately, the short term advantage gained is often offset later by inflation. This reason for changing interest rates is eliminated with independent central banks.

Another main reason that interest rates change is because of expectations of inflation. Since the majority of economies demonstrate inflation, fixed amounts of money will purchase fewer goods a year from now than they will today. Lenders expect to be compensated for this. Central banks raise interest rates to fight this inflation as necessary.

International Monetary Unit

International Monetary Unit can refer to two different things. It could be the U.S. dollar, which is the world's primary reserve currency. The International Monetary Unit is also the Special Drawing Rights, which are the currency units that the International Monetary Fund issues.

Special drawing rights are not an actual unique currency per se. They are units that are made up of a special basket of currencies. These days, these are comprised of U.S. Dollars, British Pounds, Japanese Yen, and Euros. The Special Drawing Rights, also known as SDR's, can be said to be International Monetary Units since they prove to be reserve assets for international foreign exchange. The International Monetary Fund actually allocates them to different countries. These SDR's offer the ability to get foreign currencies when a country needs hard cash for emergencies and other financial crises.

Although they are still expressed in units against U.S. dollars, the Special Drawing Rights remain the International Monetary Fund's only unit of account. They have their own currency code, XDR. They may be only little used now for an International Monetary Unit, but their utilization is growing, particularly at the insistence of Russia, China, and the United Nations.

Since the end of the Second World War, the U.S. dollar has proven to be the world's main reserve asset for foreign exchange. This makes it a primary candidate for the world's International Monetary Unit. As over sixty percent of central bank reserves are still held in dollars, it is unarguably the world's reserve currency even though many nations would like to see this changed and its share of reserves has been dropping consistently for some time now. Countries ranging from China and Russia, to Iran and Venezuela, to France have all called for a new International Monetary Unit to be established, particularly in the wake of the Financial Crisis of 2007 to 2010.

A new international monetary unit may arise to replace the dollar, but it does not look to happen any time too soon. This is mainly because no suitable replacement for it has been found yet. Euros are not yet widely enough held, though they are gaining in share of reserves each and every year. Neither Japanese Yen, nor British Pounds, nor Swiss Francs are significantly representative enough of economic spheres of influence to be a viable challenger. The special drawing rights are one possible replacement for the dollar, as would be a gold backed International Monetary Unit. Gold served this purposes for several hundred years during the gold standard era of the 1700's to 1971.

Gold is a last candidate for a new International Monetary Unit. As it has universal appeal and acceptance, it does offer a strong challenge to the dollar. Gold is a hard international monetary unit to argue with because it does not bear the liabilities of any single nation. It can not be manipulated by any single government or corporation. This makes it a likely choice as at least part of a new International Monetary Unit in the coming century, if not the sole one.

Internet Bubble

The Internet bubble is also known as the dot com bubble. This Internet bubble proved to be a spectacular asset bubble that occurred during the years of 1995-2000. It's peak turned out to be on March 10 of 2000 when the NASDAQ stock market saw a high of 5,132.52 in the middle of the trading day. In this time, stock markets of all developed countries witnessed a swift and dramatic rise in equity values. Internet stocks and other relevant fields were the drivers of this phenomenal boom. It became a boom cycle that went bust as the Internet bubble proved to be unsustainable and show cased stocks with unjustifiable values.

This Internet bubble bore numerous characteristics typical of other forms of asset bubbles. A huge number of companies started up that were Internet technology based. These dot com companies proved to be spectacular failures in many cases. Any company that had an e in front of its name, or a .com at the end of the name witnessed spectacular rises in price, regardless of their products and fundamentals. In the constant allure of the glitzy Internet stocks, reason and rational thought were exchanged for hype.

This cycle of dramatically gaining prices in stocks combined with individual investors speculating in stocks, confidence that Internet companies would certainly make money at some point, and significant amounts of available venture capital all led to a boiling point. Investors became eager to look past traditional concepts of investing such as price to earnings ratio. Instead of this, they substituted in unbridled confidence in the possibilities of technological achievements.

Even though these prices in the Internet bubble exploded spectacularly, taking the NASDAQ stock exchange down to between 1,000 and 2,000 in a year or so, the technological revolution did not die out with the bubble. The Internet bubble did give rise to the constant commercial expansion of the Internet through the advancement of the World Wide Web. Even though many of those initial companies failed, enough other ones survived to make the Internet bubble evolve into a more sustainable Internet boom that in some respects is still ongoing even in 2010.

Intrinsic Value

Intrinsic value has several meanings where finance and business are concerned. The first of these meanings pertains to companies and their underlying stock issues. An intrinsic value of a stock could be said to be the actual per share value of a stock, in contrast to its book value or price according to the stock market. Intrinsic value takes many other elements into account, such as trademarks and copyrights owned, as well as the value of the brand name. These factors are intangible in nature. This makes it hard to figure out their true worth, although it can be done. As a result of this, such items of intrinsic value are not commonly included in the stock's actual market price.

A different way of understanding intrinsic value is that the intrinsic value is the amount that a company is actually worth. Market capitalization on the other hand is the price that investors will willingly pay for a company at any given point. Intrinsic value can be calculated in varying ways, depending on the investor who is doing the calculation.

Intrinsic value is also the amount of money that a call or put option on a stock is in the money. Call options give investors the right but not the obligation to buy a stock at a certain price, while put options grant investors the right but not obligation to sell a stock at a particular price. Figuring up a call option's intrinsic value is done by simply taking the difference of the call option's strike price and subtracted from the actual price of the underlying stock.

As an example, a call option might have a strike price of $40. The stock that this option is based on could be worth $55 per share. This would give the option an intrinsic value of $15 each share, or $1,500 since stock options represent a hundred shares. Stock prices that prove to be lower than call options do not possess any intrinsic value.

Put option intrinsic values are found by taking the difference of the strike price of the put option and subtracting the price of the stock that underlies them. As an example, should a put option contain a strike price of $30, and the stock be trading at only $25, then the put option will have an intrinsic value of $5 per share, or $500 for the one hundred share option. On the other hand, if the stock market price turned out to be higher than the strike price of this put option, then the option would not contain any intrinsic value.

Intrinsic value is also the true, real worth of an asset or object. Gold and silver have intrinsic value in that people will pay you for them at any time and in any country. Conversely, paper currencies may only be said to have intrinsic value if they are linked to or backed up by a hard asset.

Investors

Strictly speaking, an investor is any person or entity that makes an investment. In the past, the word investors has acquired a far more specific meaning. In the world of business and finance, investors has come to characterize those individuals or companies that routinely buy debt instruments like bonds, or equity issues like stocks in an attempt to make financial profits. They hope to realize such gains in return for financing or providing capital to a company that is looking to expand.

Investors also relates to other types of individuals, businesses, or parties that put money into different types of investments. Although this is a less commonly used version of the word investors, it can relate to those engaging in currency, real estate, commodities, derivatives, or other personal property investments like art or antiques. An example of this would be a real estate investor. They purchase a piece of property or a house with the hopes of selling it for a greater amount of money than for what they purchased it. Similarly, commodities' investors are hoping to buy contracts or options on hard assets like gold, oil, or lumber cheaply to sell them later more dearly.

Investors are commonly buying such stocks, bonds, or other types of assets and holding on to them with the goal of realizing one of two types of returns, or in some unusual cases both types. These are capital gains or cash flow investments. Investors who are interested in capital gains are simply looking to sell an instrument or asset that they obtained at one price for a greater amount. When they do this, they realize a capital gain. Should they sell the investment for less than they purchased it, they would instead realize a capital loss. Capital gains can only be realized one time on an investment, as the investors will have sold the investment and have to look for another investment to begin the process anew once again.

Cash flow investors are alternatively looking for a repetitive income stream. They hope to achieve regular, smaller sums of passive income just from holding their investment. Dividends on a stock, royalties on an oil or gas investment, and rents from a residential or commercial realty property are all examples of cash flow investments and returns. So long as the investor owns the cash flow investment, he or she should be able to continuously count on a regular income stream.

The word investor commonly gives the connotation of a person who acquires these assets for the longer term. This stands in contrast to a day trader or even short term investor. Investors can be professional or self taught amateurs.

Investors also represent many entities other than individuals or even traditional businesses. They can be investment groups like clubs, venture capital investors who provide money to start up companies, investment banks, investment trusts such as REIT Real Estate Investment Trusts, hedge funds and mutual funds, and even sovereign wealth funds that invest on behalf of their respective nations.

IPO (Initial Public Offering)

An IPO is the acronym for an Initial Public Offering. Such IPO's represent the first opportunity for most investors to start buying shares of stock in the firm in question. Initial Public Offerings commonly generate a great deal of excitement, not only for the company involved but also for the members of the investing community.

Private companies decide to issue stock and become publicly traded companies for a few different reasons. The main two motivating factors revolve around the need to raise more capital, as well as the desire to permit the original business owners and investors to take profits on their time and investment that they originally put into starting up the company.

It is true that private companies are limited in the amount of capital that they are able to raise, since their ownership turns out to be restricted to certain organizations and individuals. Public companies have the advantages of allowing any investor to take a stake through buying stock shares on exchanges that are publicly traded. It is far easier for them to raise money as public companies.

Initial Public Offerings that go well translate to large amounts of cash for a company. They use this for future expansion and development. Those who began the company or who were initial investors typically make enormous gains at that time in compensation for their time and effort.

Initial Public Offerings take huge amounts of preliminary work. Great amounts of paper work have to be filled in and filed with the regulatory oversight groups. A prospectus has to be created for investors to study and consider. Advertising campaigns for the first shares that will be sold must be developed. On top of these tasks, the company has to continue its normal operations. Because of this, financial firms such as Morgan Stanley or Goldman Sachs are commonly engaged to perform these tasks on the company's behalf. Such a firm is called the IPO underwriting company. With enormous sized IPO's, these tasks could even be divided up between a few different IPO underwriting companies.

Contrary to what many people think, the majority of IPO's typically do not do well initially. Besides this, a percentage of the companies will not make it, meaning that all of the investment in the IPO stock could be lost. Because of this, there is great risk and often lower rewards for sinking money into Initial Public Offerings than in traditional well established companies and stocks. Many investors buy into the enthusiasm and excitement that surrounds Initial Public Offerings. Another explanation for their euphoria may have to do with believing that there is something special in being among the first investors to acquire the next possible Apple, Coca Cola, or IBM. Whatever their reasoning proves to be, investors continue to love Initial Public Offerings and the somewhat long shot opportunities that they represent.

IRA

An IRA stands for Individual Retirement Account. IRA's offer two types of savings for retirement. They can either be tax free or tax deferred retirement plans. In the universe of IRA's, numerous different types of accounts exist. These are principally either traditional and standard IRA's or Roth IRA's as the most popular types. The various IRA's are helpful to different individuals based on the particular scenarios and end goals of every person.

Standard IRA's permit contributions of as much as $4,000 every year. These are contributions that are tax deductible, giving the IRA's their primary advantage as retirement accounts. People who are older than fifty are allowed to contribute more than the $4,000 maximum for the purposes of catching up for their approaching retirement. Any money put into the IRA is used to reduce your annual income amount, which lessens your overall tax liability for the year.

The tax is really only deferred though, since monies taken from an IRA will be taxed at the typical income tax rate for the individual when they are withdrawn, even if they are held in such an account until retirement. When the money is taken out earlier than this age of 59 ½, then an extra ten percent penalty is applied as well. There are exceptions to the penalty rule though. When these early withdrawn monies are utilized to buy a home or to pay for the tuition costs associated with higher education, then they are not penalized. The typical tax rate would still apply, although the penalty is waived in these two cases. This makes IRA's a good vehicle for investments that also give you the versatility of making significant purchases with the money.

Roth IRA's are the other principal type of IRA's. The government established these types of IRA account back in 1997 in an effort to assist those Americans in the middle class with their retirement needs. Roth IRA's do not turn out to be tax deductible. The upside is that they offer greater amounts of flexibility than do the typical IRA's. These contributions are allowed to be taken out whenever you want without a penalty or extra tax. Interest that the account earns is taxed if taken out before the first five years have passed. At the end of five years, the earnings and contributions both made are capable of being taken out without having to pay either taxes or penalties. The identical housing and education allowances that permit to standard IRA's pertain to Roth IRA's. The principal attraction of Roth IRA's is that they offer tax free income at retirement time.

It is worth noting that the Roth IRA's have their particular rules that keep them from being for everybody. If your income is higher than $95,000 in a year, then you will be barred from making the full contribution, and if it exceeds $110,000, then you will not be allowed to make a partial contribution. For married, filing jointly, the limits are $150,000 for full contributions and $160,000 for partial contributions.

IRA Custodian

An IRA custodian is commonly represented by some form of a financial institution. This would likely be a brokerage or a bank. These Individual Retirement Accounts' custodians have the job of protecting your assets in your IRA. Per the rules of the Internal Revenue Service, such IRA custodians have to be financial institutions that are approved. People can not choose to perform the role of an IRA custodian. In order for institutions that are not financial in nature to perform the responsibilities of such IRA custodians, they have to receive a special approval issued to them by the Internal Revenue Service.

These IRA Custodians actually carry out the transactions that the clients request of them. They also file any and all reports, maintain all required records of anything done on the account as a custodian, and send out statements and notices for taxes, either of which may be mandated by law or the agreement for custodianship. They sometimes will disburse the assets found in the IRA as per the wishes of the client, as well as file all necessary and relevant paper work with this action. One thing that IRA custodians do not have to do is to offer legal or investment advice to you, the IRA holder. This means that you have to provide the custodian of your IRA with clear and accurate instructions which follow the code established by the IRS.

IRA custodians can be responsible for overseeing a great range of investment securities and financial instruments. While IRS rules restrict IRA money being invested into collectibles like rare coins and artworks, or even life insurance, the custodian is able to work with various different investments like franchises, real estate, tax liens, and mortgages. Still, a great number of financial institutions acting as IRA custodians will choose to restrict the kinds of investments that they will allow to be held in one of their IRA's under custodianship. It is important for owners of IRA's who wish to have their funds placed into investments that are not traditional for IRA's, such as real estate or franchises, to seek out and choose an IRA custodian who will allow and work with these kinds of investments. This is the particular reason that a real estate management firm might choose to attain IRS certification in order to obtain the permission for overseeing real estate investment IRA's.

Much of the time, IRA customers will just deposit their retirement money and assets into their account that the custodian holds and will supply them with overall guidelines for their investments. The IRS mandates fiduciary responsibility for IRA custodians. They have to place clients' interests first. This translates to practical requirements, such as not being allowed to put the IRA money into investments and projects that come with a great amount of risk, unless they have the customer's expressed consent.

IRA custodians are also involved with self directed IRA's. Self directed IRA's contain investments that are actively managed directly by the customer. The custodian only performs the actions that the customer requests in these cases.

IRR (Internal Rate of Return)

The IRR is the acronym for internal rate of return. This IRR proves to be the capital budget rate of return that is utilized in order to determine and compare and contrast various investments' profitability. It is sometimes known as the discounted cash flow rate of return alternatively, or even the ROR, or rate of return. Where banks are concerned, the IRR is also known as the effective interest rate. The word internal is used to specify that such calculation does not involve facts that are part of the external environment, such as inflation or the interest rate.

More precisely, the internal rate of return for any investment proves to be the interest rate level where the negative cash flow, or net present value of costs, from the investment is equal to the positive cash flow, or net present value of benefits, for the investment. In other words, this IRR will yield a discount rate that causes the net current values of both positive and negative cash flows of a specific investment to cancel out at zero.

These Internal Rates of Return are generally utilized to consider projects and investments and their ultimate desirability. Naturally, a project will be more appealing to engage in or purchase if it comes with a greater internal rate of return. Given a number of projects from which to choose, and assuming that all project benefits prove to be the same generally, the project that contains the greatest Internal Rate of Return will be considered the most attractive. It should be selected with the highest priority of being pursued first.

The assumed theory for companies is that they will be interested in eventually pursuing any investment or project that comes with an IRR that is greater than the expense of the money put into the project as capital. The number of projects or investments that can be run at a time are limited in the real world though. A firm may have a restricted capability of overseeing a large number of projects at once, or they may lack the necessary funds to engage in all of them at a time.

The internal rate of return is actually a number expressed as a percent. It details the yield, efficacy, and efficiency of a given investment or project. This should not be confused with the net present value that instead tells the particular investment's actual value.

In general, a given investment or project is deemed to be worthwhile assuming that its internal rate of return proves to be higher than either the expense of the capital involved, or alternatively, than a pre set minimally accepted rate of return. For companies that possess share holders, the minimum IRR is always a factor of the investment capital's cost. This is easily decided by ascertaining the cost of capital, which is risk adjusted, for alternative types of investments. In this way, share holders will approve of a project or investment, so long as its Internal Rate of Return is greater than the cost of the capital to be used and this project or investment creates economic value that is viable for the company in question.

iShares

iShares prove to be a group of ETF's, or exchange traded funds, that are run by BlackRock. The very first iShares were called WEBS, or World Equity Benchmark Shares. They were later renamed iShares.

Today iShares are traded on stock exchanges the world over. This iShares proves to be the biggest ETF issues in both the United States and the world as a whole. Most every iShares fund actually tracks the performance of either a stock market index or a bond market index. The London Stock Exchange, the New York Stock Exchange, the American Stock Exchange, the Toronto Stock Exchange, the Hong Kong Stock Exchange, and the Australian Securities Exchange, along with various other Asian and European stock markets, all trade listed iShares funds.

There are hundreds of iShares issued funds. While many of them cover large and small indexes in the United States and internationally, others deal with specialized sectors or commodities. Naturally they have funds on an enormous variety of indexes, like the Dow Jones, NYSE Composite, and the Russell 3000 in the United States markets. These cover large cap, small cap, and mid cap indexes of stocks ranked according to their dollar amounts of market capitalization.

iShares also has funds that cover a wide variety of sectors, ranging from energy funds and industrial funds, to financials funds and health care funds, to consumer staples and discretionary funds, to materials funds and technology funds, to telecommunications funds and utilities funds. Besides this, they also offer a good variety of real estate index funds for both international and United States real estate. The iShares listed funds cover a wide range of developed and developing international indexes, such as China, India, Brazil, Peru, Chile, Israel, Indonesia, Mexico, South Korea, Taiwan, Turkey, Poland, Japan, and emerging market index funds. Beyond this, they offer index funds for all of the various major regions of the world, including Africa and Middle East funds, the Americas funds, European funds, and Asian funds.

They count various global sectors of index funds in their stable too, such as a nuclear energy index fund, a global clean energy index fund, and a global timber and forestry index fund. Where bonds are concerned, iShares provides a good variety of index funds based on treasuries, government credit, corporate credit, municipal bonds, mortgages, and global bonds. They have specialty index funds like dividend stocks funds and socially responsible corporation funds. Finally, in the category of commodities, iShares offers two especially popular funds, the Gold Trust fund that trades under the symbol of IAU, and the Silver Trust fund, that trades as SLV.

iShares originally arose as a collaboration between investment bank Morgan Stanley and fund manager Barclays Global Investors in the 1990's. By the year 2000, Barclays decided to launch a major expansion of the ETF market. To this effect, they started up and marketed more than forty new funds that they branded under the name of iShares. The other funds that Morgan Stanley and Barclays had launched as WEBS were soon renamed iShares as part of the broader effort.

Keynesian Economics

Keynesian economics represents a system of economic ideas that the British economist John Maynard Keynes developed in the first half of the twentieth century. Keynes became best known for his easy to understand and straight forward arguments for the underlying causes of the Great Depression. His theories of economics found their basis in the concept of the circular flows of money. As his ideas became more and more widely accepted, they led to a range of intervening economic policies towards the end of the Great Depression, particularly in the United States.

Keynes explained all flows of money in terms of their impact on other people and entities. He said that a single person's spending contributes to the next individual's paycheck. That person spending their pay would then supply the earnings of another. This virtuous circle goes on and on and assists in maintaining a healthy economy that is working properly. As the Great Depression settled in, the natural inclination of people to save and hold their money increased. Keynes proposed that this cessation in the normally occurring circular money flow is what caused the economies of the world to grind to a screeching halt.

More than only explaining economic problems, Keynes offered solutions as well. He claimed that the best cure for this disease lay in priming the pump. With this expression, he intended for governments to intervene in order to boost their spending. They might do this by purchasing things on the open market or by growing the money supply itself. At the time of the Great Depression, such an answer did not turn out to be well received at first. Even so, the actions of American President Franklin D. Roosevelt in spending enormously on defense for the Second World War are generally credited for beginning the United States' economic revival.

Because Keynesian economics strongly makes the case for the government to jump in and help out the economy, it represented a serious break from the prior system of laissez-fair capitalism economics that predated it. This laissez-fair, or hands off, approach had endeavored to keep government out of the markets. The system argued that markets left undisturbed would find their own balance in time. Keynes' ideas represented a direct challenge to the many supporters of free market capitalism, such as the Austrian School of economics. Frederick von Hayek proved to be among its earliest founders who lived in England and represented a bitter public rival to Keynes. Their ideas on government influence in private citizen's lives battled back and forth for years in public policy debate.

Keynesian economics discourages an excessive amount of savings, which it calls an insufficient amount of consumption and spending for the economy. The theory furthermore argues in favor of a great amount of redistributing wealth as necessary. Keynes thought that giving the poorest members of society money would lead to them probably spending it, which would support economic growth.

Keynesian economics has been a major force in international economic policy since World War II. Though its influence is less in the past three decades, it has not died out. Its tenets are again gaining ground in the light of the failures that led to the financial collapse and the Great Recession.

Lease

Leases are contracts made between an owner, or lessor, and a user, or lesee, covering the utilization of an asset. Leases can pertain to business or real estate. There are a variety of different types of leases that vary with the property in question being leased.

Tangible property and assets are leased under rental agreements. Intangible property leases are much like a license, only they have differing provisions. The utilization of a computer program or a cell phone service's radio frequency are two example of such an intangible lease.

A gross lease is another type of lease. In a gross lease, a tenant actually gives a certain defined dollar amount in rent. The landlord is then responsible for any and all property expenses that are routinely necessary in owning the asset. This includes everything from washing machines to lawnmowers.

You also encounter leases that are cancelable. Cancelable leases can be ended at the discretion of the end user or lessor. Other leases are non cancelable and may not be ended ahead of schedule. In daily conversation, a lease denotes a lease that can not be broken, while a rental agreement often can be canceled.

A lease contract typically lays out particular provisions concerning both rights and obligations of the lessor and the lessee. Otherwise, a local law code's provisions will apply. When the holder of the lease, also known as the tenant, pays the arranged fee to the owner of the property, the tenant gains exclusive use and possession of the property that is leased to the point that the owner and any other individuals may not utilize it without the tenant's specific invitation. By far the most typical type of hard property lease proves to be the residential types of rental agreements made between landlords and their tenants. This type of relationship that the two parties establish is also known as a tenancy. The tenant's right to possess the property is many times referred to as the leasehold interest. These leases may exist for pre arranged amounts of time, known as a lease term. In many cases though, they can be terminated in advance, although this does depend on the particular lease's terms and conditions.

Licenses are similar to leases, but not the same thing. The main difference between the two lies in the nature of the ongoing payments and termination. When keeping the property is only accomplished by making regular payments, and can not be terminated unless the money is not paid or some form of misconduct is discovered, then the agreement is a lease. One time uses of or entrances to property are licenses. The defining difference between the two proves to be that leases require routine payments in their term and come with a particular date of ending.

Leverage

Where business and finance are concerned, leverage pertains to the concept of using investment capital, revenue, or equity to multiply any gains or losses realized. Leverage can be affected in various ways. Among the most popular means of achieving it are through purchasing fixed assets, borrowing money, or utilizing derivatives.

There are several important examples to the use of leverage. With investments, hedge funds work with derivatives to leverage their capital. They could do this by putting up one million dollar cash for their margin and using it to control twenty million dollars of crude oil. They then realize any and all gains or losses achieved by the twenty million dollar crude position.

Businesses may similarly achieve leverage on their revenue by purchasing fixed assets. In so doing, the business would boost its proportion of fixed costs. Any change in revenue would then lead to a greater change in the associated operating income.

Publicly traded corporations are also able to obtain leverage on their stock share holder equity through borrowing money. The greater amount of cash that they borrow, the lower amount of equity capital they will require. This translates to all profits and losses being distributed out to a smaller share holder base, making them proportionately bigger in the end.

There are formulas for the four main types of leverage. Accounting leverage is found by taking all assets and dividing them by all assets minus all liabilities. Notional leverage is found by taking all notional quantities of assets, adding them to all of the notional liabilities, and then dividing the result by equity. To find the economic leverage, the equity volatility has to be divided by the identical assets' unlevered investment volatility. Finally, operating leverage can be calculated through taking the revenue in question and subtracting out the variable cost, then dividing the operating income into the result.

Leverage entails significant benefits and also substantial risks. While it does allow potentially great amounts of money to be made when investments go the way of an individual or organization, it can also involve devastating losses when the investments move against the entity. As an example, a stock investor who purchases stocks with fifty percent margin will double his losses when a stock goes down. Companies that borrow excessively to increase their leverage can experience collapse and bankruptcy in a downturn in business at the same time as a company with less leverage could survive.

Not all uses of leverage entail the same degree of risk. Corporations that borrow money so that they can engage in international expansion, increase their line up of products, or modernize their plants and equipment gain additional diversification. This could provide more than just an offset for the extra risks that result from the leverage. Not all highly leveraged companies are risky either. Public utilities commonly include high levels of debt, but they are generally considered to be less risky than are technology companies that lack leverage.

Levied Taxes

Levied taxes are taxes that are forcefully collected from an individual, business, or other entity. Among the many taxes most frequently collected these days are income taxes. These taxes could be said to be levied, since the law requires that an individual's income tax is levied for the government by the company where they work.

Three main types of tax systems are in effect in the world today where income is concerned. These include progressive, proportional, and regressive tax systems. Progressive taxes levied are those that employ progressively greater rates of tax as earnings are higher. As an example, the first $10,000 that an individual makes might be taxed at only five percent, while the next $10,000 is possibly taxed at a rate of ten percent, and income above this could be taxed at a twenty percent rate.

Proportional taxes use a pre set flat rate of tax. This applies to all earnings, no matter how high or low they are. With a ten percent flat rate, everyone will pay their ten percent of income as taxes levied, regardless of what amount of money they actually make.

Regressive taxes are said to hurt the poor by shifting the tax burden to lower income earners. This type of tax levy only taxes income to a certain dollar level, such as the first $80,000. Any money made above this amount would simply not be taxed. In reality, most tax systems employ the various kinds of tax levying methods to address various forms of income.

Levied taxes also apply to corporations and businesses. The income of a company is taxed in what is known as a corporate tax. This is sometimes alternatively referred to as a profit tax or corporate income tax. With corporate taxes levied, the net income is generally the figure that is taxed. Net income refers to the difference of gross income and expenses and other allowable write offs.

With individuals, the total income for a family or individual is commonly taxed. Some deductions are usually allowed before the taxes to be levied are determined. Income may be reduced by a certain amount as a result of how many children a family has to support, as an example.

There are many other forms of taxes levied in modern capitalist countries such as Great Britain and the United States. More than two hundred different types of taxes can be identified in the U.S. alone. These include such various taxes levied as income tax, sales tax, property tax, estate tax, capital gains tax, dividends tax, gasoline taxes, leisure taxes, luxury items taxes, and so called sin taxes on items such as cigarettes and alcohol. The United States has been called the most heavily taxed society in all of world history.

Liabilities

Where a business is concerned, liabilities prove to be amounts of money that are owed by the company at any given point. These liabilities are displayed on the firm's balance sheet. They are commonly listed as items payable, or simply as payables.

There are two types of liabilities. These are longer term liabilities and shorter term liabilities. Long term liabilities turn out to be business obligations that last for greater than the period of a single year. Mortgages payable and loans payable are included in this category.

Short term liabilities represent business obligations that will be paid in less than a year. There are many different kinds of short term liabilities. They include all of the items detailed below.

Payroll taxes payable are one of these. They represent sums automatically collected from the employees and put to the side by the employer. They have to be given to the IRS and any state taxing agencies at the pre determined time.

Sales taxes payable are another short term liability. The business collects them from its customers when sales are made. They hold them until it is time to give them to the proper revenue collecting department within the state.

Mortgages and loans payable are another short term liability. These represent payments made every month on mortgages and loans. They are not large single payments or the total amount of a loan that is eventually owed, but instead represent recurring monthly obligations.

Liabilities for individuals are another type of liabilities altogether. They also represent money that has to be paid out. For people, they are debts owed, as well as monthly cash flow that goes out of the individual's accounts.

Liabilities and assets are the opposites of each other, yet people often get them confused. While assets are things that contribute positive cash flow to a person's finances, liabilities are those that create negative cash flow, or money that leaves an individual's accounts every month. For example, a house that an individual owes money on and makes monthly payments on is a liability, not an asset. The house takes money from the person in the form of monthly mortgage payments each month. For a house to be an asset, it would have to be completely paid off. Even still, if monthly taxes and insurance payments are being made, then technically it would still be a liability. Houses can only be assets really and truly when they are rented out and the rental income that a person receives is greater than all of the expenses associated with the house every month, including any mortgage payments, taxes, insurance, upkeep, and property management fees. When the net result of a property is money coming in, then it is an asset and not a liability.

Liquidity

Liquidity refers to the point that a security or asset is able to be sold or bought in a given marketplace without interfering with the price of the asset. Good liquidity is demonstrated through a great amount of trading activity. Liquid assets prove to be the kinds that are simply and quickly able to be purchased and sold. Liquidity can be summed up in a single sentence as the capability of rapidly turning an asset into cash.

Although no single means of determining liquidity exists, liquidity can be figured up through utilizing liquidity ratios. It is generally accepted that investing money in liquid assets proves to be safer and more accessible than placing your money into illiquid ones. The reason for this is that you are able to withdraw your money from a liquid investment quickly and without obstacles.

There are many types of assets that prove to be simply convertible into cash. Money Market accounts are some of the most liquid assets. Blue chip stocks turn out to be the most liquid of stocks traded.

Liquidity also has other meanings for businesses and economics. A business' capability of fulfilling its payment responsibilities is referred to as its liquidity. This is figured both with regards to the company having enough liquid assets that they are able to get to in a timely fashion.

The most liquid asset is money in your hand. This can be utilized right away for all economic functions. Among these are selling, buying, taking care of immediate needs and desires, and paying down debts.

In general, liquid assets possess many or at least a few of a number of features in common. These assets that have good liquidity are able to be sold at any point during market operating hours, quickly, and with as small a loss in value as possible. Markets with liquidity possess numerous sellers and buying who are both willing and able to transact at all times that the market is open. For markets to have deep liquidity, eager and willing parties in great numbers have to be present in a market all of the time that it is open.

The liquidity of a market has much to do with its market depth. Market depth is able to be quantified as the number of individual units that may be purchased or sold for a certain price impact. The opposite of this related term market depth is market breadth. Market breadth is quantified as the amount of price impact for every unit of such liquidity.

A given item's liquidity is measurable in terms of how frequently it is sold or purchased. This is called volume. Investments in markets with great volume like futures markets and the stock markets are generally understood to have far greater liquidity than do real estate markets. This is simply a function of stocks and futures' capability of being rapidly transacted.

There are assets that possess even liquid secondary markets. These offer greater advantages for traders, and because of this, buyers will pay a greater price for such an asset than for an asset that is similar but does not possess a liquid secondary market. This liquidity discount proves to be the lowered anticipated return or guaranteed yield on these kinds of assets. An example of this is the variance between just issued U.S. Treasury bonds and treasuries that are no longer recently issued. Both may have the same amount of time until they mature, but investors are more interested in purchased the ones that have only just been issued. Because of this, these newest ones have a higher price and lower yield.

Loan Servicing

The term loan servicing refers to the procedure of either a mortgage bank or servicing firm gathering up the regular principal and interest payments from the mortgage and loan borrowers. The amount of such service depends on the kind of loan in question and the particular terms that have been arranged between investors looking for such services and the servicing firm.

In the roaring days of the housing expansion, mortgage servicing got to be substantially more profitable than it had been in the past. Loan servicers sought out borrowers who were likely to have trouble making their payments on time. They did this with the hope of bringing in a greater number of lucrative late fees. After the financial collapse and in the Great Recession, this strategy came back to haunt them, as greater and greater numbers of homeowners defaulted on their mortgages and other types of loans.

Loan servicing outfits commonly make their money in the form of a percentage of the remaining balance on any loans that they are servicing. While the actual fees vary, they typically range from twenty five basis points down to a single basis point. This has much to do with the loan's size, amount of service necessary, and whether the loan is backed up by residential properties or commercial properties.

Loan servicers carry a certain value on their balance sheets from these loans. The current net value of the payment flow obtained in servicing the loans minus the anticipated costs for servicing them generates the asset that goes on the balance sheet. Such asset values commonly prove to be highly volatile when refinancing becomes more common. This is because the loans are commonly paid off in advance, leading to an end to the servicing fees that are collected.

A number of companies have traditionally been major players in the loan servicing field. These include Bank of America, JP Morgan Chase, Wells Fargo, and Citigroup as the biggest participants. GMAC is another major servicer. Between them they handle in excess of sixty percent of all American residential mortgage debt.

For special borrower cases that are near default or already behind, another industry of loan servicing has grown up. This is dominated by two companies. Ocwen Financial and Litton Loan Servicing, which Goldman Sachs owns, overshadow the industry. While it is the case that the big servicing companies are capable of handling borrowers who are unable or unwilling to pay, they do it inefficiently. As many as twenty-four different employees of the major loan servicing companies become involved from the first call of a collection agent down to the final foreclosure.

Loan-to-Value-Ratio (LTV)

The Loan to Value Ratio is commonly known by its acronym LTV. This loan to value ratio states the total value of the first mortgage against the full real estate property's appraised value. The formula for figuring this ratio is simply the amount of the loan divided by the property value. It is expressed as a percent. So if a borrower is seeking $180,000 with which to buy a $200,000 house, then the Loan to Value Ratio is ninety percent.

The loan to value ratio proves to be among the most critical risk factors that lenders consider when they are deciding whether to qualify borrowers for a mortgage loan on a house. The dangers of a default occurring most influence the loan officers in their lending decisions. The chances of an institution having to take a hit in a foreclosure procedure only goes up as the dollar amount of the property equity goes down. Because of this, as the Loan to Value ratio goes up, the qualification tests for many mortgage programs get significantly stricter. Some lenders will insist on a borrower who comes with a high loan to value ratio on the property in question to purchase mortgage insurance. This safe guards the lender from any default realized by the borrower, but it also raises the mortgage's total costs.

Property values used in the loan to value ratio are generally set by appraisers. Still, the most accurate value of a piece of real estate is undoubtedly that determined when a willing seller and willing buyer come together to agree on a sale. Usually, banks decide to go with the lower number when they are offered choices of a purchase price that is fairly recent or an appraisal value. Recent sales are commonly deemed to be those that happened from a year to two years ago, although every bank makes its own rules in this regard.

When a borrower selects a property that he or she will purchase with a lower loan to value ratio that is less than eighty percent, lower interest rates can many times be obtained by borrowers who are low risk. Higher risk borrowers will also be considered in such a scenario, meaning those who have prior histories of late payments on mortgages, who have lower credit scores, who have high loan requirements or higher debt to income ratios, and who have neither sufficient cash reserves nor requested income documentation. Generally, higher loan to value ratios are only permitted for those borrowers who have a reliable mortgage payment history and who possess greater credit scores. Only those buyers with the greatest credit worthiness are considered for one hundred percent financing that translates to a one hundred percent loan to value ratio.

Loans that are made to the standards of lending giants Freddie Mac and Fannie Mae and their guidelines can not have loan to value ratios that exceed or are equal to eighty percent. Any loans higher than this percentage of eighty percent must come with attached private mortgage insurance. The private mortgage insurance premiums simply go on top of the existing mortgage principal and interest payments.

Local Money

Local Money is money that is created, printed, issued, and traded by an individual community. Communities that are struggling to keep their economies going are in need of a way of boosting the local economic picture. In creating money that can only be utilized by individuals and businesses in their own local area, they attempt to address this problem.

In the United States, local money's history originated in the difficult era of the Great Depression. During this decade of the 1930's, banks were failing in numbers not seen before. This created a real shortage of currency and loans in local communities and towns. Individuals and businesses worked together to find a solution to the problem. They teamed up and created their own currencies that became known as Scrip. Utilizing this newly created local Scrip, trade and exchange continued to go on even with a shortage of banks and hard currency in the smaller towns throughout America.

Today's local money concept has made a comeback in the wake of the financial crisis and the Great Recession. Businesses began working with area banks to come up with their own local currency that could be purchased and issued to consumers in the area. In communities where local money has arisen again, a great number of businesses have signed on to the idea and consented to taking payment in the bills of this localized currency money. This is necessary in order for area consumers to feel compelled to obtain the local money in the first place.

The way that local money works in practice today is interesting. The currency is printed up and then offered by area banks in a participating community. The currency is then sold at a significant discount to its actual value. For example, $100 local money could be sold by area banks for only $95 United States dollars. The $100 local money can then by spent by the consumer at its full value in any business that takes the local money as a method of payment.

Already, over a dozen area communities throughout the U.S. have created their own local money currencies that are being honored on a fairly large scale. Not only is this helping out area businesses by keeping the locally earned paychecks in the communities, but since the currencies are sold at a five to ten percent discount to dollars, it allows struggling workers and families to stretch their incomes by using them. In communities that honor local money, they can be utilized to pay for groceries, gasoline, and even Yoga classes, as examples. Among the more successful and widely accepted local monies these days are the

Ithaca Hours of Ithaca, New York; the BerkShares in Western Massachusetts; and the Detroit Cheers in Detroit, Illinois.

The BerkShares for Western Massachusetts are a model case study of
successful local money. They can be purchased from twelve banks
throughout the area. BerkShares are accepted at in excess of three hundred seventy different businesses in the region. As the largest local
money network in the U.S, the BerkShares have so far circulated almost two and a half million dollars. Successes like these have encouraged other communities like South Bend, Indiana to begin creating
their own local currency.

Loss to Lease

Loss to lease is a phrase that is used in real estate property leasing, particularly pertaining to apartment complexes or senior assisted living
facilities. Loss to lease is also an accounting line in the books of rental
properties and apartment complexes. In both cases, it refers to income
on leases that is potentially lost through making incentive offers to
prospective tenants whom you hope to lease a unit in a property.

Examples of loss to lease are helpful to understand the concept. Some
apartments will offer one free month's rent with a six or twelve month
lease contract. The amount of this lost month's rent would be the loss to
lease figure for the leasing property and the leasing property's books.
Other examples involve loss to lease figured up on a monthly basis.
Should the potential revenue from rent amount to only $500 when the
market rate for rental is $550, then the loss to lease comes out to be $50
per month.

Cash flow is the part of a rental property books where loss to lease
most commonly appears. When required, it can be figured up using a
simple formula. The scheduled base rental revenue is determined. This
figure has the potential market rent subtracted from it to come up with
the Loss to Lease result.

The interesting thing about loss to lease is that it has no meaningful
impact on a rental property or apartment complex's cash flow bottom
line. Instead, it only represents an accounting number. Loss to lease
does not offer any advantages to a company or individual when they
are figuring up and filing their taxes either, since it does not represent
any actual real or tangible loss in income, only loss in potential income,
or hoped for income.

Macroeconomics

Macroeconomics refers to the division within economics that concentrates its study on the workings of large national economies, or even regional economies, in their entirety. This field proves to be extremely general as a result. It is mostly concerned with big picture measurements like the rates of unemployment, as well as with the developing of models whose purpose is to detail the various indicators' correlations. An opposite to macroeconomics might be said to be microeconomics that focuses on the activities of individuals and businesses instead of bigger pictures and scales. Macroeconomics and microeconomics are considered to be complimentary studies.

Because of the Great Depression that occurred in the 1930's, the study of macroeconomics evolved into a practical area of economics on which economists might concentrate their efforts. Up to that point, economists did not distinguish between the activities of individuals and businesses and an entire national economy. The most influential developers of macroeconomics proved to be those economists who made it their business to relate what had caused the Great Depression. The British economist John Maynard Keynes is among the chief of these economists who developed the study.

Until just a few decades ago, Keynes' ideas on macroeconomics overshadowed the entire field. Followers of Keynesian thought depended on the concept of aggregate demand, or total demand, to grapple with hard questions in macroeconomics, like the way to explain what stood behind particular unemployment levels. Today, Keynesian models are not the underlying philosophy of macroeconomics any longer, as neoclassical economics has successfully challenged it. Still, the presently used models bear great influence of the Keynesian precursors.

To date, no one economic philosophy has come up with a single model that is able to correctly and totally reproduce the ways that economies literally work. This causes different economists to have varying understandings of economics. Because of this, gaining an understanding of macroeconomics involves studying the ideas of each major economic school of thought.

As a result of the field of macroeconomics, governments have taken proactive approaches to managing economic cycles and changes. They do this through governmental policies that are utilized to create changes with the goals of either avoiding or lessening the impacts of economic shocks, such as depressions. This management of large national economies is affected in practical terms through two types of government policies. These are monetary and fiscal policies. Monetary policies involve the governmental control of the nation's money supply and the national interest rate levels. Their goals are both stable prices with low inflation and low unemployment levels.

Fiscal policies are amounts of spending that a government engages in, as well as taxes that they collect, to influence the economy. For example, the government can expand the economy by spending a good deal more money than it collects in tax revenues. It might similarly contract economic activity by spending less money than it actually brings in from taxes. Besides this, a government can stimulate the economy by cutting tax rates, or shrink the economic activity levels by raising tax rates.

Margin Trading

Margin trading is the practice of buying investments on margin. This is accomplished through borrowing money from your broker in order to buy stocks. Another way of understanding margin trading is taking out a loan from your broker to buy greater amounts of stock shares.

Margin trading generally requires a margin account. Margin accounts differ from cash accounts that only allow you to trade with the money that your account contains. Brokers have to get a signature from you in order to open up a new margin account. This could be as an extension of your existing account and account opening forms or as a separate and new agreement. Minimum investments of $2,000 are necessary to open such a margin account. Some brokers insist on larger amounts. Whatever the final margin requirement deposit is, it is called the minimum margin.

After the margin account is up and running, you are able to purchase as much as fifty percent of a stock with margin trading money. The money that you use to buy your part of the stock is called initial margin. Margining up to the full fifty percent is entirely optional. You might borrow only fifteen or twenty percent instead.

Margin trading loans can be held for as long a period as you wish, assuming that you continue to meet the margin obligations. A stock maintenance margin has to be maintained while the loan is outstanding too. This maintenance margin is the lowest account balance that can be held by the account in advance of the broker making you deposit additional funds. If you do not meet this minimum or resulting margin call for extra funds, then the broker has the right to sell your stocks in order to reduce your outstanding loan.

Borrowing money from your broker is not done for the sake of charity. Interest has to be paid on the loan. Also, the marginable securities in the account become tied up as collateral. Unless you pay down the loan, interest charges will be applied to the loan balance. These interest amounts can significantly increase the debt level in the account with time. Higher debt levels in your account lead to still higher interest charges. Because of this, buying stocks on margin is typically utilized only for shorter time frame investments. This is true since the greater amount of time that you hold the margin loan in the investment, the higher a return you will require in order to break even on the margin trade. When you maintain such a margin based investment over a long time frame, it becomes difficult to turn a profit after the expenses are cleared.

It is also important to remember that not every stock qualifies for purchase using margin. The rules pertaining to which stocks can be purchased with margin are set by the Federal Reserve Board. In general though, Initial Public Offerings, penny stocks, or over the counter traded stocks are not allowed to be purchased utilizing margin as a result of the daily volatility and trading risks associated with such kinds of stocks. Besides this, each brokerage can restrict whichever other stocks that they wish.

Maturity

In the world of business and finance, maturity stands for the last payment date of either a loan or some other form of financial instrument. It is also known as the maturity date. On this maturity date, both the outstanding principal and any remaining associated interest are owed and expected to be rendered for final payment. If they are not paid on the maturity date, such loans or instruments are considered to be in default.

A fixed maturity pertains to a kind of financial instrument where the loan will have to be paid back on a pre set date. Included in fixed maturity instruments are variable rate loans and fixed interest rate loans or other kinds of debt instruments. Besides these, redeemable preferred shares of company stocks fall under this category of fixed maturity instruments. The key to fixed maturities is that they must have a particular maturity date spelled out in their terms. This maturity date is much like a redemption date.

Other instruments do not come with a set fixed maturity date. These kinds of loans go on indefinitely, until the point that a lender and borrower get together and agree on the loan being paid down. These instruments and loans are sometimes referred to as perpetual stocks. Other financial instruments may include a range of potential dates of maturity. These types of stocks may be repaid at any time that suits the borrower, so long as it is within the time range that is provided to them.

Another form of maturity is the serial maturity. Serial maturities mostly pertain to bonds that companies issue to borrow money for a variety of purposes, including expansion into new markets or developing and marketing new products. With serial maturities, all of the bonds are actually issued at one time. Their classes describe the various redemption dates on them, which are generally staggered away from each other.

Maturity is also used by financial news media to discuss securities that have maturities, such as bonds themselves. This abbreviation for these kinds of investments is commonplace. They might claim that the yields declined on twenty year maturities. This would mean that bond prices which are due to reach full maturity in twenty years rose while their actual yields fell, since bond prices move inversely to the direction of their associated yields.

All types of bonds may be referred to using this short hand form of calling them maturities. This could include corporate bonds, Federal Treasury bonds, and also local government municipal bonds. All of these bonds have specific dates of maturity on which they will repay their principal. Preferred stocks also could be thought of as maturities, since they similarly possess set dates on which they are redeemed. They are not commonly referred to by this abbreviation though.

MERS

MERS stands for the Mortgage Electronic Registration Systems. It is also a privately owned and operated company that maintains this electronic database and registry whose purpose is to follow the ownership of and servicing rights to American mortgage loans.

This MERS represents a revolutionary way of vastly simplifying the means of keeping track of how both mortgage servicing and ownership rights can be originated, sold, and followed. The Real Estate finance industry actually created it. MERS boasts that it does away with the requirement to create and record assignments as both commercial and residential loans are being exchanged.

The mortgage banking industry got together to come up with a way to simplify the process of working with mortgages through utilizing e-commerce to reduce and even eliminate paper. The mission of the company and its database lies in registering literally all mortgage loans within the U.S. on the MERS system.

MERS actually performs its role on behalf of the servicer and the lender in handling county land records. Loans that are registered on the MERS system can not have problems with future assignments since MERS is always the nominal mortgagee, regardless of the number of times that a mortgage servicing is sold. MERS is approved to be original mortgagee by all of the major lending outfits, including Freddie Mac, Fannie Mae, Ginnie Mae, the VA, the FHA, and both Utah and California Housing Finance Agencies, along with each of the Wall Street ratings agencies.

Many groups benefit from the existence of the MERS registry. This includes mortgage servicers, originators, wholesale lenders, warehouse lenders, retail lenders, settlement agents, document custodians, title companies, investors, insurers, and country recorders. MERS claims that the consumer benefit as well, though this has been in question until recently.

Ironically, a recent situation has arisen surrounding MERS that may actually benefit many consumers in the end. They are embroiled in the middle of a scandal surrounding original titles and signed promissory notes. Part of what they accomplished in their paperless process led to the loss of such critical original signature documents that the majority of states require for enacting mortgage foreclosures. MERS is now right in the middle of a number of legal challenges resulting from the sub prime crisis and going on in most states around the country. Their right to begin the process of foreclosure has been called into account, since they lack these required original signed documents.

This means that their role in the early days of setting up the system that helped with the buying and selling of mortgages may come back to haunt them and the entire mortgage industry as a whole in the end. Should judges rule these legal suits in favor of the homeowners who took out the mortgages, then it is widely believed that the losses that the banking industry in America suffers from will be so great that they will require substantial amounts of re-capitalization.

Middle Class

In the United States, the Middle Class is a broadly defined social group found throughout America. There are no exact definitions of what comprises the middle class. Depending on whose standard you use, the middle class in the U.S. is made up of from twenty-five to sixty-six percent of families.

The middle class in America have been responsible for many of the country's greatest accomplishments. Middle class people are known by characteristics of creativity, coming up with concepts, and consultative abilities. Most middle class people have either obtained a college degree or at least been through some years of college education.

Middle class values are central to the recognized American way of life. These values center around sticking to intrinsically held ethics and beliefs, independence, and innovation. Middle class people prove to be more politically motivated and active than do the other demographics throughout American society.

The income of the middle class ranges widely. It can be from around the national median income to over $100,000 per year. This means that the standard of living for middle class people can similarly vary greatly, dependent on the size of the household in question. This means that families with two incomes that have many members can earn more than a smaller family in the upper middle class that only has one income, even though the latter's standard of living would be considerably higher.

The middle class in the United States remains the most influential group in American society. They are responsible for the vast majority of teachers, writers, voters, editors, and journalists. The majority of trends within the United States begin with the middle class.

The middle class also pay the majority of the taxes within the U.S., making them an extremely critical group economically. The top twenty-five percent of earners, the overwhelming majority of whom are considered to be middle class, pay eighty-five percent of all taxes in the United States. Meanwhile, the bottom fifty percent pay only three percent, while the wealthiest one percent pay up to thirty-seven percent of the total share of taxes.

Even though the Middle Class are considered to be indispensable to American society and the economy, their ranks are dwindling with time. Data on income demonstrates that the American Middle Class have benefited from much slower growth in income than the top one percent of wealthy wage earners, according to data going back to 1980. This stands in contrast to the rise in income seen in the years after World War II, when the income of the middle class grew at the same pace as did the income of the rich. In the years since then, the rich have out gained the middle class considerably.

As an example, from 1979 to 2005, the after tax earnings of the top one percent grew inflation adjusted by 176% as opposed to only sixty-nine percent for the top twenty percent of wage earners as a whole and only twenty-nine percent for the top forty percent of workers. As a percentage of total gross yearly household income, the top one percent currently make over nineteen percent of all earnings, representing their greatest share of the wealth since the late 1920's.

Further proof that the critical middle class is shrinking is revealed by the June 2006 Brookings Institution survey. It demonstrated that the neighborhoods of middle income Americans as a percent of all metropolitan neighborhoods have decline dramatically over a thirty year period. From 1970 to 2000, this percentage decreased from fifty-eight percent to forty-one percent. According to this data, the middle class have already fallen well below the significant half of the country's population that it always represented in the past.

Monetarism (Milton Freedman's Economics)

Monetarism is an idea that Milton Freedman developed and expounded upon. It centers on the idea found in monetary economics that money supply changes lead to huge impacts on short term national outputs and on long term price levels. It argues that the goals of monetary policy are most effectively achieved when the money supply is carefully and appropriately expanded in line with actually output growth.

Milton Friedman started out as a believer in Keynesian economics. Later in his career, he determined that it had major problems and he began to criticize it on a variety of levels. He wrote a book with Anna Schwartz that proved to be extremely influential. In this book, "A Monetary History of the United States 1867-1960," Friedman proposed that inflation is everywhere and always a monetary phenomenon. Because of this now generally accepted truth, he strongly recommended a policy to be practiced by the central banks, or the Federal Reserve, of maintaining supply and demand equilibrium of money. This money supply should only increase with demand and accompanying productivity growth.

The roots of monetarism come from two radically opposed concepts. The hard money policies of the end of the nineteenth century were merged with some of the monetary ideas held by John Maynard Keynes who argued for money supply that was driven by demand. Keynes concentrated on the stable value of a currency that had been threatened by a lack of sufficient money supply that then led to currency collapse. Friedman concentrated instead on price stability to control and keep down inflation. This proves to be the perfect equilibrium of demand and supply for money. Friedman took these diametrically opposed concepts and wove them together into a new theory of Monetarism.

In the 1960's and 1970's, this Monetarist school of thought for monetary demand being a stable function found significant traction in the work of David Laidler. Other influential monetarists include former U.S. Federal Reserve Chairman Alan Greenspan, who showed his Monetarism bias in his own policies and ideas. Some central banks have attempted to orient their monetary policy around appropriate targets for money supply. The European Central Bank is the chief of these Monetarist idea central banks.

Monetarism is not entirely without its critics. The neo Keynesians propose that money demand and supply are closely interrelated. Other conservative economists maintain that monetary demand is not predictable. Nationally known economist Joseph Stiglitz makes the case that the relationships that exist between the growth of the money supply and inflation are weak at times when inflation is actually low.

Money Supply

Where business and economics are concerned, the money supply proves to be the complete quantity of money that is available throughout the economy at any given moment in time. Money can be defined in a few different ways. The commonly accepted definitions are comprised of both circulating currency and demand deposits. Demand deposits are the assets of depositors in banks that are easy for them to access, such as checking accounts.

The statistical data on money supply is recorded and made available to the public by the government. In some countries, the central bank publishes such information. Analysts are always interested in any changes to the money supply total, since it has great impacts on inflation levels, prices, and the business cycle.

There are now several different measurements of money supply published within the U.S. These range from narrow to broad money supply totals. While narrower calculations only measure the most liquid of assets that are easy to spend, such as currency itself and checking account deposits, other broader measures include assets that are not so liquid, such as certificates of deposit.

The MB is the complete monetary base as it pertains to all currency. It proves to be the money supply figure that is the most liquid. M1 is the measure that leaves out bank reserves. M2 is the measurement that is given as the main economic indicator in figuring how high inflation will become. Both money and its near substitutes are included in this category. M3 used to be the main figure for money supply in the Untied States, until the Fed elected not to release it any longer after 2006. It included the M2 measure plus longer term deposits.

Inflation commonly results from changes to the money supply. The evidence demonstrates the direct correlation between the growth of the money supply and longer term rising prices. This is particularly the case when the money supply increase is rapid within an economy.

The latest example of how the growth of the money supply can ruin a currency and destroy an economy is demonstrated by Zimbabwe. This African country witnessed dramatic increases in the national money supply and then became a victim of hyperinflation, or a dramatic gain in prices. Because of this, the money supply has to be responsibly controlled and overseen.

The money supply is actually controlled through monetary policy. Central banks such as the Fed determine the money supply in part through their reserve ratios that they make banks observe with percent of deposits kept on hand. They can also adjust it with the interest rates that they set for the country.

Many critics have pointed to the rapid growth in the money supply of U.S. dollars in the years of the financial crisis and the Great Recession as dangerous. From the years of 2007-2010, the dollar money supply has been grown by in excess of three hundred percent. At the same time, the economy has a whole has barely grown. This is the consummate recipe for inflation, and many economists have suggested that you will see high inflation, and potentially even hyperinflation, within the United States in the next several years as a direct result.

Mortgage

Mortgages are loans made on commercial or residential properties. They commonly use the house or the property itself as collateral. These mortgages are paid off in monthly installments over the course of a pre determined amount of time. Mortgages commonly come in fifteen, twenty, and thirty year periods, though both longer ones and shorter ones are available.

A variety of differing mortgages exist. All of them have their own terms and conditions that translate into advantages and disadvantages. Among the various mortgage types are fixed rate mortgages, adjustable rate mortgages, and balloon payment mortgages.

The most common kinds or mortgages, especially for first time home buyers, prove to be fixed rate mortgages. This is the case because they are both simple to understand and extremely stable. With such a mortgage, the regular monthly payments will be the same during the entire life of the loan. This makes them very predictable and manageable. Fixed rate mortgages have the advantages of protection against inflation, since the interest rate is locked in and can not go up with the floating interest rates. They allow for longer term planning. They come with very low risk, since you are always aware of both the payment and interest rate.

Adjustable rate mortgages, also known as ARM's, have become more popular since they begin with lower, more manageable interest rates that result in a lower initial monthly payment. The downside to them is that the interest rate can and likely will go up and down in the loan's life time. Factors to consider with ARM's are the adjustment periods, the indexes and margins, and the caps ceilings, and floors. The adjustment period is the one in which the interest rate is allowed to reset, commonly starting anywhere from six months to ten years after the mortgage begins.

The interest rates change based on the index and margin. The interest rates are actually based on an index that is published, whether it is the London Interbank Offered Rate, or LIBOR, or the U.S. Constant Maturity Treasury, or CMT. The margin is added to this index to determine the total new interest rate on your mortgage. The amount that these ARM rates are capable of going up or down in a single adjustment period and for the life of the loan is called a cap, a ceiling or a floor.

The third common type of mortgages is balloon reset mortgages. They come with thirty year schedules for repayment, with a caveat. Unless you pay are willing to allow the mortgage to reset to then current interest rates at the end of either a five year or seven year term, then your entire balance will be due at this point. This gives you the benefits of the low monthly payment plan as a person with a thirty year loan would have, yet you will have to be willing to pay off the whole mortgage if you do not take the reset option when the term is up. Because of this, many people refer to this type of a mortgage as a two step mortgage.

Mortgage Broker

A mortgage broker is a firm or sole proprietorship that performs a role as an intermediary between banks and businesses or individuals who are looking for mortgage loans. Even though banks have always vended their own mortgage products, mortgage brokers have gradually taken a larger and larger share of the loan originating market as they seek out direct lenders and banks that have the specific products that a customer wants or needs.

Nowadays, sixty-eight percent of all loans begin with mortgage brokers in the United States, making them by far and away the biggest vendors of mortgage products for banks and lenders. The remaining thirty-two percent of loans come from banks own direct marketing efforts and retail branch efforts. Mortgage broker fees are separate from the bank mortgage fees. They are based on the loans' amounts themselves and range from commonly one to three percent of the total loan amount.

Mortgage brokers are mostly regulated in order to make sure that they comply with finance laws and banking rules in the consumer's jurisdiction. This level of regulation does vary per state. Forty-nine of the fifty states have their own laws or boards that regulate mortgage lending within their state's borders. The industry is similarly governed by ten different federal laws that are applied by five federal agencies for enforcement.

Banks find mortgage brokers to be an ideal means of bringing in borrowers who will qualify for a loan. In this way, a mortgage broker acts as a screening agent for a bank. Banks are furthermore able to shift forward a portion of the fraud and foreclosure risks to the loan originators using their contractual legal arrangements with them. In the originating of a loan, a mortgage broker will do the footwork of collecting and processing all of the necessary paper work associated with real estate mortgages.

Mortgage brokers should not be confused with loan officers of a bank. Mortgage brokers are typically state registered and also licensed in order to work as a mortgage broker. This makes them liable personally for any fraud that they commit during the entire life span of the loans in question. Being a mortgage broker comes with professional, legal, and ethical responsibilities that include proper disclosure of mortgage terms to consumers.

Mortgage brokers come with all kinds of experience, as do loan officers, who are employees of banks. While loan officers commonly close more loans than mortgage brokers actually do because of their extensive network of referrals within the bank for which they work, the majority of mortgage brokers make more money than loan officers make. Mortgage brokers generate the lion's share of all loan originations within the country as well.

Mortgage brokers are all represented by the NAMB, which is the acronym for their group the National Association of Mortgage Brokers. The NAMB's mission is to represent the industry of mortgage brokers throughout the U.S. It also offers education, resources to members, and a certification program as well.

Municipal Bonds

Municipal bonds prove to be counties', cities', and states' debt obligations. They issue these in order to raise money against future tax revenues for building highways, schools, sewer systems, hospitals, and numerous other public welfare projects.

When you as an investor buy a municipal bond, you are actually loaning a state or local government or agency money. They agree to pay you back your principal, along with a certain sum of interest that is generally paid out twice a year. The principal is commonly given back on the pre arranged maturity date of the bond.

The advantage that is most commonly touted to municipal bonds is their tax free nature. The truth is that not every municipal bond actually provides income which is tax free on both state and federal levels. Many municipal bond issues are exempt from taxes from the state and local authorities but still have to pay taxes on earning to the federal government. Municipal bonds that come without any federal taxes as well are generally known as Munis. These Munis prove to be the most appealing bonds for many investors since they are generally exempt from all Federal, state, and local taxes too. Besides this, Munis are commonly investments made in the local and state infrastructure, impacting your daily quality of life and that of your community. Projects including highways, hospitals, and housing are all covered by these types of municipal bonds.

Municipal bonds can also be further subdivided into one of two general categories. These are general obligation bonds and revenue bonds. With a general obligation bond, the interest and principal that is owed to you is commonly backed up by the issuer's own credit and faith. They typically come underpinned by the taxing power of the issuer. This can be based on their limited or unlimited powers of taxing. General obligation bonds usually come approved by the voters who will pay the taxes that support their repayment.

Revenue bonds on the other hand are backed up by specific revenues for the project in question. Their interest and principal payment amounts have supporting revenues that come from tolls, rents from the facility that they build, or charges to use the facility that is built. Many different public works are built with revenue bonds. These could be airports, bridges, roads, sewage and water treatment plants, subsidized housing, and even hospitals. A great number of such bonds come issued by authorities which are specifically launched to create such bond issues in the first place.

Municipal bonds and notes commonly come with minimum investment amounts. These are typically denominated by $5,000. They can come in multiples of $5,000 increments as well. If you want to buy a municipal bond, you can buy them directly off of the bond issuer when they come out on the primary market, or alternatively off of other bond holders after they have come out, from the secondary market.

Mutual Funds

Mutual funds prove to be collective investment pools that are managed professionally. They derive their sometimes enormous capitals from the contributions of many different investors. These monies are then invested in a variety of investments and securities comprised of bonds, stocks, other mutual funds, money markets, and commodities like silver and gold.

Mutual funds all have a fund manager. His responsibility is to sell and buy the holdings of the fund according to the guidelines spelled out in the particular mutual fund's prospectus. U.S. regulations require that all mutual funds registered with the governing SEC, or Securities and Exchange Commission, make distributions of practically all income and net gains made from selling securities to the investors minimally once a year. The majority of these mutual funds are furthermore overseen by trustees or boards of directors. Their job is to make certain that the fund is properly managed by its investment adviser for the investors of the funds ultimate good.

There are really a wide variety of different securities that mutual funds are permitted by the SEC to purchase. This is somewhat limited by the objectives spelled out in the prospectus of the fund, which is comprised of a great amount of useful information on the fund and its goals. While cash instruments, stocks, and bonds are the more common types of investments that they purchase, mutual funds might also buy exotic types of investments like forwards, swaps, options, and futures.

The investment objectives of mutual funds explain clearly the types of investments that the fund will purchase. As an example, if a fund's objective claimed that it was attempting to realize capital appreciation through investing in U.S. company stocks regardless of their amount of market capitalization, then it would be a U.S. stock fund that purchased U.S company stocks.

Other mutual funds purchase specific market sectors or different industries. Utilities, technology, and financial service funds are examples of this. Such a fund is called a sector fund or specialty fund. There are also bond funds that purchase different kinds of bonds, like investment grade corporate bonds or high yield junk bonds. They can invest in the bonds issued by government agencies, municipalities, or companies.

They might also be divided up according to whether they purchase long term or short term maturities of bonds. These funds may also buy bonds or stocks of either domestic companies or global companies, or even international companies outside of the United States. Index funds are another type of mutual fund that attempts to match a certain market index's performance over time. The S&P 500 index is an example of one on which index mutual funds are based. With this type of index fund, the mutual fund would find derivatives based on the S&P 500 stock index futures so that they could match the index's performance as identically as possible.

To help investors better understand the type of fund that they are getting into, the SEC came out with a particular name rule in the 40' Act that makes funds actually invest in minimally eighty percent of securities that actually match up with their name. So a fund called the New York Tax Free Bond Fund would have to use eighty percent or more of its funds to purchase investments of tax free bonds that New York State and its various agencies issued.

NASDAQ (National Association of Securities Dealers)

The NASDAQ is the acronym for the National Association of Securities Dealers Automated Quotation Systems, though the organization has dropped the Automated Quotation Systems part of the name as obsolete. This NASDAQ is the country's second largest stock exchange. It represents the principal rival to the NYSE, or New York Stock Exchange, which is the largest stock exchange in the country and only one larger than it.

The NASDAQ is also the largest equity securities trading market in the U.S. that is based on an electronic screen. When market capitalization, or the value of its stock per share multiplied by the number of outstanding shares, is considered, it is the fourth largest trading exchange in the world. The NASDAQ actually records a higher trading volume than does any competing electronic stock exchange on earth with its actively traded 2919 ticker symbols.

NASDAQ became established in 1971 by the NASD, or National Association of Securities Dealers. The system originally represented the successor to the OTC, or Over the Counter traded market. It later developed into an actual stock exchange of sorts. By 2000 and 2001, the NASD sold off the NASDAQ into the NASDAQ OMX Group, who presently own and operate it. Its stock is listed under the symbol of NDAQ since July 2 of 2002. The FINRA, or Financial Industry Regulatory Authority, oversees and regulates the NASDAQ stock market exchange.

The NASDAQ made major contributions to the world of electronic stock exchange trading as the first one of its kind on earth. When it began, it started out as a computer bulletin board system that did not literally put buyers and sellers in touch. Among its great achievements, the NASDAQ proved to be responsible for decreasing the spread, or the bid and the asking prices' difference for stocks. Many dealers disliked the NASDAQ in the early days, as they made enormous profits on these higher spreads.

In subsequent years, the NASDAQ evolved into a typical stock exchange through adding volume reporting and trade reporting to its new automated trading systems. This exchange became the first such stock market in America to advertise to the public. They would highlight companies that traded on the NASDAQ, many of which were technology companies. Their commercials closed out with the motto the stock exchange for the nineties and beyond, that they eventually changed to NASDAQ, the stock market for the next one hundred years.

The NASDAQ is set to become a trans Atlantic stock exchange titan with its purchase of the Norway based OMX stock exchange. This will only enhance its European holdings that presently include eight other stock exchanges throughout Europe. Besides its NASDAQ stock exchange in New York City, the group possesses a one third stake in the Dubai Stock Exchange in the United Arab Emirates. With its double listing arrangement in place with the OMX exchange, the NASDAQ OMX is set to become the major competitor for NYSE Euronext in bringing in new listings.

Net Operating Income

Net Operating Income can refer to two different concepts. It may be used in regards to companies and corporations, or to properties and their annual incomes. Where companies are concerned, Net Operating Income, also known by its acronym NOI, is the income after deducting the company's operating expenses. It is figured up in advance of taking off interest and income tax deductions. When this number proves to be a positive number, it is called net operating income. If the number turns out to be a negative value, then it is referred to as a Net Operating Loss, also known by the acronym of NOL. Many analysts like to look at the Net Operating Income as a realistic picture of how a company is performing. They feel that this number is more difficult for management to manipulate than are other numbers in the income statements of a company.

Pertaining to properties, Net Operating Income equals the annual gross income minus the expenses for operating. In this respect, the gross income is comprised of real income from rentals as well as other incomes like laundry receipts, vending receipts, parking charges, and every type of income that is related to properties. Operating expenses prove to be the expenses that are encountered in the typical maintenance and operating of the property in question. Among these expenses are insurance, maintenance, repairs, utilities, management fees, property taxes, and supplies. Some costs are not deemed to be operating expenses, such as capital expenditures, interest and principal payments, income taxes, depreciation, or amortization of the points on a loan. So, calculating the Net Operating Income on a property involves first taking the various forms of annual gross income and adding them all up. Then the operating expenses should be taken and added up. Finally, the operating expense total is subtracted from the operating income total to achieve the Net Operating Income figure.

In real estate, Net Operating Income is utilized within two critical real estate ratios. The Capitalization Rate, also know as the Cap Rate, is employed to come up with an estimate of the actual value of properties that produce income. For example, maybe a property being considered for purchase possesses a market capitalization value of ten. Coming up with the market cap rate is achieved by considering the financial information from the sales of properties that produce income and are similar in a particular market.

The other important real estate ratio that relies on Net Operating Income is the Debt Coverage Ratio, also know as the DCR. The Net Operating Income proves to be a critical component of this DCR ratio. Investors and lenders alike utilize the debt coverage ratio to determine if a property has the capability of covering both its mortgage payments and operating expenses together. A result of one is deemed to be the break even point. The majority of lenders want at least a 1.1 to 1.3 ratio in order to contemplate making a commercial loan to a given property. The higher this debt coverage ratio works out to be in a banks' opinion, the safer the loan will ultimately be.

Net Worth

Net worth is a figure that represents a business, an individual, or another group's difference between the assets that they have and the liabilities that they owe. Figuring up this net worth is done by first taking all of the entity's debts and obligations and then subtracting that number from the entire sum of assets. If the total of all of these assets is greater than the sum of all of the debts and obligations, then a positive net worth results. Otherwise, when the debts are greater than the assets, then the entity has a negative net worth.

When you sit down to determine the net worth figure, every asset should be totaled in the operation. There are many different kinds of assets. These are comprised of cash in the bank, holdings of stocks, real estate, bonds, and other types of investments, and major possessions like vehicles. Correctly figuring out the different assets' values is done with the use of the up to date fair market value, not the cost paid for the item when it is purchased.

You must also correctly add up the total of debts and obligations when you are attempting to get a correct net worth value. Liabilities cover many different obligations, like a car payment, mortgage, total of credit card debt outstanding, and any other forms of loans that have balances left on them. Both every asset and liability must be measured in order to come up with an accurate net worth.

Knowing your present net worth is very useful and meaningful. If you are able to cover all of your outstanding debt obligations simply by selling of all of your assets, then you have a financial condition that is fairly stable and in order. If your assets are more than sufficient to cover all of your obligations, then your finances are in greater shape. Most businesses and people seek to reach a point that they have actual positive net worth.

There are a few benefits from having a correct understanding of your net worth. It is essential that your present assets' value is greater than your present debt load. A person who owes more money than they actually own presents a profile of a person who is not an especially good credit risk. Without a positive net worth, many lending institutions like banks will think twice about providing you with the most advantageous loan rates offered. This is because they feel that you present more of a risk to lend money.

It is also good to know where your net worth stands because it is a helpful beginning point for your general financial planning. Should you discover that you hardly have sufficient assets with which to cover your present amount of debts, then this is a good sign that you should not engage in any other purchases until later, after you have eliminated several of your debts. This means that if you occasionally figure up your net worth, then you will comprehend not only where you stand now, but also when you will be in a better position to purchase a new car.

Note (promissory)

Promissory notes are negotiable instruments that are called notes payable in accounting circles. In such promissory notes, an issuer writes an unlimited promise that he or she will pay a certain amount of money to the payee. This can be set up either on demand of the payee, or at a pre arranged future point in time. Specific terms are always arranged for the repayment of the debt in the promissory note.

Promissory notes are somewhat like IOU's and yet quite different. Unlike an IOU that only agrees that there is a debt in question, promissory notes are made up of a particular promise to pay the debt. In conversational vernacular, loan contract, loan agreement, or loan are often utilized in place of promissory note, even though such terms do not mean the same things legally. While a promissory note does provide proof of a loan in existence, it is not the loan contract. A loan contract instead has all of the conditions and terms of the particular loan arrangement within it.

Promissory notes contain a variety of term elements in them. Among these are the amount of principal, the rate of interest, the parties involved, the repayment terms, the date, and the date of maturity. From time to time, provisions may be included pertaining to the payee's rights should the issuer default. These rights could include the ability to foreclose on the issuer's assets.

A particular type of promissory note is a Demand Promissory note. This specific kind does not come with an exact date of maturity. Instead, it is due when the lender demands repayment. Generally, in these cases lenders only allow several days advance notice before the payment must be made.

Within the U.S., the Article 3 of the Uniform Commercial Code regulates most promissory notes. These negotiable forms of promissory notes are heavily used along with other documents in mortgages that involve financing purchases of real estate properties. When people make loans in between each other, the making and signing of promissory notes are commonly critical for the purposes of record keeping and paying taxes. Businesses also receive capital via the use of promissory notes that are sometimes referred to as commercial papers. These promissory notes became a finance source for the creditors of the firm receiving money.

Promissory notes have functioned like currency that proved to be privately issued in the past. Because of this, such promissory notes that are bearer negotiable have mostly been made illegal, since they represent an alternative to the officially sanctioned currency. Promissory notes go back to well before the 1500's in Western Europe. Tradition claims that the very first one ever signed existed in Milan in 1325. Reference is made to some being issued between Barcelona and Genoa back in 1384, even though we no longer have the promissory notes themselves. The first one that we still have dates back to 1553 where Ginaldo Giovanni Battista Stroxxi issued one that he created in Medina del Campo, Spain against the city of Besancon.

NYSE (New York Stock Exchange)

The NYSE is the acronym for the world's largest stock exchange, the New York Stock Exchange. With a market capitalization of companies listed on it totaling at $11.92 trillion dollars in August 2010, it also possessed an average day trading value of around $153 billion in 2008. By market capitalization, the NYSE has no rivals for size.

The New York Stock Exchange is owned and operated by the NYSE Euronext company. This outfit came into being in 2007 when the NYSE merged with the completely electronic Euronext stock exchange. Four rooms make up the trading floor of the NYSE that is found at 11 Wall Street. Its main building is found at 18 Broad Street on the corners of Wall Street and Exchange Place. This building became a National Historic Landmark back in 1978, along with its sister 11 Wall Street Building.

Occasionally known as "the Big Board," the New York Stock Exchange allows for sellers and buyers of stocks to exchange shares in all of the companies that are listed for public trading. Its trading hours prove to be 9:30 AM to 4:00 PM on Monday to Friday. Holidays are spelled out in advance by the exchange itself.

The NYSE has always operated as an in person trading floor since its inception in 1792. Today, this works in an auction format that is ongoing. Floor traders here are able to make stock transactions for investors. They simply gather together surrounding the particular company post where there is a specialist broker working as auctioneer in open outcry format to get buyers and sellers together and to oversee the auction itself. This specialist works directly for the company that is an NYSE member and not the exchange itself. These specialists will commit their own money to assist the trades about ten percent of the time. Naturally, they also give out information that serves to bring together sellers and buyers.

In 1995, NYSE began making the automation transition for the auctions. This started with hand held computers that were wireless. Like this, traders were capable of executing and getting orders electronically. This ended a 203 year tradition of paper based trades.

From January 24 of 2007, most every stock on the NYSE is able to be traded on the electronic Hybrid Market. With this ability to send in customer orders for electronic confirmation immediately, orders can also be sent to the floor for auction market trade. More than eighty-two percent of the NYSE order volume came to the floor electronically in only the first three months of that first year.

Only those who own one of 1,366 actual seats on the exchange are permitted to trade shares directly on the exchange. Such seats are sold for enormous sums. The highest price paid for one amounted to $4 million in the tail end of the 1990's. The highest price ever paid adjusted for inflation proved to be $625,000 in 1929, which would amount to more than six million dollars in terms of 2010 dollars. Since the exchange became a public company, the seats have been instead sold in one year licenses.

Offshore Account

Offshore accounts are accounts that you have in a bank that is located in another country. The term originally came from banks and accounts that were found in the Channel Islands, which were literally off shore from Great Britain. Interestingly enough, the majority of offshore banks and offshore accounts are still found on islands to this day.

Individuals and businesses might use offshore accounts for a variety of purposes. The popular conception of offshore accounts is that spies and criminals utilize them as places to store their cash. In fact, most offshore accounts are completely legitimate. People and even businesses have them as places to deposit their money, make investments, or use as trading accounts. When they are used as trading accounts, the person utilizes them to place online trades in stock markets.

Offshore accounts can also be employed to hide assets from governments and taxes, even though this is not the case for most such offshore accounts. A number of offshore banking accounts exist, such as HSBC Offshore Banking in Gibralter, Barclays Offshore Banking in the island of Jersey, and Griffon Bank in the island of Dominica in the Caribbean. These accounts provide all types of services for the banking needs of people and businesses, one of which is Internet banking.

Among the advantages of offshore accounts is privacy. Offshore banking institutions keep offshore account information secret. Such banks are forbidden to declare this information concerning the status of the account or any of its particulars to any individual or entity who is not the account holder. The only exception to this is when offshore banks believe the holder of an offshore account may be using the account for illegal purposes like drug trafficking, support of terrorism, or criminal money laundering.

Another good reason for putting your money into an offshore bank account is because they typically offer better interest on money. It is a well known fact that offshore banks provide better interest rates for their customers. Such rates depend on the location and the offshore bank in question. Reasons for higher interest rates have to do with the lower operating costs in these islands or other locations, as well as the higher interest rates in the prosperous countries where they are based.

Tax advantages prove to be another motivating factor for offshore banking and having offshore accounts. A number of countries will provide tax benefits to investors who are foreigners in order to attract their money. While this is different for every location too, many offshore banks and their hosting countries will not levy taxes on investment returns and interest earned in such offshore accounts.

Operating Expenses

In the world of business and corporations, operating expenses is the term that pertains to the continuous costs of running a business. This makes operating expenses the expenses for everything happening behind the scenes. Such operating costs include any expenses incurred for the literal operation of the business.

You occasionally see the words operating expenses written as OPEX. This is especially true in internal memos and documentation that are relevant to the earnings of a company. The most frequent operating expenses are those having to do with employee benefits and salaries. These commonly make up the biggest individual expenses for a corporation. Other operating costs could be office supplies, marketing budgets, licensing and legal fees, raw material expenses, costs of research and development, accounting fees, and office utilities.

Another key operating expense is depreciation. Depreciation proves to be the quantity of value that diminishes in an asset over a period of time. This means that accounts can take equipment, vehicles, and other assets and subtract out the lower value off of the initial value to come up with depreciation as assets gradually lose value. This depreciation can be counted as an operating expense so long as the asset is still employed by the business in its operations.

Some expenses are deemed to be capital expenses instead of operating expenses. This is generally the case for single event expenses, like buying replacement equipment for completely depreciated existing equipment. This division of costs allows both the firm and its investors to have a more realistic snap shot of for what the money is used before it is able to be put to profits. When you are self employed, then you may count both CAPEX and OPEX as business expenses.

Operating expenses have to be included in the annual reports of both not for profit outfits and corporations that are publicly traded. This kind of information commonly comes with charts that compare the operating expenses of several years. In this way, a reader is able to obtain a good understanding of how the expenses are progressing with time.

By tracking operating expenses in an ongoing fashion all year long, the information is easily at hand for a company to include it in their reports. Accountants, or alternatively programs that do financial management, are generally used to help with operating expense tracking and calculation. When operating expenses go up and down every year, investors will want to know why this is the case. Detailed records provide good explanations for the final numbers to satisfy the questioning parties. Corporate treasurers are generally responsible for answering these queries and coming up with answers.

Origination Fees

Origination fees are also known as activation fees. These are the costs pertaining to setting up an account with a mortgage broker, bank, or other firm that will go through the tasks of collecting and processing all documents and requirements for getting a loan, in particular a mortgage on a house.

These origination fees are generally amounts that are pre determined for any new account. Origination fees can range from half a percentage point to two percentage points of the entire loan total. This variance has to do with where the loans come from, off of either the prime or the subprime loan market. On a subprime mortgage for $200,000, the origination fee would likely amount to two percent, equaling four thousand dollars in this particular case.

The average origination fee comes in at approximately one percent of the total mortgage loan dollar amount. This fee goes to the firm that originates and processes your loan. It defrays their expenses that arise from developing, putting together, and finally closing on your mortgage.

The rise of the Internet has allowed for an alternative compensation scheme for companies that put together and originate mortgages. While the vast majority of mortgage brokers and banks still charge these loan origination fees, there are some Internet based brokers who use a different model. These entities do no charge origination fees at all; instead they pass the savings directly on to you the customer. The way that they get paid is by selling your loan to an investor once it is closed. The investor pays them a premium for the packaged loan, which covers the origination fees, and the online mortgage broker is compensated for his or her work and time.

The origination fees can be deducted from taxes. The year that the transaction closed and the origination fees were charged, they can be used to reduce actual income on income tax forms. The Internal Revenue Service permits this reduction to income no matter who pays the origination fees, meaning that a person who employs a broker that does not charge them origination fees will still be able to deduct the fees that the investors who later buy the loan are subsequently paying to the mortgage broker. This means that if you take out a $200,000 mortgage, then you are able to deduct the $2,000 in loan origination fees, even if you did not have to pay them, but an investor in the loan did instead.

Origination fees are listed on the HUD-1 Settlement form. They are tallied beneath the sub-heading of lender charges. Discount points that are used to bring down interest rates either permanently or temporarily are also listed on this form under the category.

OTC (Over The Counter)

OTC is the acronym for Over the Counter. In the business and financial world, Over the Counter trading is also known as trading off of the exchange. Such OTC trading goes on when financial instruments of various kinds, including stocks, commodities, bonds, or derivatives, are traded literally between the buying and selling party themselves, without having an exchange in the middle of the transaction. Over the Counter trading can be said to be the opposite of exchange trading. Exchange trading happens in facilities or over electronic market places that are specially created for the trading of these instruments. Stock exchanges and futures exchanges are the places that exchange trading takes place and Over the Counter trading does not.

Within the United States, Over the Counter stock trading is done via market makers who ensure that there are markets in both Pink Sheet and OTCBB, or bulletin boards, securities. They do this through the utilization of quotation services that are between dealers, like Pink Quote, run by the Pink OTC Markets, and OTC Bulletin Board for the OTCBB. While Over the Counter stocks typically do not either list or trade on any form of stock exchange, stocks that are listed on exchanges may be traded on the third market over the counter.

OTCBB quoted stocks have to follow the reporting rules as set out by the United States SEC, or Securities and Exchange Commission, regulatory body. Pink Sheet stocks are not governed by such reporting requirements. Still other stocks that are traded as OTCQX meet different disclosure guidelines that they are permitted to work under in the OTC Pink sheet markets.

OTC can also relate to contracts created between two entities. In these contracts, the two parties concur on the way that a specific trade will be settled at a certain future point. These typically come from investment banks and go out to their own clients. Good examples of these types of OTC arrangements are swaps and forwards. Such contracts are typically arranged over the phone or via computer. Derivative OTC contracts fall under the governance of an agreement provided by the International Swaps and Derivatives Association. This type of OTC market is sometimes called the Fourth Market.

In the Financial Crisis of 2007-2010, many of these OTC derivative contracts created and wreaked havoc in international financial markets specifically because they were traded over the counter, and no one exactly knew what risk and credit were entailed in the contracts that totaled in the tens of trillions of dollars and were made between mysterious partners. To address this critical problem, the NYMEX, or New York Mercantile Exchange, set up a mechanism for clearing many of the most frequently traded energy derivatives that were previously traded only OTC. Now, many of these customers can simply hand over the trade to the exchange's clearing house ClearPort. This removes the dangers associated with both performance and credit risk that were previously seen in these OTC transactions. Other exchanges are endeavoring to do the same thing to try to take derivatives and credit default swap contracts away from the shadowy world of Over the Counter trading. The G20, or Group of Twenty Industrialized and Industrializing nations, is considering ways of rewarding parties for bringing such OTC derivative transactions onto regulated exchanges as well.

Paper Assets

Paper assets have three different meanings depending on whether you are discussing business, investments, or fiat currencies. Where business is concerned, paper assets are assets that you can not easily use or change in to cash. These paper assets possess extremely low liquidity, meaning that they are difficult to sell too. The term in this case literally arises from assets that are valuable on paper, or that have a paper only value.

In investments, paper assets mean something entirely different. They refer to assets that are representations of something. Paper assets in investments literally are pieces of paper that define ownership of an asset. Classic examples of investing paper assets prove to be stocks, currencies, bonds, money market accounts, and similar types of investments. For paper assets to have a tangible value, there must be a working financial system in order to back them up and exchange them. In the cases where a financial system collapses, paper assets commonly sharply decline along with it. The majority of Americans have placed an overwhelming percentage of their money in paper assets, and as the Financial Crisis of 2007-2010 showed, this makes them extremely vulnerable to economic calamities.

Paper assets stand apart in contrast to hard assets. Hard assets contain actual value in the nature of the item itself. There are many forms of hard assets, but among the most popular are gold, silver, diamonds, oil, platinum, land, and other such physical holdings. While financial collapses can cause a set back for the value of hard assets, these types of assets almost always hold up far better than do paper assets.

Many people are shocked by the fact that the U.S. dollar is also a paper asset, as are all Fiat currencies in the world except for the Swiss Franc. These paper currencies are no longer backed up by the long running gold standard. Instead, they only have value because their respective issuing governments, as well as the underlying currency users, say that they do. The Swiss Franc is a lonely exception. The Swiss constitution requires that for every four paper or electronic currency Swiss Francs in existence, there must be one Swiss Franc worth of gold in the Swiss National Bank vaults. Since the Swiss only value their gold holdings at around $250 per ounce, and gold has been trading between $1,300 and $1,400 per ounce for some time now, the Swiss actually have a greater gold backing to their currency than one hundred percent.

Paper Investments

Paper investments can be several things. Where businesses are concerned, paper investments turn out to be investments in commercial paper. Commercial paper investments prove to actually be money market instruments that companies and banks sell to raise money. There are many large issuers with good credit who offer these types of paper investments to interested investors. They represent inexpensive other sources of short term funding as opposed to standard bank loans.

Commercial paper investments come with a fixed maturity of from one day to two hundred and seventy days. These types of paper investments are generally regarded as extremely secure, although they are unsecured loans. The companies that take advantage of them are commonly utilizing these short term operating funds for working capital or inventory purchases.

Corporations like to utilize commercial paper because they are able to quickly and effectively raise significant sums of money without having to get involved with costly SEC registration through selling paper investments. This can be done through working with independent dealers, or on their own efforts directly to investors. Institutional buyers commonly prove to be significant buyers of these types of paper investments.

Such notes come with amounts and maturity dates that can be specifically crafted to meet particular needs. The key features of these types of paper investments are that they are of short term maturity, commonly ranging from only three to six months of time. They liquidate on their own, with no action being required by the investing party in question. There is little to no speculation involved in their intended use as well. This gives them an appeal of clarity.

Offering this type of paper investments offers several advantages for the issuer as well. The issuer is able to access cash at rates that are lower than those offered at the bank. Companies taking advantage of commercial paper are able to leave open reserves of borrowing power at their area banks. Finally, they are capable of getting cash on hand which will allow them to benefit from trade creditors who offer special discounts for those who pay for supplies and other needs with cash.

Where traditional investments are concerned, paper investments also prove to be investments whose value is stated on and represented by paper. A number of different kinds of popular investments in the United States qualify as paper investments. These include stocks, bonds, mutual funds, certificates of deposits, and money market accounts. Shares of stock are pieces of paper that relate a certain percentage of ownership in a publicly traded company.

Most any type of investment that does not have a physical component of the investment associated with it is considered a paper investment. Commodities, as well as futures and options on futures that permit you to take delivery of the underlying commodities if you wish, represent examples of investments that are not only paper investments. These types of investments, along with real estate holdings, are considered to be physical, or hard, investments.

Passive Income

Passive income refers to money that, once it is arranged and established, does not require additional work from the person getting it. A variety of different types of passive income exist. Among them are movie, music, book, screenplay, television, and patent royalties. Other samples of passive income include click through income, rental income, and revenue from online advertising.

Activities that lead to passive income have something in common. They usually need a great amount of money, time, or both invested in them upfront to get them started. There are financial means to establishing passive income as well. You could purchase a rental property or choose to invest in a partnership or other form of company where you are a silent partner. The income that you derive from these investment activities is deemed to be passive.

Various other kinds of passive income do not need a great deal of financial investment made in them, but instead require great amounts of effort, time, and even creativity to achieve. More than a year can be required to either build up a popular website that can contribute passive income from advertising or to write a great novel. Making money from such passive income that is actually profit may take longer.

Books are a good example of how long it can take to actually make money from passive income. Publishers generally get to recover all of their printing and promoting costs, as well as any advance monies given to authors, before royalties are created and paid. Books that sell poorly could turn out to pay the author little to nothing.

Websites have a different set of challenges for their creators. There has to be more than simply good content to make money from them. They must similarly rank high in the search engine results for the necessary amount of visitors to find and go to the website. Unless a great number of visitor hits are recorded on a website, the passive income that is generated will be negligible or even none.

People are willing to put in such a huge amount of time with little assurance of results because they know that the passive income generating activity will create money for them around the clock for years to come, if it is successful. This means that passive income money is constantly being made, even when the person is asleep or on vacation. If you are able to get one passive income project up and running well, then you can attempt others. This way, you might hope to develop a few different income streams that result in a significant annual revenue which can even support you.

Many investors believe that passive income is the most superior kind that you can achieve. This is why rental properties can be so popular. Even though they can require a significant amount of maintenance work and tenant management, they can provide substantial income once several such properties are owned and made profitable.

Pension Entitlements

Pension entitlements are the monies that have been promised to employees who are guaranteed a pension by the company for which they work. The majority of newly issued pensions anymore come from Federal, state, and local government employees. Some companies still offer pension entitlements to their employees who serve a minimum number of years with the firm, such as from twenty to thirty years.

These companies are becoming fewer and farther between as more and more corporations switch over to matching 401K retirement plans that cost them far less money and entail significantly lesser liabilities every year. This is because with pre set limit matches to 401K contributions, companies can know for certain how much money they will have to come out of pocket, whereas with pensions, it has much to do with how long the retirees live.

Pension entitlements are at risk as they become larger every year. Many companies are struggling to keep up with their pension entitlements as their retiring employees live longer and longer. Because of the danger to failing pensions that many retirees count on, the PBGC was set up. This entity acronym stands for Pension Benefit Guarantee Corporation.

The government created this entity in the Employee Retirement Income Security Act in 1974. Today, it safe guards in excess of forty-four million American retirees and workers pensions, covering the pension entitlements against default from the companies underlying them. These are held in greater than twenty-nine thousand multi employer and private single employer defined benefit pension plans.

The PBGC does not derive money from the general tax revenues in protecting the pension entitlements. Insurance premiums that Congress sets are paid by the sponsors of defined benefit plans, assets from pension plans that PBGC trustees, investment income of the PBGC, and recoveries made from companies who are no longer handling their own plans.

As a result of the financial crisis of 2007-2010, many private pension funds have suffered disastrous losses. In 2008 alone, this amounted to tangible losses of in excess of twenty-six percent. Even though the markets recovered somewhat, many pension funds had locked in their losses by selling the underwater investments. As a result of these terrible financial events, even more pension entitlements in the United States are now under funded.

In order to help make up for these, businesses will have to make substantially larger contributions in the future. It remains to be seen if the Pension Benefit Guarantee Corporation will be able to keep up with and cover all of the unfunded pension entitlements that have been promised to retirees and workers. Some experts have speculated that the PBGC itself will require bailouts in the hundreds of billions of dollars in the near future.

PMI (Private Mortgage Insurance)

PMI is the acronym for Private Mortgage Insurance, also known some-times as Lenders Mortgage Insurance. PMI proves to be insurance that is paid to a lending institution that is required much of the time when an individual gets a mortgage loan. Such insurance is used to cover any losses that arise if a person is not capable of paying back their mortgage loan.

Should the lender not be able to recoup all of its costs in foreclosing on and selling the mortgaged property, then PMI insurance covers the re-maining losses that exist on the balance sheet of the bank or other lender. The general rates for this Private Mortgage Insurance turn out to be around $55 each month for every $100,000 that is actually financed. On a $250,000 loan, this amounts to $1,875 each year in premiums.

Private Mortgage insurance yearly costs range though. They are usually given out in comparison against the entire loan's value. This depends on a number of factors, such as loan type, loan term, actual coverage amount, amount of home value that the person finances, the premium payment frequency that might be monthly or yearly, and the individ-ual's credit score. While PMI can be paid in advance with closing costs, it can also be worked into the loan payments with single premium PMI.

Private Mortgage Insurance is generally only necessary when the down payment proves to be smaller than twenty percent of either the ap-praised value of the property or alternatively of the sales price. When then loan to value ratio is greater than eighty percent, you can expect to be required to carry it. As the principal is reduced with monthly pay-ments, or the home value rises through real estate appreciation, or a combination of the two occurs, then this Private Mortgage Insurance might not be required any longer. At this point, the home owner is al-lowed to discontinue paying for the PMI insurance.

There are some banks and lenders who will insist that PMI be paid for minimally for a pre fixed period of time, such as two to three years. This is regardless of whether the principal value of the property ex-ceeds eighty percent in a shorter amount of time. Banks do not have to permit a person to cancel this insurance legally until the loan has amor-tized down to a Loan to Value ratio of seventy-eight percent of the orig-inal price for which the house is purchased.

A cancellation request must originate from the mortgage servicer. They must send it to the issuing company that made the PMI policy in the first place. Many times, such a mortgage servicer will insist on a current home value appraisal being done in order to ascertain the actual loan to value ratio.

Premiums paid for mortgage insurance were not tax deductible according to the Internal Revenue Service in the past. In 2007 this changed. Now all PMI premiums are considered to be fully reducing of your income for the year in question.

Ponzi Scheme

Ponzi Schemes prove to be frauds surrounding investments that are related to the pay out of returns to investors in the scheme that are covered using contributions from new investors. The individuals who run Ponzi schemes are able to attract newer investors through boasting of tremendous opportunities that will guarantee terrific investment returns, typically with little to no risk.

With a great number of these Ponzi Schemes, the managers of the scheme concentrate their efforts on constantly bringing in new sums of money in order to be capable of giving out the payments that they promised investors from earlier time periods. Besides this, they utilize the new money for their own personal expenses. Rarely does any energy actually go into real investment opportunities and strategies.

Ponzi schemes always fail at some point in time. This eventually happens since there are no real earnings to distribute. Because of this problem, Ponzi schemes need constant money flowing into them from newer investors in order to survive. As attracting newer investors becomes more challenging, or if a great number of currently involved investors request their money back, then the Ponzi Scheme will likely fall apart.

Ponzi Schemes actually earned their name from a famed early con artist Charles Ponzi. He became famous after he tricked literally thousands of well to do New Englanders into pouring their money into his speculation in postage stamps in the 1920's. The allure of his scheme proved to be hard to resist, since bank accounts were paying only five percent annual returns while he offered investors incredible returns of fifty percent in only ninety days. In the early days, Charles Ponzi really did purchase a small quantity of international mail coupons to support his investment scheme. Before long, he decided to employ the money that came in to cash out earlier investors.

The most successful Ponzi Scheme of all time proved to be the one run by Bernie Madoff. Madoff ran an over thirty year, over thirty billion dollar investment scheme that tricked thousands of investors out of their money. Madoff proved to have a different angle on his Ponzi scheme in that he did not offer his investors who were short term amazing returns. Rather than this, he sent out fake account statements that constantly demonstrated moderate but always positive gains, no matter how turbulent the market proved to be.

Bernie Madoff is presently undergoing a one hundred and fifty year sentence in federal prison for his activities. His investment advisory company began back in 1960 and did not come down until the end of 2008. All during the years that his scheme ran, he served as Vice Chairman of the National Association of Securities Dealers, and even as a member of the board of governors and chairman for the NASDAQ stock market.

The Securities Exchange Commission is ultimately responsible for discovering and prosecuting Ponzi Schemes. They typically utilize emergency actions to freeze assets while they break up the schemes. In 2009 as an example, the SEC actually pursued sixty different Ponzi schemes, the highest profile one of which turned out to be Robert Allen Stanford's $8 billion Ponzi scheme.

Portfolio

In the world of business and finance, a portfolio stands for an investment collection that a person or institution holds. People and other entities put together portfolios in order to diversify their holdings to reduce risk to a manageable level. A number of different kinds of risk are mitigated through the acquisition of a few varying types of assets. A portfolio's assets might be comprised of stocks, options, bonds, bank accounts, gold certificates, warrants, futures contracts, real estate, facilities of production, and other assets that tend to hold their value.

Investment portfolios may be constructed in various ways. Financial entities will commonly do their own careful analysis of investments in putting together a portfolio. Individuals might work with the either financial firms or financial advisors that manage portfolios. Alternatively, they could put together a self directed portfolio through working with a self directed online broker such as TD Ameritrade, eTrade, or Scott Trade.

A whole field of portfolio management has arisen to help with the allocation of investment money. This management pertains to determining the types of assets that are appropriate for an individual's risk tolerance and ultimate goals. Choosing the instruments that will comprise a portfolio has much to do with knowing the kinds of instruments to buy and sell, how many of each to obtain, and the time that is most appropriate to purchase or sell them.

Such decisions are rooted in a measurement for the investments' performance. This usually pertains to risk versus return on investments and anticipated returns of the entire portfolio. With portfolio returns, various types of assets are understood to commonly return amounts of differing ranges. Portfolio management has to factor in an individual investor's own precise situation and desired results as well. There are investors who are more fearful of risk than are other investors. These kinds of investors are termed risk averse. Risk averse portfolios are significantly different in their composition than are typical portfolios.

Mutual funds have evolved the act of portfolio management almost to a science. Their fund managers came up with techniques that allow them to prioritize and ideally set their portfolio holdings. This fund management reduces risk and increases returns to maximum levels. Strategies that these managers have created for running portfolios include designing equally weighted portfolios, price weighted portfolios, capitalization weighted portfolios, and optimal portfolios in which the risk adjusted return proves to be the highest possible.

Well diversified portfolios will contain many different asset classes. These will include far more than just stocks, bonds, and mutual funds. They will feature international stocks and bonds to provide diversification away from the U.S. dollar, as well as foreign currencies and hard asset commodities such as real estate investments, and gold and silver holdings.

Portfolio Income

Portfolio income proves to be money that is actually brought in from a group of investments. The portfolio commonly includes all of the various types of investments that an investor owns. These include bonds, stocks, mutual funds, and certificates of deposit. These various financial instruments earn a variety of different types of passive income, such as dividends, interest income, and capital gain distributions. Such portfolio income returns are generated by the holdings of the various investment products in the portfolio.

Portfolio income varies with the types of investments that an investor picks. You as an investor will commonly look at two different factors when assembling a portfolio for portfolio income. These turn out to be the money that the investment itself will produce, which is also known as an investment's return, and the investment's risk level that it contains.

As an example, stocks are frequently deemed to be investments with considerable risk, yet the other side of the risk return equation is that they provide income from a company's dividends, or distribution earnings returned to the shareholders, as well as an increase in the stock price as the stock value gains with time. Certificates of deposit and bonds create interest income that is paid out on the investment that you hold. Still different kinds of investments produce other types of income, although this depends on the characteristics of the investment in question.

To maximize the portfolio income while reducing the amount of risk involved, individuals commonly choose to invest in numerous different kinds of investments. This is known as diversifying your portfolio and portfolio income. This way, you can combine both safer investments that provide lower real returns with riskier investments that offer greater investment returns. Your total collection of investments is the portfolio that makes your portfolio income for you.

This portfolio income is also classified as passive income, or income that does not require you to perform any work in order to make the money. The upfront investment actually creates the income without you having to be actively involved in the money making process. This stands in contrast to incomes that are earned through active involvement, or active income that you must expend both energy and time to create.

The ultimate goal for you with your portfolio income will probably be to build up enough of it that you are capable of living off of only the income that the portfolio generates. Once this point is reached, you would be able to not receive a payroll check any longer. Instead, you would support yourself in retirement from the dividends, interest, and capital gains created by the investments in the form of portfolio income. The best and safest way to do this is to only draw on the portfolio income itself, without drawing down the original principal.

By not touching the investment principal, you allow your portfolio and resulting portfolio income to build up over time. If you do not take out the portfolio income, then the total value of the portfolio will grow faster with time, allowing you to compound your investments for retirement. It is critical to have enough money saved for retirement that you do not need to take out this principal to support yourself. Sufficient portfolio income should be generated to cover the monthly retirement expenses. In this way, you will not be reducing your principal and risking the very real danger of your portfolio running out of money while you are still alive to need it.

Preferred Stock

Preferred stock is referred to as preference shares or preferred shares as well. Preferred stock is the name used for a particular equity security which exhibits both characteristics of a stock equity as well as an instrument of debt. Because of this, preferred stocks are commonly deemed to be hybrid types of instruments. In the claims on a company's assets in the event of default or bankruptcy, preferred stocks prove to be higher ranking than mere common stocks, yet subordinated to bonds.

Preferred stocks have a number of interesting properties. They typically come with a dividend that is often fixed. They also enjoy preference versus common stocks where dividend payments are concerned and at any liquidation of the company's assets. A downside to preferred stocks is that they do not include voting rights as do common stock shares. Some preferred stocks offer convertible features that turn them into common shares of stock at a certain time. There are preferred stocks that may be called in early at the wishes of the issuing company. All terms for a preferred stock are listed out specifically in the Certificate of Designation.

Since preferred stocks are somewhat like bonds, the big credit rating companies all rate them for quality of credit. Preferred stocks generally garner lower ratings than do bonds, as the dividends of preferred stocks are not guaranteed as are bonds' interest payments. Preferred stocks are also subordinated to all of the creditors, making them less secure.

Dividends are a key feature of preferred stocks and the main motivating factor in acquiring them. Preferred stocks come with dividend payment preference over other shares. While this does not guarantee that the stated dividends will be paid, the company has to pay such dividends to the preferred share holders before they are allowed to issue any common stock shares' dividends.

These dividends for preferred stocks might be either noncumulative or cumulative. Cumulative preferred stocks mandate that companies who neglect to cover stated dividends up to the full rate must cover them fully at a later date. In each passing dividend time frame, the dividends continue to accumulate. This might be on an annual, semi annual, or quarterly basis.

Dividends that are not paid on time are labeled dividends that have passed. These passed dividends for cumulative stocks are called dividends that are in arrears. If a stock does not possess these cumulative features, then it is called a straight preferred stock, or a noncumulative dividend stock. With these types of non cumulative preferred stocks, the dividends that become passed simply vanish for good if they are not paid on time.

Besides these preferred stock features, they have various other rights. Some types of preferred shares do include a particular group of voting rights for the approval of unusual events like the ability to issue and sell extra shares, to approve the company to be sold, or even to choose the board of directors' members. In general, preferred stocks do not have voting rights. Many preferred shares also come with a liquidation value that states what sum of money was put into the issuing corporation as the shares became issued.

Prospectus

In the world of finance and investments, a prospectus proves to be a legal document. This document is utilized by businesses and institutions who must describe in great detail the type of stock or bond securities that they are issuing for potential buyers. Such a prospectus generally offers great information to investors concerning stocks, mutual funds, bonds, and even other types of investments. The information contained in a prospectus will be reports like the financial statements of the company, a detailed description of their business, biographies of directors and other officers along with their pay packages, lists of properties and assets, and information concerning any lawsuits with which they are involved. When stocks are first being issued as in an IPO, or initial public offering, such a prospectus is given out to the interested parties of investor prospects by brokerages and underwriters. This prospectus should always be read by an interested investing party in advance of putting capital into their security. This is especially important so that you will know the risks that are inherent in the company's business and their stock or bond issue in advance of becoming involved with their securities.

In the U.S., securities may not be offered to the public until after a prospectus has been first placed on file with the SEC, or Securities and Exchange Commission. This is a component of a registration statement. Once the SEC states that the registration is in effect, the stock or bond issuing company is then allowed to utilize the prospectus to help finalize the shares of stock or the bonds in question. The SEC examines a prospectus to ensure that is maintains the appearance of abiding by the disclosure rules.

Some corporations are allowed to work with a simplified prospectus to issue stock and bond securities. These companies must be up to date with their Form 10-K filings with the SEC for a given amount of time, keep their level of market capitalization over a minimum amount, and engage in some procedures. Some scenarios do not mandate that an offering has to be SEC registered. In these cases, a prospectus is called either an offering circular or offering memorandum.

A good example of this is the offerings of municipal securities. These turn out to be exempted from the majority of federal security laws. Such municipal types of issuers usually make up a disclosure document type that is referred to as the official statement instead. This would not offer the depth and scope of a standard prospectus, but will still contain a great deal of helpful and useful information on the particular offering.

Companies generally do not have the time to put together a prospectus entirely on their own. Since this is the case, they commonly engage the help of an issue manager who is also the underwriter of the new issue. These issue managers are also known as book running managers.

Put Option

Put options are financial contracts that are entered into by two parties, the buyer of the option and the seller, or writer, of the option. They are generally called simply puts. A purchaser is able to establish a long position in a put option by buying the right to actually sell the instrument that underlies the put. This is done at a particular price called the strike price and is only valid with the options' seller for a certain amount of time. Should you as the buyer of the option choose to exercise your rights, then the seller has to purchase the associated instrument off of you at the price that was set in advance, whatever the present market price proves to be. In consideration for the buyer gaining this option, you pay an option premium amount to the seller of the option.

Put options are a form of insurance against loss. This is because they offer a guaranteed price and purchaser for a given amount of time for an associated instrument. Put option sellers also benefit when they obtain profits for selling you options that you do not choose to exercise. Options are almost never exercised if the instrument's market value stays above the strike price within the put option contract time frame.

You as a buyer of a put option also have the ability to make money. This is done by selling the associated instrument for a higher price and buying back the position for a significantly lower market price. When an option is not sold or exercised, it expires worthless, representing a total loss of the premium paid for it.

When you purchase a put, you do so with the idea that the associated asset price will decline by the expiration date. The other reason for taking on such a put option is to safe guard a position that you own in the asset or security. Purchasing a put option provides an advantage as compared to selling a stock short. The most that you can lose with a put option is the money that you have paid for it, while those who sell short have an unlimited loss potential. The downside to a put is that the gain potential is restricted to a certain amount. This turns out to be the strike price of the option minus the spot price of the associated asset and the premium that you pay for the option.

A seller or writer of a put feels confident that the associated asset price will go up or remain the same but not decline. Sellers of puts engage in this activity in order to collect premiums. A writer of a put has a limited loss equal to the strike price of the put minus the spot price and the premium that has already been obtained. Put options can similarly be utilized to reduce a risk in the option seller's investment portfolio. They can be part of complicated strategies called option spreads.

A put option that is not covered by owning the underlying security or asset is referred to as a naked put. In these types of put scenarios, the investor might hope to build up a position in the stock that underlies the options so long as they can get a cheap enough price. If you the buyer do not exercise these options, then the seller of the put gets to keep the premium that you paid for the option, representing a profit to the seller.

Should the associated stock's actual price be lower than the strike price of the option when the expiration date comes, then you as a buyer have the ability to exercise the put option in question. This makes the seller of the put option purchase the associated stock at the strike price of the option. You as a buyer would profit to the amount of the difference found between the market price of the stock and the strike price of the option. Yet, should the price of the stock prove to be higher than the strike price of the option on the expiration day, this option becomes worthless. The loss to the owner of the option is restricted to the money that you paid for it, which then becomes the profit to the put option seller.

Quantitative Easing

Quantitative easing is the policy where the government purchases bonds and financial instruments by printing money in order to stimulate the economy. Quantitative easing proves to be a monetary policy that the Federal Reserve and other central banks around the world utilize in order to grow the money supply. They do this by boosting the cash reserves in the banking system. This is accomplished via purchasing the government's issued bonds in order to raise their prices.

Since prices and interest rates of bonds move inversely, higher bond prices lead directly to lower long term interest rates. Quantitative easing is commonly employed only after other more traditional means of dominating the supply of money have not worked. These other methods involve lowering discount rates, bank interest rates, and even interbank interest rates to around zero.

Once these traditional means have failed to stimulate the economy, the Fed then steps into the market and directly buys financial instruments. The assets that they purchase include agency debt, government bonds, corporate bonds, and mortgage backed securities, which they purchase from banks and institutions. This entire process is called open market operations. By depositing electronically created money into the banks' accounts, the banks gain additional reserves that permit them to create still additional money from thin air. The Fed hopes that this multiplication of deposits accomplished through the fractional reserve banking system will allow greater amounts of loans to be made to businesses and individuals in order to stimulate the economy.

This quantitative easing policy is not without its risks. It could be too effective or not sufficiently effective, should banks decide to hoard their extra money to boost their capital reserves. This is particularly the case in an environment of rising defaults in the banks' mortgage and other types of loans' holdings.

Recent examples of quantitative easing abound. This subtle form of printing money became more and more common as the financial crisis of 2007 to 2010 grew worse. In these years, the United States engaged heavily in it, tripling the world wide dollar reserves by creating money both at home and abroad. Other Central Banks, such as those of Great Britain and the European Union, similarly engaged in the practice to help mitigate the effects of the crisis and resulting Great Recession. These countries and economic blocks had all already lowered their interest rates to zero or near zero amounts, and they found quantitative easing to be their best remaining option for restarting economic growth.

Rate of Return

In the worlds of finance and business, the rate of return, also known by its acronym ROR, proves to be the ratio of money lost or gained pertaining to an investment and the sum of money that is originally invested in it. This rate of return is also called the rate of profit or more commonly the return on investment, or ROI. The sum of money that is lost or gained could be called the loss or profit, interest, or even net loss or net income. Regarding the money that is actually invested, it is sometimes called the capital, asset, or principle. It is also referred to as the cost basis of an investment. Rate of return or Return on Investment is commonly stated as a percentage and not a fraction.

This rate of return is one measurement of how much cash is made or lost as a direct result of the investment in question. It quantifies the amount of income stream or cash flow that moves from the investment itself to the investor as a percentage of the original amount that the investor put into the investment. Such cash flow that accrues to the investor comes in a number of forms. It might be interest, profit, capital gains and losses, or dividends received. These capital gains and losses happen as the investment's sale price is greater or less than its initial purchase price. The use of the term cash flow includes everything except for the return of the original invested money.

Rates of return can be figured up as averages covering a number of different time periods. They may also be determined for only one time frame. When these calculations are being made, it is important not to mix up annualized and annual rates of return. Annualized rates of return prove to be geometric average returns figured up over several or even numerous periods. Annualized returns might be the investment return on a period less than or greater than a year, for example for six months or three years. The rates of return are then multiplied out or divided in order to come up with a one year rate of return that can be compared against other annual rates of return. As an example, if an investment possessed a one percent rate of return per month, then this might be more appropriately expressed as an annualized rate of return of twelve percent. Or, if you had a three year rate of return amounting to fifteen percent, then you could say that this is a five percent annualized rate of return.

Annual rates of return are instead returns figured up for single time frame periods. These time frames are commonly one year periods running from the first of January to the last day of December. Alternatively, they could cover any year long period, regardless of what month and day they started and ended.

Real Estate

Real estate turns out to be a phrase that is used legally to describe property and the structures on such property. It refers to the land and the residential, commercial, or industrial structures on the land. Other improvements to the property can also be covered by the term, such as wells, fences, and other immobile objects fixed on the property. The natural features of the property are also included in the phrase, like lakes, streams, and trees. Real estate can be natural land, residential property, commercial property, and even industrial property.

Real Estate is governed by real estate law. This represents the legal codes and regulations that have to do with real estate in a given jurisdiction. It covers such elements as the specifics of transactions of residential and commercial real estate. Real estate attorneys practice this form of law.

Realtors are the principal professionals who work in the field of selling real estate. Realty is the term that pertains to realtors and their firms. Real estate and realty companies are often equated with real property. This stands in contrast to personal property and personal property law.

As real estate property has developed and become more complex, it has evolved into an important part of business. This is referred to as commercial real estate. Commercial real estate can be buildings and office spaces used by businesses. Buying real estate is an expensive proposition requiring large investments. As every type and zoning of land has its own characteristics, the real estate industry has developed into a variety of different fields. There are people who specialize in valuing different kinds of real estate and helping the transactions to come together.

Many different types of real estate related businesses have developed as a result. Brokers are third parties who collect a fee in exchange for mediating real estate transactions between two different entities or individuals. Appraisers perform professional level evaluations of properties. Developers improve a land's value, typically by building or rebuilding structures on it.

Property managers handle the management of a given property on behalf of the owner. Real estate investors handle real estate investments. Real estate marketers handle the promotion and sales aspects of any property business. Corporate real estate people deal with the real estate portfolios of a company in support of its main businesses. Relocation servicers function to move businesses or individuals to a different part of the country or internationally from one real estate property to another.

The different types of real estate involve specialists in the various branches of real estate. In each of the different fields, real estate businesses commonly focus on a single type of real estate. This might be residential realty, commercial property realty, or industrial property realty. Construction businesses are involved significantly with sometimes either one branch, or sometimes even two or all three branches of real estate. They develop and build real estate to an end user's specifications.

Recession

A recession is literally defined as the declining of the nation's GDP, or Gross Domestic Product, by a smaller amount than ten percent. This drop in GDP has to occur over greater than a single consecutive quarter in a given year. Gross domestic product stands for the total of all goods and services that a country produces, or the actual total of all business, private, and government spending on the categories of investment, labor, services, and goods.

The terms recession and depression are typically confused and sometimes used interchangeably. They are quite different from each other. Recessions are typically less severe than are depressions. Recessions are generally corrected in significantly less time and with less economic pain for individuals. Depressions furthermore involve drops in GDP of greater than ten percent.

There is no universal consensus on what makes a recession within an economy. Most economists agree on a few different factors that are commonly involved in causing such recessions. Prices might decrease substantially, or alternatively they could go up substantially. The decrease in prices shows that people are spending smaller amounts of money, and this will cause the Gross Domestic Product to go down. Conversely, higher prices can diminish the amounts of public and private spending, similarly causing the Gross Domestic Product to decrease.

As much as governments, individuals, and businesses hate recessions, many economists feel that they are normal for economies to go through, particularly mild ones. They claim that such economic pull backs are a built in part of society and economics. Prices go up and down, and spending and the amount of consumption similarly decreases and increases over time as well. Still, natural decreases in spending are not sufficient to provoke a recession into occurring. Some other factor changes suddenly and leads to sharp spikes or drops in real prices.

For example, the early 2000's recession came about as a result of the dot com industry suddenly and precipitously decreasing in activity. One day, the demand that they had anticipated turned out to be far less than expected. This created enormous failures of companies and significant layoffs that led to production decreases and finally spending cuts. This dot com drop created a shock effect on the gross domestic product, leading to a significant fall in production and output as spending dropped.

The recession had ended by 2003, yet the consequences of it turned out to be dramatic and can still be felt. High paying jobs suddenly disappeared, only to be outsourced to foreign countries. These jobs will likely never return to the United States. Still, as the Gross Domestic Product began growing again, the recession was deemed to have ended. This does not change the fact that numerous individuals still feel the impact of it in their own personal lives.

Similarly, the Great Recession that you saw stem from the financial collapse of 2007-2010 came about as a sudden seizure in the banking industry and credit markets. It has led to the highest levels of real unemployment since the Great Depression, reaching nearly twenty percent when measured by the formula that had been used until President Bill Clinton changed it. Even though this recession has been called over, the unemployment levels have not declined meaningfully. This means that for several more years at least, a great amount of economic pain and hardship will continue to be felt by those countless millions who have lost their jobs in the recession.

Refinance

When the word refinance is used, it is referring to the act of refinancing, or canceling out a currently existing debt with another debt that a bank or refinance company issues under alternative terms. By far and away the most popular refinancing that pertains to consumers is for mortgages on houses. Debt replacements that are performed in conditions of financial distress are also known as debt restructuring.

Home owners might choose to refinance their mortgage for a variety of reasons. It can assist them in meeting a range of end goals. You as a home owner might be interested in lowering your monthly payments on the mortgage through attaining a better interest rate or lengthening the terms of the loan.

You could lessen the amount of interest that you pay during the loan's term and expand the equity build up by going through a refinance to get a loan with a shorter life. You could also decrease your exposure to the risk of rising interest rates through obtaining a fixed term loan in place of a balloon mortgage or adjustable rate mortgage. Finally, you might be interested in drawing out home equity in order to do debt consolidation or to cover the costs of major expenses that you are encountering elsewhere.

The act of refinancing eliminates the original mortgage loan. This is then replaced with a new loan. There are many factors that you will have to decide in obtaining this new loan. This includes what type of loan is most ideal for the circumstances, which lender you will utilize, which term and rate are most advantageous, and the fees that you feel are reasonable. Because of these complicated decisions that must be made, consumers should seek out advice in their refinancing. If you do not possess a clear comprehension of all that is involved with the refinancing procedure, then you could accidentally put your house or your finances in danger.

There are risks associated with refinancing. These are principally penalty clauses that are also known as call provisions. When you pay off a mortgage loan early, these penalties would be triggered along with closing fees. The refinancing itself will entail transaction fees. All of these fees should be figured up and considered before you begin a project to refinance your home loan. This is especially the case since all of the fees together may eliminate any potential savings that you hoped to realize through the refinancing.

Another possible downside to refinancing loans is that they may provide you with lower payments every month on the same amount of money to be repaid. In this case, you will pay a greater amount of interest throughout the loan term. You would also pay on the debt for a great number of additional years over the original mortgage's terms. This is why it is so important to determine not only the upfront charges, but also the variable and ongoing costs involved in refinancing as a factor in the decision on whether to pursue it or not.

Repayment Penalty

A repayment penalty is commonly associated with paying back a loan before the end of its term. If you are contemplating paying off your loan balance in advance of its due date, then you should be aware that a number of loans come with these repayment penalties for liquidating the balance early. Different types of loans utilize different names for these same fees. Repayment penalties can also be called redemption charges, early redemption fees, prepayment penalties, or financial penalties.

The fees associated with repayment penalties vary depending on the loan in question. These repayment penalties are commonly stated as a percentage of the balance that is outstanding when prepayment is offered. Alternatively, they might be figured up as a certain number of months of interest charges. In general, when they are figured up using months of interest, they are comprised of one to two months' interest in fees. The sooner in the loan's life that you choose to repay the loan, the greater amount of charge you can expect to pay. This is because the anticipated interest portion of the loan comprises a great part of the repayment earlier in the loan's time frame. Early repayment penalties might increase the total cost of your loan significantly.

If you wish to avoid a repayment penalty in paying off your loan in advance of the term's end, then you will have to be aware of the loans that come with these fees and the ones that do not. Even if you change a currently existing loan into a loan for debt consolidation, you will have to cover the early repayment penalty if one is in the terms. The only way to avoid early repayment penalties is by selecting loans that specifically do not have ones attached to them. It is ironic that some of the least expensive loans out there do not include repayment penalties for early pay off actions.

Another factor of repayment penalties involves a gradual disappearance of the provision over time. With many mortgages, these repayment penalties gradually go down over the years of the mortgage. After the fifth year, the majority of repayment penalties no longer even apply. In many cases, repayments of as much as twenty percent of the original balance are permitted in a given year without you having to be penalized.

Besides this, there are different kinds of penalties for repayments. Penalties that only apply to your refinancing of the mortgage are called soft penalties. Penalties that include the sale of the house and a refinancing are known as hard penalties.

Repayment Split

A repayment split refers to the ways that payments are allocated on a split mortgage. These repayment splits might allow you to take out a mortgage where part of the loan is a fixed rate loan, while the remainder of the loan is a variable rate, set against a tracking rate for the life of the loan. Home buying borrowers are able to fix their rate at twenty-five percent, fifty percent, or even seventy-five percent of the total mortgage amount. The balance of the loan then tracks a certain rate, like the Prime Rate or Bank of England base rate alongside the fixed part of the loan.

The interest rate charged varies along with the percentage of the mortgage balance that is at a fixed rate. For example, with only twenty-five percent of the home loan balance fixed, the fixed part of the rate might amount to 3.49% interest. If the split is done at a fifty percent rate of split, then the interest rate might instead be at 3.69% on the fixed rate. With seventy-five percent of the mortgage total fixed, the interest rate on the fixed portion could come in at 3.99% instead. These sample rates assume a loan to value ratio of only seventy percent, meaning that a thirty percent down payment would be expected. With only a twenty percent down payment made, the rates would likely be a half percentage point higher. The interest rate on the balance of the loan total is variable and is adjusted periodically. The repayment split then determines which portion of the payments applies to which interest rate balance. This form of repayment split and split mortgage is most commonly seen in Great Britain.

A second way that repayment splits are used has to do with split mortgages that involve first and second mortgages. This split mortgage technique is commonly used in America to reduce the amount of the principal mortgage to no more than eighty percent of the purchase price so that Private Mortgage Insurance will not be required. With this technique, a second mortgage or home equity line of credit to the amount of five to ten percent of the home purchase price is used to come up with enough cash to keep the first mortgage to eighty percent or less. In this version of the split mortgage, the repayment split refers to which portion of the payments goes against the first mortgage and which against the second mortgage.

Residual

Residual refers to residual income. Residual income can have several different meanings depending on the context that you use. For an individual, residual income proves to be the money that remains at the end of a month after all financial responsibilities for the month are covered.

These include living costs, taxes, and housing costs. Where business is concerned, residual incomes are the operating income that is additional as compared to the typical minimum amount of operating assets that are controlled. Residual income furthermore refers to passive income that is earned. In this form of the term, it relates to all income that is created as a result of activities that are indirect. These might include royalties, rental income, investment portfolio returns, website revenues, or passively managed businesses, all of which qualify as residual income.

The word residual is a variation on the word residue. Residue means anything that stays behind because of some other substance or cause. So, residual income proves to be additional money made because of another activity like penning a novel and collecting royalties for the sale of every book.

Rental incomes are residual as they remain from the action of buying a house and then renting it to a tenant who pays you a monthly rental fee. Work is involved in this activity, although a property management company can do it on your behalf. The rewards for this rental project can be significant, as you enjoy the continuous rental stream as well as any increases in the value of the real estate property underlying it. Rental income can be utilized to pay for potentially an entire mortgage.

Income from investment portfolios is similarly considered to be residual income. Both dividends and interest are acquired as an additional, passive benefit of possessing stocks, bonds, mutual funds, and other instruments. This residual income is not guaranteed from these investments, but it is common for investors.

A form of residual income that is growing in popularity these days is website, or Internet based, revenues. Internet revenues are commonly those that you make from having advertising on a given website. The dollar value of the advertising is mostly based on the number of visitors to the page. A significant amount of start up work is required to create the website and get it highly ranked on the major search engines. After this, you can see continuous monthly profits that you earn as a result of the advertising, which builds up a residual income. This amount of money could be as little as a few dollars a month to possibly thousands of dollars per month.

A last form of residual income can result from a business. If your company becomes large enough, you may be able to hire a manager to run it. The income that supports you while the manager runs the business is then considered residual income.

Return on Equity

Return on equity proves to be a useful measurement for investors considering a given company. This is because it takes into account three important elements of a company's management. This includes profitability, financial leverage, and asset management. Looking at the effectiveness of the management team in handling the three factors gives you as an investor a good picture of the kind of return on equity that you can expect from an investment in such a company.

Return on equity is very easy to calculate. You can figure it up by collecting two pieces of information. You will need the company earnings for a year and the value of the average share holder equity for the same year. Getting the earnings' figure is as simple as looking up the firm's Consolidated Statement of Earnings that they filed with the Securities and Exchange Commission. Alternatively, you might look up the earnings of each of the last four quarters and add them up.

Determining share holder equity is easiest by looking at the company's balance sheet. Share holder equity, which proves to be the difference of total liabilities and total assets, will be listed for you there. Share holder equity is a useful accounting construct that reveals the business assets that they have created. This share holder equity is most commonly listed under book value, or the quantity of the share holders' equities for each share. This is also an accounting book value of a corporation that is more than simply its market value.

To come up with the return on equity, you simply divide the full year's earnings by the average equity for that year. This gives you the return on equity. Companies that produce significant amounts of share holder equity turn out to be solid investments, since initial investors are paid off using the money that the business operations generate. Companies that create substantial returns as compared to the share holder equity reward their stake holders generously by building up significant amounts of assets for each dollar that is invested into the firm. Such enterprises commonly prove to be able to fund their own operations internally, which means that they do not have to issue more diluting shares of stock or take on extra debt to continue operating.

The return on equity can also be utilized to determine if a corporation is a cash generating machine or a cash consuming entity. The return on equity will simply show you this when you compare their actual earnings to the share holder equity. You can learn at almost a glance how much money the company's present assets are producing. As an example, with a twenty percent return on equity, every original dollar put into the company is creating twenty cents of real assets. This is also useful in comparing subsequent cash investments in the company, since the return on equity percentage will demonstrate to you if these extra invested dollars match up to the earlier investments for effectiveness and efficiency.

Reverse Split

A reverse split is also known as a reverse stock split. Reverse splits are used to reduce the total outstanding number of a given company's shares. This action boosts the value of its stock and the resulting earnings per share. Not everything concerning a stock changes in a reverse stock split. One thing that remains the same is the market capitalization. Market capitalization refers to the value price of the total outstanding number of shares.

A reverse split works by a certain process. In this scenario, a company involved will actually cancel out the presently existing shares for every share holder. They will replace these with a smaller number of new shares. These new shares will be issued in an exact proportion to your original stake in the company.

Such a reverse split proves to be the exact opposite of a stock split. Reverse splits can also be called stock merges, since they literally reduce the total number of outstanding shares and proportionally increase the price per share. Companies commonly issue the reverse split shares according to an easy to understand ratio. You might receive one new share for every two old shares, or possibly four new shares for every old five ones that you owned.

Looking at an example of the way that a reverse stock split actually works is helpful. Say that a company in which you own stock shares decided to affect a one for ten reverse split. If you had one thousand shares of the company, then you would only own one hundred shares of the resulting issue. This would not change the value of the shares that you held though, as the price of the shares would increase by ten times. If the shares had been worth only four dollars per share, now they would be valued at forty dollars per share.

There are several reasons why companies choose to do a reverse split of their stock shares. They might feel that the actual price per share of their stock is so low that it is not appealing to new investors. Some institutions are only allowed to buy shares that trade at a certain minimum value, such as five dollars per share or higher. Reverse stock splits can also be used to reduce the number of share holders, since they can force smaller shareholders to be cashed out, which means that they no longer possess any shares of the company. In this case, you would receive the value of your shares in cash.

There is a negative connotation associated with engaging in reverse stock splits. Because of this reason, they are not done lightly by companies. A company might find that its share price has declined so precipitously that it becomes in danger of having its shares de-listed from the stock exchange. They could quickly boost the share price with the reverse split. Stocks that have undergone a reverse split will usually have the letter D added to the end of their symbol tickers.

A board of directors for a given company is allowed to perform a reverse split without consulting with its share holders to obtain their approval. The Securities and Exchange Commission also does not have any say over such reverse stock splits. They are instead regulated by a state's corporate laws and the company's own articles of incorporation, along with the company's by laws.

ROI (Return on Investment)

ROI is the acronym for return on investment. This return on investment is among the most often utilized methods of determining the financial results that will arise from business decisions, investments, and actions. ROI analysis is used to compare and contrast both the timing and amount of investment gains directly with the timing and amount of investment costs. Higher returns on investment signify that the results from investments are positive when you compare them against the costs of such investments.

Over the past couple of decades, this return on investment number has evolved into one of the main measurements in the decision making process of what types of assets and equipment to buy. This includes everything from factory equipment, to service vehicles, to computers. ROI is similarly utilized to determine which budget items, programs, and projects should be both approved and allocated funds. These cover every type of activity from recruiting, to training, to marketing. Finally, return on investment is often employed in choosing which financial investments are performing up to expectations, as with venture capital investments and stock investment portfolios.

Return on investment analysis is actually used for ranking investment returns against their costs. This is done by setting up a percentage or ratio number. With the vast majority of return on investment calculation methods, ROI's that are higher than zero signify that the returns on the investment are higher than the associated expenses with it. As a greater number of investments and business decisions compete for funding anymore, hard choices are increasingly made using the comparison of higher returns on investment. Many companies believe that this yields the better business decision in the end.

There is a downside to relying too heavily on the return on investment as the only consideration for making such business and investment decisions. Return on investment does not tell you anything regarding the anticipated costs and returns and if they will actually work out as fore-cast. Used alone, return on investment also does not explain the poten-tial elements of risk for a given investment. All that it does is demon-strate how the investment or project returns will compare against the costs, assuming that the investment or project delivers the results that are anticipated or expected. This limitation is not unique to return on investment, but similarly plagues other financial measurements. Be-cause this is the case, intelligent investment and business analysis also relies on the likely results of other return on investment eventualities. Other measurements should also be used along side the return on in-vestment to help measure the risks that accompany the project or in-vestment.

Wise decision makers will demand more from return on investment figures than simply a number. They will require effective suggestions from the person making the return on investment analysis. Among these inputs that they will desire are the means of increasing an ROI's gains, or alternatively the means for improving the ROI through decreasing costs.

Roth IRA

A Roth IRA is a particular type of Individual Retirement Account. These Roth IRA's prove to be special retirement plans that are given favorable tax treatment. The tax laws of the United States permit tax reductions on restricted amount savings for retirement accounts.

Roth IRA's are different from other IRA's in several ways. Among the chief of these is that tax breaks are not given on monies that are put into the plan and account with a Roth IRA. Instead, these tax breaks are given out on the money and its investment gains when they are taken out of the account at retirement. This chief appeal of Roth IRA's is that they provide completely tax free income at retirement.

Other Roth IRA benefits over traditional forms of IRA's exist as well. The restrictions placed on the kinds of investments that they are al-lowed to contain are fewer. You can turn them into gold IRA's and an-nuity account IRA's. Roth IRA's can also contain all of the usual forms of investments that IRA's contain, such as mutual funds, stocks, bonds, and certificates of deposit. More unusual investments such as real es-tate, mortgage notes, derivatives, and even franchises are allowed to be purchased with Roth IRA's. These investment choices do depend on the capability and allowance of the Roth IRA trustee, or firm with which the plan is set up. Roth IRA's also permit you to make un-penalized withdrawals of all direct contributions that you make, after the first five years of the account have and plan have passed, which is certainly not the case with traditional IRA's.

These distributions, or withdrawals, are not taxed because they are taxed before the contributions are made. The penalties are waived for principal, as well as interest and earnings in the account, if the distributions are for purchasing a house or for disability or retirement withdrawal uses. If there is not a justified reason for the distribution, then the account earnings and income made above contributions will be taxed.

All IRA's contain specific limits on the dollar amount of contributions that the government permits. This amount changes per year, and is set through the year 2011 now. Presently, you can put $5,000 per year into Roth IRA's. There are income restrictions that govern whether you are allowed to make this full contribution as well. Individuals who make less than $106,000 are permitted to make full Roth IRA contributions, and those who make under $121,000 may make a partial contribution. Married couples who file together are allowed to earn less than $167,000 to make their full contribution to the Roth IRA, while those who make under $177,000 can do a partial contribution.

Roth IRA conversions from traditional IRA's have been allowed by the IRA in the past, although with certain income restrictions. Beginning in 2010, this policy changed. Now the IRS permits any persons, regardless of how much money that they make, to convert their traditional IRA's into Roth IRA's.

Run on the Bank

A run on the bank is the vernacular expression for a bank run. Runs on the banks actually happen as a result of many bank customers deciding to take out their deposits at one time. They do this out of fear that the bank is either broke or on its way to becoming insolvent. When runs on the banks get started, they have a tendency to create their own terrible momentum that leads to a self fulfilling prophecy. The more customers who take out their money, the greater the odds of bank default become, which leads to still more customer deposit withdrawals. If this happens long enough, it will likely upset a bank's finances to the point that the bank encounters bankruptcy as a result.

Runs on the bank can often lead to bank panics. These financial crises result from a large number of banks experiencing bank runs all at once. If the bank panics are not dealt with swiftly and convincingly, then a systemic banking crisis can develop. In such a banking crisis that is system wide, it is not uncommon to witness practically all, or even all, of a country's banking capital disappear.

Once this occurs, numerous bankruptcies follow, many times ending up in a deep and painful economic recession or even depression. Bank runs created a great amount of the economic damage that you saw done in the Great Depression. Associated costs of fixing the mess related to a systemic banking crisis are enormous. Over the last forty years, these expenses around the world have averaged fully thirteen percent of the respective countries' Gross Domestic Products in fiscal costs, leading to losses of economic output that averaged twenty percent of Gross Domestic Product.

Runs on the bank are able to be prevented with a few different strategies. Withdrawals can be suspended. More effectively, deposit insurance systems can be put in place, like the one that the Federal Deposit Insurance Corporation operates in the United States. The Central Bank may also help out banks by performing the function of the lender of last resort in times of banking crises. Such strategies are commonly effective, but not always. Even when countries possess deposit insurance, the bank depositors could still be fearful that they will not have instant access to their bank held deposits while the bank is reorganized by the FDIC.

The reason that runs on the bank are able to happen in the first place is because of the fractional reserve banking system. Modern day banks only keep a small percentage of their demand deposits in cash on hand, typically ten percent in developed nations. The rest of these deposits are tied up in loans that have longer terms than demand deposits. This leads to a mismatch of assets and liabilities. Though some banks keep better reserves than others do, no modern bank keeps sufficient reserves in its vaults to handle the majority of their deposits being withdrawn at a single time.

SEC (Securities and Exchange Commission)

The SEC is the acronym for the Securities and Exchange Commission. This Federal government agency actually governs the buying and selling of stock securities and other types of related investments. The SEC also works to safe guard investors against impropriety and fraud. They encourage the development of the market with the end goal of keeping America in the first place as the world's leading economic giant.

The Securities and Exchange Commission came into existence in 1934. The stock market crash in 1929 prompted a tremendous regulatory response where the national government observed that it had to oversee and monitor investments within the U.S. The SEC is headquartered today in Washington D.C. Its staff is comprised of five commissioners who are appointed, as well as the personnel working in eleven different regional offices throughout the country. They work together to create, amend, and enforce the laws that regulate investments in the country.

The SEC has various critical missions. Among the most significant one is their role in ensuring that the markets are transparent. To do this, they significantly regulate securities trading within the U.S. Companies are required to turn in a variety of legal financial documents during the year so that investors may obtain a true picture of the total financial health of the firm in question.

The documents are kept on file in a database that is available to the public. Anyone who is interested is allowed to inspect them by logging on to the SEC's website and working through their system of electronic documentation. The SEC has great powers that it exercises in enforcing the rules. It is able to mandate company audits if it has suspicions of illegal behavior. Those it finds in violation of its rules may be brought by the SEC to court.

In keeping with the SEC's mandate to help safe guard investors, they monitor the trading of stocks and the individuals responsible for selling them. This means that exchanges, their dealers, and all stock brokers are required to work through the Securities and Exchange Commission. They can be subjected to inspection from time to time to be certain that they are properly taking care of their customers. Consumers have the right to report practices that are unfair to the SEC directly. If you are an investor, you ought to avail yourself of the SEC's wide range of documents on the various publicly traded corporations that they keep in their database on their website.

The SEC additionally governs companies that are interested in undergoing Initial Public Offerings in order to become public companies. Such interested firms have to file a significant quantity of documents with them first. To help them accomplish this, the SEC engages a big staff. Their document database includes regulations and directions for filing such documents. Consultation help is available if companies run into difficulties.

The SEC also promotes education. If you are an investor who wants to learn more about safe investing, then simply go to their website. They have workshops and publications on the site to help all investors. This is in addition to all of the companies' documents kept on file there.

Seller Financing

Seller Financing turns out to be a loan that a business or property seller offers to the buyer. When seller financing is provided, the buyer generally gives a down payment amount to the seller. The balance of the purchase price is paid to them using installment payments that are typically monthly. This is accomplished at a certain time of the month and for an interest rate that the two parties agree to, until the loan itself has been completely paid back.

Seller provided financing is not governed by any regulatory body or set of laws. Because this is the case, for a seller and a buyer both to protect their interests, a purchase agreement that is legally enforceable in a court of law needs to be drafted by an attorney. The two parties, buyer and seller, can then sign this agreement to make the transaction fully legal.

There are many benefits offered in pursuing seller financing. Both the seller and the buyer of a real estate property can realize significant closing cost savings that typically amount to thousands of dollars. The interest rate, loan conditions, and repayment schedule may also be negotiated with seller financing. Borrowers are not forced to go through a loan qualification process via a loan officer or underwriter either. Private Mortgage Insurance is also not required to be paid. Buyers are able to make specific requests as part of the condition of buying the property too, like having the appliances included in the sale.

Sellers also receive benefits when they provide seller financing. They might end up with a better return on the investment if they get their equity payments with interest. They similarly might be capable of obtaining a better selling price and interest rate. They could choose to sell the property in "as is" condition, meaning that they will not be required to cover the costs of any repairs that the property needs. Finally, the seller is capable of picking out the security documents that he or she believes best serve the interests of getting the loan paid off, such as deeds of trust, mortgages, or land sales documents.

There are some downsides to seller financing that should be carefully considered as well. While the buyer might make the payments on time, the seller could choose to not pay off more senior financing on the property, which would cause the property to be foreclosed on. Besides this, the buyer might not be given the title to the property if there are problems tying up the property title, even when he or she paid off the loan as per the agreement. The buyer also does not benefit from the safeguards offered by mortgage insurance, home inspections, or appraisals that will ensure that he or she is not paying too high a price for the house.

The seller also encounters risks with seller financing. If the seller does not get an accurate picture of the buyer's ability to pay for the property, then he or she might suffer through a foreclosure. This foreclosure can require as long as a year to complete. Finally, the seller might accept a smaller down payment and then find that the buyer later abandons the property and payments since he or she puts a limited investment into the property.

Selling Short

Selling short, or short selling, is a strategy used in trading stocks. In the selling short process, you borrow the shares of the stock in question from your stock broker. You then turn around and sell the stock shares borrowed for a certain price that the market offers. Your hope is that the price of the stock will drop, so that you can buy back the stock shares for a lesser amount. This creates a profit for your transaction. The practice is buying low and selling high done in the reverse order.

If the price of the stock drops, then this process of short selling makes you money. The down side to it is that when the price of the stock instead rises, then you lose money. Detractors of selling short claim that you can subject yourself to an unlimited amount of risk, since stock prices could rise without stopping. This means that you could potentially lose more than the amount of money that you invest if a given stock that you sold short took off and ran away without you closing out the transaction. Profits are limited by the distance of the stock price to zero, since a share's price can never decline below zero.

Such selling short trades are closed out by repurchasing the shares that you sold short earlier. When it is time to close out the transaction by buying back the shares, this is called covering. The other names for this process are buy to cover or simply cover.

There are risks involved in selling short stocks. The biggest risk is that the stock could go up indefinitely. For example, you might sell short ten shares of IBM's stock at $100 per share. This means that you have put a thousand dollars into the trade. If the stock later declined to ninety, then you would realize a gain of one hundred dollars. If instead it rose to $130 before you covered it, then you would lose three hundred dollars. While the lowest that the IBM shares might decline is to zero, potentially making you as much as one thousand dollars in profits, they could also rise to three hundred dollars, losing you two thousand dollars.

Short sellers can also fall victim to a short squeeze. As the stock price that you have shorted rises, some investors who shorted it will choose to limit their losses by buying the stock back. Still other investors may have no choice but to buy back the shares in order to satisfy any margin calls on their declining valued position. All of this buying back to cover creates a bigger increase in the price of the stock. The final outcome is a large move up in the price of the stock that creates significant losses for those who continue to be short the stock.

Short Sale

Short sales are real estate sales where the money received from the sale is not sufficient to cover the balance that is owed on the property loan. This commonly happens as a result of borrowers being unable to keep up with the mortgage payments for their home loan. In this case, the bank or other lending institution will likely determine that it is in their best interest to take a reasonable loss on the sale of the property instead of pressuring the borrower to make the payments that he or she can not afford.

Both parties come together and agree on the short sale process, since it permits them both to stay out of foreclosure. Foreclosure is a negative outcome for the two parties, as it lowers credit scores of borrowers and costs banks in expensive fees. Borrowers must be careful, since a short sale agreement does not always absolve the borrower from having to cover the additional balance left on the loan. This remaining balance is called the deficiency.

The process of a short sale starts with the two parties concurring on a short sale being the best option to resolve a mortgage that the borrower is unable to keep up with as a result of financial or economic difficulties. The home owner actually sells the house in question for an amount that he or she is able to realize, even though it is less than the remaining loan balance. They give the money to the bank or lender. This is really the most economical answer for the problem in this scenario, since short sales are less costly and quicker than foreclosures that damage both lender and borrower.

Banks commonly employ loss mitigation departments. Their job is to contemplate the short sales that are possible or likely. Most of them work with criteria that they have set up in advance. In the difficult days following the financial crisis of 2007-2010, they have become more flexible and willing to entertain offers from borrowers. The banks will usually decide on how much equity is in the house by ascertaining the likely selling price that they will be able to receive either through a Broker Price Opinion, appraisal, or Broker Opinion of Value.

Even when Notice of Defaults have been sent out to borrowers beginning a foreclosure process, many banks will still consent to short sale requests and offers. They have become more understanding and accepting of short sales in the wake of the financial crisis than they ever were before. This means that for the countless borrowers who own houses on which they owe more than they are worth and who can not sell them, there is a better option open to them than foreclosure.

Stock Split

Stock splits occur when corporations decide to expand the number of underlying shares in the company. They do this by setting out a ratio for the stock split. They might say that for every one share of stock, there will now be two, which would double your existing shares. This would be called a two to one stock split. If you had one hundred shares of the stock before the split that were trading at twenty dollars per share, then you would possess fifty shares of the stock trading at ten dollars each share after the split occurred. The value of the total shares owned does not change as a result of a stock split, only the amounts of shares that you possess and the per share price of the stock in question. In either case, they would still be worth two thousand dollars.

Companies mostly engage in stock splits because of a liquidity motivation. There are many companies that feel that more expensive stocks keep investors from buying them. By splitting the shares, the price of the shares declines proportionally. They hope that this will result in a scenario where greater quantities of shares of the stock are then purchased and sold. The downside to this argument is that the higher volume of the shares traded could cause larger drops and increases in the price of the stock, which leads to greater volatility in the share prices.

While numerous investors believe that stock splits are beneficial, there is no real evidence to support this feeling. Stocks do not automatically rise back to the price that they maintained in advance of the split. The extra shares do not result in greater amounts of dividends being realized by the investors either, since each share then represents proportionally smaller earnings, assets, and dividends of the company involved in the split.

While most companies go through stock splits as the price rises, a select few have steadfastly refused to do so. Berkshire Hathaway proves to be the most famous case of this. In the 1960's, it traded at only $8 each share. In recent decades, you have seen its value jump up to $150,000 per share. The Washington Post has also seen its non splitting shares trade upwards of six hundred dollars each. The shareholder base of both companies has remained consistent and stable as a result of not splitting the stock shares.

Stocks

Stocks are financial instruments that are issued by publicly traded corporations. These shares of stocks prove to be the tiniest portion of ownership that you can acquire in a company. Even by owning a single share of a company's stock you are a small part owner of the firm.

Owning shares of stock gives you the privilege of voting for the underlying company's board of directors, along with other critical issues that the company is considering. Should a company decide to distribute earnings to share holders as dividends, then you will get a portion of them.

With the ownership of stock, your liability in the company is only limited to the value of your shares. This means that should a company lose a lawsuit and be forced to pay an enormous fine or judgment, then you can not be made to contribute to it. The company's creditors also can not pursue you if the company runs into financial trouble and goes bankrupt.

Two different types of stock shares exist. These are common shares and preferred shares. The vast majority of shares that are issued are common stock shares. These are the shares that members of the public hold most of the time. They come with full voting rights and also the possibility of receiving dividends that the company pays out.

Preferred stocks come with fewer voting rights but give preferential treatment for dividend payment. Preferred stock issues are paid out before common share dividends. Companies that offer preferred stock typically pay dividends on both classes of shares anyway. Preferred stocks also have a higher claim on the assets of a company if it fails.

Liquidity is a feature of stocks that should always be considered. Common stock shares are almost always more liquid than are preferred shares. Large companies offer the greatest amount of liquidity in the trading of their stocks. Because of the depth of the stock markets, you are able to purchase and sell the shares of practically all companies that are publicly traded at any time that the exchanges are working.

When you purchase a stock, you are looking for two different kinds of gains. Cash flow or passive income with stocks comes from the dividends that they declare and pay out. Capital gains appreciation is realized when you buy a stock at a lower price than the price that you get when you later sell it. While cash flow dividends are smaller payments that are realized on a generally quarterly basis, capital gains turn out to be larger one time returns made when you sell the underlying stock shares investment. At this point, you would no longer own the stock and you would have to purchase another stock in order to work towards cash flow gains from dividends, as well as other possible capital gains.

Strategy

Where businesses are concerned, strategy proves to be both the scope and direction that a business pursues over a longer term time frame. Strategy gains a business or other organization advantages through optimally deploying and utilizing all types of resources in competitive environments. Strategy is utilized to fulfill the needs that markets experience and to live up to the expectations and anticipation of the share holders in the firm or stake holders in the organization.

Strategy covers many components of a company. It pertains to the direction, or place that a firm is trying to arrive at over a longer time frame. Strategy explores the markets that are most effective for businesses to become involved with, as well as the types of activities that they should pursue in these markets, known as the scope of a business. Strategy seeks to determine what advantage a business can acquire, or how it might operate more efficiently and effectively than the various competitors in the markets.

Businesses are also interested in a number of other elements with strategy. They are concerned with the resources that they will need to compete in these markets. Resources for a business can include facilities, technical abilities, contacts, finance, specific skills, and particular assets. Companies also look into strategy as it pertains to the external environment of the business and its abilities to compete effectively. Finally, a firm must consider the wishes and expectations of the share holders in the business with their strategy.

Strategy can be found on three main levels of a business or organization. These run from the entity at the highest level on down to the individual employees who work within the company or group. Corporate strategy is the macro level. It deals with the entire scope and purpose of a business in achieving the expectations of share holders. Investors are commonly involved and consulted with in the development of corporate strategy. Corporate strategy is typically outlined specifically within the corporate mission statement.

The different business units also have strategy, referred to as Business Unit Strategy. This level of strategy worries about the ways that the company is competitive in specific markets. Strategic decisions at this view involve choices and ranges of products, the ways of gaining an advantage over the competition, satisfying the business' customers, and creating and discovering different opportunities on which the business or organization may capitalize.

Finally, operational strategy works with the ways that all parts of the company in question are arranged to work together in order to provide both business units and corporate strategy direction. With operational strategy, processes, resources, and people are concentrated on in particular.

Strategy of a business or organization is handled and created in the processes of strategic management. Strategic management simply goes through the thought process to make strategic decisions. There are three core parts of strategic management. These are strategic analysis, strategic choice, and strategy implementation.

Sub-prime Mortgage

A sub-prime mortgage is one where the home loan that the bank or lending institution makes is offered to the category of consumers who are considered to possess the riskiest credit. Sub prime mortgages are actually sold on a different market than are prime mortgage loans. Sub prime mortgage borrowers are determined through a combination of factors, such as the credit rating of the borrower, the documentation offered for the loans, and the borrower's debt to assets ratio. Besides this, sub-prime mortgage are also deemed to be those that do not fulfill the prime mortgages' standards and guide lines offered by Fannie Mae and Freddie Mac, the two biggest issuers of mortgages within the United States.

A universally agreed upon definition for sub-prime mortgages does not exist today. In the U.S., sub-prime mortgages are commonly considered to be those where the associated borrower possesses a FICO credit rating score that is less than 640. This phrase became a part of pop culture in the credit crunch that occurred in 2007.

The original sub-prime mortgage program began in 1993. At this time, some lenders started offering sub-prime mortgages to borrowers classified as high risk, who possessed credit that was less than ideal. Traditional lenders showed wariness towards sub-prime mortgages and borrowers. They tended to shy away from people who had impaired credit histories. Sub-prime mortgage borrowers commonly have information on their credit reports that argue for greater percentages of defaults. These include too much debt, a track record of not paying debts or missing payments, recorded bankruptcies, and low amounts of experience with debt.

Around twenty-five percent of the American population is grouped into this category of sub-prime borrowers who qualify for the category of sub-prime mortgages. Because of this, proponents of sub-prime mortgages argued that they allowed a large number of people to gain access to credit who would not otherwise have experienced the opportunity to purchase and own a home. Borrowers with less than perfect credit who can demonstrate enough income are able to qualify for sub-prime mortgages. This proves to be the case even if their credit scores are lower than 640.

The lenders who participate in sub-prime mortgages take significant risks in so doing. This is because people who have a credit score of less than 620 statistically possess a significantly greater rate of defaulting on their mortgages than do those people with much higher scores over 720. Lenders compensate for the risks associated with offering sub-prime mortgages through several different means. One of these is by charging higher rates of interest. They also collect late fees for any customers who do not keep up with their payments. These greater interest rates and fees help to reward lenders who take the risks of the higher default rates, and who also incur costs for collecting and keeping up with these -mortgage accounts. As an example of their potential danger, sub-prime mortgages proved to be among the main causes of the Financial Crisis of 2007-2010.

Sub-prime Mortgage Crisis

The sub-prime mortgage crisis proves to be a still going financial and real estate crisis. It continues to revolve around the steep decline that you saw in American housing prices, the resulting increase in numbers of mortgage delinquencies and finally foreclosures, and the ultimate fall of securities that are backed up by these sub-prime mortgages.

The problems began with the fact that around eighty percent of all United States mortgages that banks gave out to sub-prime borrowers, or people with less than perfect credit, turned out to be adjustable rate types of mortgages. Housing prices actually reached their highest point in the middle of 2006 and then began sharply falling. This caused refinancing of interest rates on mortgages to be harder to obtain. The double edged sword of adjustable rate mortgages resetting at their higher rates started, causing an enormous number of delinquencies and finally foreclosures in mortgages.

The greater problem came as these mortgages underlay a number of financial securities that many financial firms held in huge numbers. They saw most of their value disappear in the following months. Investors around the world then began to dramatically cut back on the quantities of collateralized debt obligations and other mortgage securities that they bought. Besides the damage that increasing sub-prime mortgage delinquencies and foreclosures created themselves and for the investments based on them, this sub-prime mortgage crisis led to a fall in the ability of the banking system to engage in lending. This caused significantly tighter credit and lower rates of growth throughout the developed world, in particular in Europe and the United States, that are still plaguing the industrial countries.

Ultimately, the sub-prime mortgage crisis arose as a result of easy up front loan terms which banks made to borrowers. Both the borrowers and the banks felt confident that the loans could be easily refinanced into better terms as needed, since housing prices were steadily rising over a long term trend. Financial incentives were provided to sub-prime mortgage originators.

This coupled, with fraud that borrowers and lenders engaged in, significantly boosted the quantities of sub-prime mortgages to customers who should have received standard conforming loans or who should not have received loans at all. When the easy interest rate terms expired, the majority of sub-prime loan holding consumers could not refinance at the better rates in which they had believed. The interest rates reset higher, dramatically increasing the monthly mortgage payments.

Home prices started falling to the point that homes were no longer even worth as much as the original mortgage, meaning that they could not be sold to pay off the mortgage obligation. Instead, the borrowers' best interest lay in going through foreclosure and walking away from the hopelessly underwater homes. This continuous epidemic of foreclosures that began with the sub-prime mortgage crisis is still a major continuous part of the world wide financial and economic crisis. The foreclosures are still taking away wealth from consumers and sapping away at the damaged banks' balance sheets.

Tariff Programs

Tariff programs are tariff regimes that apply to imports. Tariffs prove to be taxes that governments put on goods that are imported. Every nation has its own tariff programs and amounts. There are five principle tariff types in any tariff program. These are revenue, specific, ad valorem, protective, and prohibitive.

Revenue types of tariffs are those that boost government revenues. A revenue tariff would be one set up by a country that does not grow oranges but imposes tariffs on the import of oranges. This way, that government makes money when any business chooses to import and sell oranges.

Ad valorem tariffs are those that a government places as a percent of the value of imports. An example of such a tariff is fifteen cents for each dollar value. This contrasts with specific tariffs that do not revolve around the imported goods' estimated value. Instead, they are levied as a result of the specific quantity of the goods in question. Specific tariffs can be figured up based on the volume of the goods that are imported, on their weight, or on any other form of measurement applicable to goods.

Tariffs that are prohibitive in nature turn out to be the ones that stop a business from importing a good at all. These tariffs might be used on goods that a government does not wish brought into the country. This might be for safety, health, or moral reasons.

Protective tariffs are set by a government in order to ensure that the sale price of goods that are imported do not destroy a local industry. These are employed to protect domestic markets from foreign competition. Higher tariffs will permit local companies that may not be so efficient to compete effectively against the foreign competitors within the local domestic markets. While protective tariffs have their time and place in building up the local firms and economy, they can have unintended consequences. They might cause an item to be so costly that companies have to charge more for their related products.

A good example of this pertains to the prices of gasoline. As they rise excessively through tariffs, companies involved in shipping, like trucking companies, have no choice but to charge retail businesses higher prices for getting their products to them. The retail businesses will then respond by increasing the prices of their goods to compensate for the greater costs of transportation. They have to do this to make the same level of profit that they did in the past. The final result will be that consumers bear the brunt of the tariff by having to pay higher prices for their products and goods.

All countries employ tariff programs for one reason or another. They may not apply them evenly to every import or industry, but they will utilize them somewhere. Sometimes countries choose not to put tariffs on goods being imported. This is known as free trade in these cases. Free trade is believed by many economists to permit higher levels of economic growth. Critics say that without tariff programs, economies will be forced to rely on global markets instead of their own local markets.

Term Life Insurance

Term life insurance is a form of life insurance. It offers coverage for a preset and limited amount of time that is called the relevant term. The coverage provided is a fixed rate of payment coverage. Once the term expires, the individual's coverage at the rate of the premiums that were charged before are not assured any more. The client will be forced to drop their term life insurance coverage or to get a different coverage with varying payments and terms. Should the person who is insured die within the term, the death benefit amounts are paid out to the insured person's beneficiary. This term life insurance proves to be the most affordable means of buying a major dollar value of death benefit coverage based on the premium cost charged.

Term life insurance turns out to be the first type of life insurance created, and it stands in contrast to permanent forms of life insurance like universal life, whole life, and variable universal life. These coverage types promise an individual pre set premiums that can not go up for the person's entire life. People do not usually employ term insurance for strategies involving charitable giving or their needs for estate planning. Instead, they are thinking about a need to replace an income if a person passes away on his or her family unexpectedly.

A great number of the permanent life insurance policies also offer the advantage of increasing in value during the person's contract. This cash value can then be withdrawn when certain conditions are met by the policy holder. Generally, withdrawing these cash amounts closes out the policy. Beneficiaries of permanent life insurance products get the insurance policy face value but not the cash value upon the holder's death. Because of this, financial advisers will suggest that people purchase term life insurance for their insurance needs and then invest the money saved over permanent products in retirement accounts that provide tax deferred contributions and investment gains, like 401k's and IRA's.

Like with the majority of insurance policies, term life insurance pays out claims for the insured, assuming that the contract is current and the premiums are paid as due. Assuming that a claim is not filed, the premium is not given back to the policy holder. This makes term life insurance like home owners' insurance policies that pay claims if a home becomes destroyed or damaged as a result of fire, or like car insurance policies that pay drivers if they have a car accident. Premiums are not refunded when the product is no longer required. Because of this, term life insurance like these other products only provides risk protection.

Title Deed

Title deeds are a form of legal documents. They are utilized to demonstrate that a person owns a certain property. Title deeds are used most often to provide proof of home or vehicle ownership. Title deeds might also be given out on other kinds of property. Title deeds give owners privileges and legal rights. To transfer a property's ownership to another individual, a title deed is required.

Title deeds generally come with detailed descriptions of the property to which they are attached. They are made specific enough so that they can not be mixed up with other properties. They also include the individual's name who owns the piece of property. More than one person can be named as an owner on a title deed. Proof that the title deed is recorded with the appropriate office is provided by the presence of an official seal. Title deeds are commonly signed by the property owner and a person who witnesses the signature, such as a clerk or area government official.

Having a title deed does not mean that a person keeps the car in his or her possession. You can loan a car to a relative to use, even though they are not on the title. If you purchase a car using a loan, then the bank will have the title for its security, even though you would keep the car. You might purchase a house and rent it to a tenant. Although the tenant would not have the title deed, he or she would still possess and occupy the house. The title deed is useful for forcefully retaking possession in any of these scenarios.

When you sell a property, the old title deed is invalidated and a new one is given out that has the new owner's name on it. You might also add another person to a title deed by working with a title company for a property, or the Department of Motor Vehicles for vehicle titles. You have to fill in a request in writing before you receive a new title deed with the other names added to it. Once a person's name has been added to a title deed, they legally control the property along with the original title deed owner.

Title deeds have to be kept safe. As official legal documents, they are not easy to replace when stolen or lost. It is a smart idea to keep title deed copies separate from the original to have proof of ownership while an official replacement title deed is being issued. Physical possession of title deeds allows a person to start a transfer of ownership, so they must be kept where they will not be stolen and then subsequently utilized to transfer your property to another individual.

Toxic Assets

Toxic Assets is a coined phrase for those financial assets which saw their actual value plummet. Toxic assets do not have well working markets anymore, making them difficult or impossible to sell for a price on which the owner will agree. The term arose as a popularly coined phrase during the financial crisis of 2007-2010. Toxic assets proved to have a major part in causing the financial crisis.

As toxic assets' markets seize up, they are called frozen markets. Many markets for these toxic assets froze up starting in 2007. The problem only continued to grow exponentially worse in the second half of the following year 2008. A number of elements combined to lock up the markets for toxic assets. These assets had values that proved to be extremely vulnerable to the worsening economic situation. As uncertainty only grew in this scenario, finding a value for toxic assets became more difficult. In the resulting frozen markets, banks and similar lending institutions chose not to unload these assets for greatly diminished prices. The reason for it lay in their fear that such drastically lower prices would force them to mark down all of their holdings, so that they became insolvent or bankrupt.

Typically, toxic assets are able to clear when the supply and demand of them reach the point that buyers and sellers will come together. This did not occur in the financial crisis starting in 2007. As a number of the financial assets simply hung around on banks' balance sheets, experts declared that the markets had broken down.

Another way of putting this is that because banks would not write down the prices on the assets, the price of them proved to be overly high. Buyers knew that these assets were now worth far less than the selling banks hoped to realize for them. This kept the sellers' price expectations far higher than buyers were willing to pay.

Toxic assets mostly arose as a result of banks and other investment banks deciding to pour enormous sums of money into new and complex financial assets like credit default swaps and collateralized debt obligations. These highly leveraged assets had values that turned out to be extremely vulnerable to a variety of economic conditions like the rates of default, prices of houses, and liquidity of financial markets. These toxic assets threatened to destroy the entire financial system and did manage to take down a number of venerable institutions like Bear Stearns, Lehman Brothers, and Washington Mutual Bank, the country's largest savings and loan institution. As a result of the carnage created by these highly leveraged, speculative investments in toxic assets, experts have named them financial weapons of mass destruction.

Trade Balance

Trade balances are used to describe the difference between the value of goods and services that are exported versus those that are imported into a country. Countries might have positive trade balances, where they export a greater value than they import. They might also have negative trade balances, or trade deficits, when they import a larger value of goods and services than they export. Positive trade balances create cash stockpiles and investment surpluses. Nations like Singapore, South Korea, Taiwan, and most of the Gulf Oil states like Saudi Arabia, Kuwait, and the United Arab Emirates continuously run positive trade balances. Negative trade balances create currency outflows or government debt that must be issued and sold domestically or exported as payment for the extra imports. Countries like the United States and Great Britain commonly run negative trade balances.

Positive trade balances are beneficial and constructive to a nation. They can be run forever in theory, so long as other countries continue to purchase their goods and services at high levels. Negative trade balances, or trade deficits, are harmful to a country over long periods of time. They can not be carried on forever, since eventually the negative trade balance running countries will reach a point that they have spent all of their money covering the imports or issued an amount of debt that finally becomes unsustainable and undesirable to investors any longer.

The United States' trade balance specifically refers to the differences between the value of American goods and service exports versus goods and services imported into the United States. This trade balance proves to be among the largest Balance of Payment components. America's Balance of Payments is constantly pressuring the U.S. dollar's value. These deficits minimally bring down the value of the currency for a country that continuously runs them.

Trade balances are reported in the United States and other advanced economies. The problem with such reports is they commonly come out some time after the data is current. This means that most of the information contained within such trade balance reports has already been anticipated and affected the markets. The Foreign Exchange markets do move based on these trade balance reports though, since trade balance data helps to form or support foreign currency trends. To this FOREX market, the Trade Balance report has proven historically to be among the most significant released from the United States.

Trade Deficit

Trade deficits are unfavorable balances of trade. With a trade deficit, a greater valued amount of goods and services are being imported than are simultaneously being exported. This stands in contrast to trade surpluses that occur when a larger amount of goods and services are exported by a nation than are imported in return. Trade deficits are also called trade gaps. These trade deficits and trade surpluses are a part of the balance of trade, or net exports, which proves to be the total difference between imports' and exports' tangible value within a country's economy during a particular time frame. The balance of trade results from the relationship of the country's exports and imports.

Economists have held varying opinions on how negative or non important that trade deficits might be. Some have said that issuing paper money not backed by anything other than faith and credit of a government in exchange for valuable produced goods is not a bad thing. Professor Milton Freedom, the founder of monetarism, is one of the main proponents of this particular point of view. He felt that what would likely happen is that high exports would raise the U.S. currency value, while high imports would lower the U.S. dollar value.

Friedeman said that the worst case scenario for running trade imbalances would be that easily and inexpensively printed U.S. dollars would leave the country in order to pay for the excess imports versus exports. Friedman claimed that this produced the same result as if the country that earned the dollars through exports simply set them on fire and did not send them back to America. His policies became influential in the late 1970's and early years of the 1980's.

Other influential investors and businessmen have made opposite arguments. Warren Buffet is perhaps the greatest investor in American history. He claims that the constant U.S. trade deficit proves to be the biggest financial threat facing the national economy. He says that it is worse than the enormous annual national budget deficit and consumer debt levels together.

Buffet has said that other countries in the world own three trillion dollars more of America than we own of their countries. This investment imbalance has only increased since Buffet made these arguments nearly five years ago. Buffet and his followers are so worried about the imbalanced trade deficit that they have suggested instituting import certificates as an answer to the American problem and to bring balanced trade back to the country.

Treasuries

Treasuries refer to United States Treasury Securities. These Treasuries are United States government debt that is actually issued and sold by the Department of the Treasury via the Bureau of Public Debt. The U.S. government uses its Treasury securities to finance the enormous and rising debt of the Federal government. In common and investor vernacular, these treasury securities are commonly simply called Treasuries.

Four different kinds of treasury securities exist. These are Treasury notes, Treasury bills, Treasury bonds, and TIPS, or Treasury Inflation Protected Securities. Other types of treasury securities are not marketed. These are comprised of savings bonds, Government Account Series debt given to trust funds that the government manages, and SLGS, or State and Local Government Series. The former marketable Treasury securities prove to be extremely liquid and also are traded significantly on the secondary market. The latter mentioned non marketable Treasury securities are only sold to subscribers. They may not be transferred back and forth via market sales.

The vast majority of U.S. Treasuries are actually held by other countries. As of January 2010, the top five largest holders of American Treasuries turn out to be China with $889 billion, Japan with $765.4 billion, the combined oil exporting nations with $218.4 billion, the United Kingdom with $206 billion, and Brazil with $169.1 billion. China and Japan combined hold an enormous $1.6 trillion worth of U.S. Treasuries.

These and other foreign countries have become such a large component of U.S. Treasuries debt purchases that many economists have grown afraid. They fear that since foreign nations now account for such a great percentage of U.S. Treasuries that should they decide to stop purchasing them, the U.S. debt and economy might simply collapse. The possibility that this is true has caused many observers to believe that the two economies of the United States and China are inextricably linked. Both countries are afraid of what would happen if the Chinese slowed their purchases of U.S. Treasuries. When Hillary Clinton, the U.S. Secretary of State, visited China earlier in 2010, she insisted that Beijing monetary authorities keep buying United States Treasuries. Her argument centered on the hope that this will pump the American economy back up, which would stimulate Chinese goods' imports back home.

China has demonstrated its frustration over the possible decline in value of its U.S. Treasuries holdings too. The Chinese Premier Wen Jia Bao has expressed concern and a warning that the Chinese holdings of U.S. Treasuries could be downgraded and devalued if Washington can not get its runaway debt under controlled.

Treasury Bills

Treasury Bills prove to be among the largest category of United States issued Treasuries. They are also called T-Bills for short. Treasury Bills have maturities of a year or less. They never pay investors interest before they mature, making them somewhat like zero coupon bonds. The government instead sells Treasury Bills at a face value discount, which causes there to be a positive yield to maturity. Numerous economists and ratings agency consider Treasury bills to be the lowest risk investments that American and foreign investors can purchase.

T-bills come issued with varying maturity dates. These typical forms of weekly Treasuries can have four week maturity dates, thirteen week maturity dates, twenty-six week maturity dates, and fifty-two week maturity dates. Every week, the government runs single price auctions for its Treasury bills. The quantity of thirteen week and twenty-six week Treasury bills available for purchase at auction are actually announced every Thursday. They are then offered on Monday and issued on the next Thursday.

Four week T-bill quantities get announced Mondays for next day auctions. The bills become issued on Thursday. Fifty-two week bills become announced only on the fourth Thursday, to be auctioned the following Tuesday and issued that Thursday. Associated purchase orders have to be received before 11 AM on Monday auctions at Treasury Direct. Minimum purchases for these T-bills are a reasonable $100, marked down from the former $1,000 minimum. The Treasury redeems T-bills that mature every Thursday. The biggest buyers of T-bills prove to be financial institutions such as banks, and primary dealers in particular. These Treasuries in their individual issue all get one of a kind CUSIP numbers.

Sometimes the Treasury cash balances are lower than usual. At these times, the Treasury often opts to sell CMB's, or cash management bills. They sell these in much the same way as T-bills, at auction with a discount. Their main difference lies in their irregular amounts and shorter terms of fewer than twenty-one days. They also possess different week days for auction, issue, and maturity. As these CMB's mature on the identical week day as typical T-bills, commonly Thursdays, they are termed on cycle. When they instead reach maturity on another day, they are known as off cycle.

Treasury bills are regularly sold on the secondary market too. Here, they are both quoted and sold via annual discount percentages, known as a basis. The secondary market trades these T-bills heavily.

The Treasury has modernized its means of offering T-bills to investors recently. Treasury Direct is their means of selling T-bills over the Internet, so that funds can be taken out and then deposited straight to the individuals' bank accounts. This permits investors to make better rates of interest on their savings than with simple bank account interest.

Underwriting

Underwriting refers to a means of determining if a consumer is eligible or not for a particular kind of financial product. These products vary depending on the person's or business' requirements. They might include home mortgages, insurance coverage needs, business mortgages, lines of credit, or financing for venture start up projects. The bank or other financial institution undergoing the underwriting evaluation procedure will look into the odds of the business transaction successfully providing them with a profit in exchange for their offer of financial help.

As banks and insurance firms go through the underwriting process, two different things will occur. The first of these is showing an interest in the project that the borrower is proposing for finance. They demonstrate this by offering the financial aid that the customer is requesting. Next, with a bank or institution underwriting an insurance policy, residential or commercial mortgage, or venture, they are looking to make money on their investment one day in the future. They might either gather these profits at one time in the form of a lump sum at a future date or little by little in monthly payments. In these underwriting activities, compensation is expected, which is commonly paid via finance charges or other fees.

Underwriters contemplate more than simply the amount of risk that an applicant demonstrates. They also consider the potential risk that working with the new customer might bring to other customers of their company. In order to ensure that the bank or firm does not suffer too much harm to keep up with commitments made to already existing clients, they have developed underwriting standards.

Insurance companies heavily rely on underwriting in performing their business. Health insurance is one example of this. Health insurance providers seriously look into the past and present health of a person applying. Sometimes their underwriting will show that they need to exclude various pre-existing conditions for a certain amount of time when they insure the person. Other times, underwriting will reveal a medical history that demonstrates too much risk for the company. In this case, a health insurance company will refuse to provide the requested health insurance coverage. Their goal is to not insure individuals who they believe will need significant medical treatment over time, so that they can provide a solid financial backing for their existing clientele.

In business, underwriting is commonly employed to determine if new ventures should be given financing. An example of this might be a company that has created a new technology that it wishes to sell. These underwriters will consider how marketable the product appears, the applicant's marketing plan, the expense of creating and selling the new items, and also the odds of the company realizing profits on every piece that they sell. Sometimes, underwriters of these business ventures will express an interest in having shares of stock in the start up company as a portion of their payment for services. Other times, they will only require a set interest rate for the dollar amount invested.

U.S. Treasury Bonds

U.S. Treasury bonds are bonds that the United States government issues so that it is capable of paying for Federal government projects. When a person or business purchases a Treasury bond, they are actually loaning the Federal government money. Like with all loans, the principal is paid back along with a set rate of interest. Treasury bonds carry the full faith and credit guarantee of the United States government. This translates to them having very low risk, as the government is always able to print extra money to repay the loan. Another benefit to U.S. Treasury bonds lies in their being tax exempt from local and state taxes. You would still have to pay Federal taxes on all money that you make in interest.

The primary market is where the government markets its Treasury bonds through auctions. You might also buy them on the secondary market using a broker. While the government does not charge fees for partaking in their auctions, brokers likely will expect to receive fees for selling you a U.S. Treasury bond. The Treasury bonds are marketable securities since you are able to sell or buy them once you have obtained them initially. They are considered to be extremely liquid too, since the secondary market for them is very active. The prices for Treasury bonds both at auction and via the secondary market are set by their interest rates. Today's Treasury bonds can not be called back by the government before maturity, which means that you continue to receive interest until they mature.

Treasury bonds are not without their downsides. Should interest rates rise while you have a Treasury bond, then your money will be making lower interest than it might in another investment. If the interest rates were to increase, then the bond's resale price would also go down. Inflation that goes up also cuts into the Treasury bonds' interest that they pay. With practically no risk of the U.S. government defaulting on these bonds, Treasury bonds pay a low return on investment, so higher inflation rates will wipe out all or most of the interest profits as they lower the real worth of the principal and interest repayments.

If you are interested in becoming involved in government auctions to buy the Treasury bonds straight from the Federal Reserve Bank, then you can do so. Simply open a Treasury Direct Account. The government does not charge fees for such an account until it has in excess of $100,000. For these larger accounts, they collect tiny maintenance fees.

Besides Treasury bonds, the government also sells two other kinds of securities. These are Treasury bills and Treasury notes. Treasury bonds are distinguished from these other two types by their length of time till maturity. Treasury bonds do not mature until from twenty years to thirty years elapse. They do make coupon payments of principal and interest in every six month period, like with Treasury notes. Thirty years maturities prove to be more common than do the twenty year maturities with these Treasury bonds.

Vacancy Rate

Vacancy rates turn out to be statistics that are gathered and maintained on availability of homes for sale, rental properties, and hotels. When you see high rates of vacancy, this is evidence that a market is struggling. Lower vacancy rates are hoped for as they demonstrate that properties are in demand and vacancies do not stay open for much time. Government agencies and other companies that focus on economic analysis maintain the records on vacancy rates. If you are contemplating moving into a new community, then you will find that vacancy rates are worth contemplating.

Where housing is concerned, vacancy rates add up all housing units that can be lived in but are not presently occupied. The agencies compiling the vacancy rates then express this as the percent of available to be lived in housing that is presently vacant. Vacancy rates cover houses, townhouses, apartments, and other forms of housing. As vacancy rates prove to be lower, it becomes more difficult for individuals to obtain housing. This is because the types of housing that they want may not be available either for sale or rent on a regular basis.

The vacancy rate statistics can be found on various kinds of housing arrangements. This differentiates on vacancy rates between townhouses, apartments, and single family homes. Landlords read these vacancy rates to be appraised of the rental situation, since changes in this number impact how much rent they can charge tenants. If landlords' tenants are constantly leaving, causing high rates of turnover, then they may wrestle with high vacancy rates personally.

When you see high vacancy rates in housing, it indicates that economic recession or depression is evident. High rates of vacancy can also happen if a great number of individuals leave a particular community, causing significant quantities of homes to lie vacant. Developers incorrectly estimating how strong a market is for housing in a local community might also cause them. Another factor that leads to higher vacancy rates proves to be rents that are high. When individuals can not pay an area's rent, then they will look for other places to live. Hotel vacancy rates demonstrate the strength or weakness of an area economy more profoundly, since high hotel vacancies mean tourism in the area is down.

Businesses are concerned with commercial vacancy rates. These are commonly figured up separate from residential vacancies. In the business vacancy rates figure are commercial buildings like factories and warehouses, and also empty retail storefronts and offices. Lower rates mean that people are supporting the businesses by spending their dollars in those areas. When consumers see a large number of empty storefronts, even when the economy is doing well, it will discourage them from frequenting that plaza or area.

Any individual who wants to see the vacancy rates for a given community can get them. A good place to start looking is at a local government office and in census data. Besides this, Realtors commonly maintain statistics on area vacancy rates, as do Internet sites that keep demographic information on different communities.

Velocity of Money

The velocity of money proves to be the speed at which money is changing hands. When the velocity of money is higher, then money is rapidly going from one hand to the next. This allows for a comparatively smaller amount of the money supply to cover a significant number of purchases. Conversely, if the velocity of money turns out to be lower, then the money is going from one hand to the next at a slower rate. This requires a greater supply of money to cover the same quantity of purchases.

The velocity of money is never the same. Such velocity will change along with the preferences of consumers. Besides this, it goes up and down as prices or money's real value fall or rise. Should the real value of money prove to be lower, then the levels of prices are higher. A greater quantity of bills would have to be utilized to pay for purchases. Assuming that money supply is constant, velocity of money has to go up to be able to pay for all purchases. The velocity of money also shifts as the Fed changes the money supply. These changes might cause price levels and money's value to stay the same.

The velocity of money turns out to be the single most critical factor in determining the impacts of any changes to the money supply. As an example, pretend that you buy a piece of pizza. The waiter takes the money that he is paid from this transaction and employs it to pay for dry cleaning. The dry cleaner owner next uses the money to wash his car. This goes on again and again until finally the bill is removed from circulation. Since bills can stay in circulation for literally decades, one bill will generally allow for a vast number of multiples of its face value to be transacted along the way.

The equation that demonstrates how velocity of money relates to the money supply, output, and the price level is expressed as M times V equals P times Y. In this equation, M represents the money supply and V stands for velocity, while P represents the price level and Y is the amount of output. Since P times Y yields the country's Gross Domestic Product, you could also say that V equals GDP over M, or velocity is Gross Domestic Product over money supply. In practice, the equation tells you that a certain Gross Domestic Product level that contains a tinier money supply will require a higher velocity of money so that all purchases can be funded. This means that velocity will go up in this scenario.

Velocity of money equations can also be altered to give percent changes in velocity of money equations. With velocity of money equations, you might employ them to measure the impact that any changes in the velocity, money supply, and price level have on one another. Only the output, represented by Y, would be fixed in such changes, since quantity of output does not change in short time frames.

Venture Capital

Venture capital refers to the process of investors purchasing a portion of a start up company. Firms or individuals that engage in this are called venture capitalists. They pour money into a firm that offers a high rate of growth but that also contains high risk. The typical venture capital investment time frame generally proves to be from five years up to seven years. Such investors anticipate getting a profit back on their investment through one of two ways. Either they hope to sell their stake in an Initial Public Offering to the public, or they hope to sell the company outright.

Investors who involve themselves in venture capital investments often wish to obtain a certain percentage of the company's ownership. They might also request being given one of the director's seats. This makes it easier for the investors to ask to be given their funds back either through insisting that the company be sold or reworking the deal that they made in the first place.

Venture capitalist investments are comprised of three different kinds. One of them is early stage financing that might be broken down into seed financing, first stage financing, or start up financing. Seed financing means that a tiny dollar amount of venture capital is paid to an inventor or other entrepreneur who wants to open a business. This might be employed to come up with a business plan, do market research, or bring on a good management team.

First stage financing is the type needed as companies look to boost their capital so that they can begin full scale operations. Start up financing instead is venture capital distributed to a business that exists for under a year. In this stage, a product will not be on the market already, or will only just have been put on the market for sale.

A second type of venture capital investments is known as expansion financing. Expansion financing is comprised of both bridge financing as well as second and third stage financing. Bridge financing refers to investments that only receive interest and are short term. They are mostly employed for company restructurings. They might also be utilized to cash out early investors.

Second stage financing proves to be investment money for the purpose of growing a company already up and running. While such a company may not yet demonstrate actual profits, it is producing and selling merchandise. It also possesses inventories and accounts that are expanding.

Third stage financing is investments that venture capitalists make in companies that have at least broken even on costs or are even starting to demonstrate profits. In this case, venture capital is employed to grow the business further. For example, third stage financing could be utilized to develop more or better products, or to purchase needed real estate.

Still a different popular version of venture capital investing is known as acquisition financing. In this type of venture capital, the investment goes into gaining a stake in or the entire ownership of a different company. Management could also choose to use this venture capital to buy out yet another business or product line, whatever its development stage proves to be. They might acquire either a public or a private company in this way.

Volatility

Volatility in investments has to do with the possibility of stocks or other investments undergoing a dramatic gain or loss in price and value in a certain amount of time. Investors consider the volatility of stocks and other investments when they decide to buy more shares of the asset, sell their current holdings, or to buy shares of a new offering. Whatever an investment's volatility proves to be, investors' goal should always be to make the highest return that they possibly can for the lowest chances of experiencing losses.

Volatility is caused by many different elements. With stocks, a great concern is how stable the assets of a company are that underlie the stock itself. A sudden loss of confidence in a public company would also likely cause a sharp decline in the price. The stock price drop and accompanying volatility is actually created by the public's perception of something within the company, like changing leadership or a coming acquisition. In fact the stock might come back in a relatively short time frame as the public decides that the company is stable after all. But such factors might be more troubling and enduring, causing the volatility of the stock to become too high. When such volatility persists, many investors will decide not to buy additional shares or even to sell off the ones that they hold.

The overall conditions of a market can also influence investment volatility. As the stock market all around shows higher signs of volatility, individual investments will likely suffer the same fate. This stock market wide volatility can occur as consumers become worried about the whole economy, or if political situations force investors to take more conservative trading positions. Should such impacts grow sufficiently significant, then even stable stocks can become lightly traded while investors sit on the sidelines to watch for the troubling issues to get resolved. In the meanwhile, the stocks and their underlying options might make dramatic rises and drops in price from higher volatility.

Volatility is a fact of life that investors have to be capable of handling. Still, some stocks and investments demonstrate higher degrees of volatility than do others. Investors can gain an insight into this amount of individual volatility that an investment might have thorough looking into its historical levels of price and accompanying volatility. Using this data with projected trends in the economy and markets, investors can get a good picture of the amount of an individual investment's volatility to determine if they are comfortable with it before they invest in the offering.

Wages

Wages are financial considerations given out to employees as payment for their time and effort of labor. Wages also refers to the compensation given to workers paid by the hour, whereas salary is the word used to describe compensation given out to employees. Compensation, like wages, proves to be monetary payments that employers give out to employees in exchange for their services that they provide the employer or company.

Wages can be determined by supply and demand market forces in capitalist economies. In other countries, wages can be impacted by different elements like the social structure, tradition, and seniority, as they are heavily in Japan. A number of nations have chosen to set up a minimum wage that ensures that a floor on the value of particular types of labor is maintained.

The word wage is a derivation of words that meant to make a promise in the form of money. The medieval French word Wagier stood for pledging or promising, specifically in the situation of a bet. The word Wadium from the Latin of the late period refers to a pledge being given.

Within the U.S., the majority of employees and hourly workers' wages are determined by either the interaction of market forces or collective bargaining. Labor unions actually negotiate the wages of their members in such collective bargaining. The U.S. also has its Fair Labor Standards Act that creates a minimum wage in Federal law that all states have to observe. Besides this national minimum, many cities and fourteen different states have established their own minimum wages which are greater than the national minimum. With some state government and federal government contracts, a prevailing wage exists that employers have to observe. This is mandated by the Davis Bacon Act or similar legislation within a given state.

Some activists are not satisfied with these wage levels. They have pursued the concept of getting a living wage rate passed. These types of wages would be based on the costs of living and other needed items, causing a living wage rate to be significantly greater than the presently established minimum wages actually are.

Wages are reported to the IRS and employees with W-2 forms sent out by employers. Employees must also state their wages accurately on their tax returns each year. Wages are the starting point for figuring out the amount of taxes that you owe the Internal Revenue Service every year. Wages are reduced by the allowable deductions before an adjusted income is derived for taxing purposes.

Wealth

Wealth proves to be the abundant possession of material things or other resources that are considered to be valuable. People, areas, communities, or nations who control these assets are said to be wealthy. The word for wealth comes from the old English word 'Weal' and 'th', which means 'the conditions of well-being'.

The ideas of wealth have great importance for every part of the study of economics. This is particularly the case with development economics. Since the definition of wealth often depends on the situation in which you use it, no universally accepted definition for wealth exists. Different individuals have expressed a number of varying ideas of wealth in differing scenarios. Stating the concept of wealth often involves ethics and moral issues, because the accumulation of wealth is viewed by many people as the highest goal.

Wealth is not evenly distributed throughout the world. In the year 2000, world wealth estimates ranged around $125 trillion. The citizens of Europe, North America, and a few high income Asian countries have ninety percent of all of this wealth. Besides this shocking statistic, only one percent of all adults on earth possess forty percent of the planet's wealth. This number declines to thirty-two percent when wealth is calculated according to purchasing power parity, or equivalency of what it buys from one country to the next.

Wealth and richness are two separate words that are used interchangeably. They mean slightly different things. Wealth describes gathering up resources, whether they are common or abundant. Richness relates to having such resources in abundance. Wealthy countries and people possess many more resources than do poor ones. The word richness is similarly employed to describe peoples' basic needs being fulfilled through sharing the collective abundance. Wealth's opposite proves to be destitution, while richness' opposite is known as poverty.

Wealth is a concept that requires a social contract of ownership to be set up and enforced. Ideas of wealth are actually relative. They range from not only one society and people to another, but even between varying regions or areas of the same society or nation. As an example, having ten thousand dollars throughout all of the United States does not make a person among the richest in any area of the country. But this amount in desperately poor developing nations would represent a huge quantity of wealth.

The idea of wealth changes in different times too. Thanks to the progress of science and machines that save labor, even the poorest in America today benefit from a higher standard of living than the wealthy used to enjoy not so long ago. Assuming this trend continues, then the wealthiest people's standard of living today will be considered poor in the future.

Welfare

Welfare is a social program that the government uses to attempt to provide for its citizens' well being. This could happen with social security, social welfare programs, or even government sponsored financial aid. Corporate welfare is generally described as the government directly supporting companies instead of permitting the free market to close down inefficient businesses. Governments that grow their welfare programs excessively find that they are called welfare states.

Any type of program that has the government giving services or money directly to citizens in need of help can be called welfare. This means that lots of government programs are forms of welfare, even when the citizens and critics do not realize it. Still others say that still more welfare programs are needed to adequately take care of people's needs.

Social welfare provisions are what the majority of people are describing when they talk about welfare. These programs offer minimum income standards to those who have lost their jobs, are old, or are disabled. The government feels an ethical obligation to help these individuals who could not live without help. By allowing them a chance to find work again, the government ultimately helps out the economy and nation as a whole.

As an example of welfare, those who have lost their jobs can get welfare assistance in the form of unemployment as they are seeking replacement work. This is offered as cash assistance and sometimes as food stamps. If you become disabled and can no longer work, then you are able to obtain the same type of help, even though you do not have to look for work to be eligible.

A great number of countries today feature national health care programs. These prove to be enormous welfare systems. In these systems, every group in the country is able to access medical care when they need help. The U.S. does not yet have a functioning universal health care system set up, though one has been passed by congress and President Obama for the future.

A free universal welfare system that runs throughout the U.S. is free schooling until the end of high school. The government pays for all associated costs, even food and transportation when it is required. Because most critics do not consider free public education to be welfare, there is little controversy surrounding it.

World Bank

The World Bank proves to be an institution in international finance. It offers developing countries of the planet leveraged loans to help out with funding capital programs. The goal of the World Bank is to cut down on poverty. Every decision that the organization enacts is required to be carried out with the objectives of encouraging international trade, foreign investment, and facilitate capital investment.

The World Bank should not be confused with the World Bank Group. The World Bank is two of the five organizations within the World Bank Group. These two groups that make up the World Bank are the IDA, or the International Development Association, and the IBRD, or International Bank for Reconstruction and Development. The World Bank Group is also made up of MIGA, or the Multilateral Investment Guarantee Agency; the IFC, or International Finance Corporation; and the ICSID, or International Center for Settlement of Investment Disputes.

The World Bank's two organizations are widely supported by the nations of the world. The International Development Association contains one hundred and sixty-eight members, while the International Bank for Reconstruction and Development is comprised of one hundred and eighty-seven countries. Exclusively members of the IBRD may belong to the various other organizations in the World Bank. All IBRD members are supposed to belong to the IMF, or International Monetary Fund, as well.

The year 2010 saw significant revisions to the allocated votes of members of the World Bank. Developing countries, especially China, gained a larger voice. The nations that possess the biggest voting power currently are the United States at 15.85%, Japan at 6.84%, China at 4.42%, Germany at 4%, Great Britain at 3.75%, and France at 3.75%. These changes are called the Phase Two of the Voice Reform. They also gave major votes percentages to countries such as India, Brazil, Mexico, and

South Korea. To come up with the extra votes, the voting percentages of the majority of developed nations declined. Russia, the United States, and Saudi Arabia's votes did not change.

The World Bank focuses on reducing the poverty found in the poorest developing countries in the world. They do this analyzing a nation's economic and financial condition and comparing it against a snap shot of many local groups in the country. Then, the World Bank comes up with unique strategies for addressing the problems of the given country. After this, the country's government lays out their biggest priorities for reducing poverty, so that the World Bank can line up its help to work together with this government.

Besides giving out money to the poorest countries on the earth, the World Banks heads several other initiatives. They are managers of the Clean Technology Fund. They also run the Clean Air Initiative.

Yield

In business and finance, yield is the word that states the quantity of cash that comes back to a security's owners. Yield is measured independently of variations in price. It proves to be a percentage of total return. Yield is used for measuring the return rates of fixed income investments, such as bonds, bills, strips, notes, and zero coupons; stocks, including common, convertible, and preferred; and various other insurance and investment hybrid products like annuities.

Yield can mean different things in varying situations. It is sometimes figured up as an IRR, or Internal Rate of Return, or alternatively as a ratio. Yield describes an investment owner's entire return or a part of the income.

The end result of the many differences in yield is that they can not be compared one against the other. This is because they are not all the same from one branch of finance and investments to another. You could see numerous different formulas for figuring up yield used by different investments and groups.

Bonds are a classic example of this. Nominal yield is also known as coupon yield. This proves to be the face value of a bond divided into the annual interest total. Current yield instead is those interest payments over the bond's price on the spot market. A yield to maturity is the internal rate of return on the bond cash flow, including the bond principal when maturity arrives plus the interest received, and the purchase price. Finally, a bond's yield to call is the bond's cash flow internal rate of return if it is called in by the company at their earliest opportunity.

Bonds yields are unusual in that they vary inversely to the price of the bond. Should a bond price decline, then the yield will rise. If instead the rates of interest drop, then the bond's price will go up in general.

Some securities come with real yields. TIPS are a primary example of this. A real yield means that the face value of the instrument will be adjusted upwards compared to the CPI inflation index. The real yield would then be set against this principal that is adjusted to make certain that an investor makes a better return than the rate of inflation. This ensures that his or her purchasing power is protected. TIPS are one rare investment that will not allow investors to lose money if they purchased them in the auction and keep them until they mature, either as a result of deflation, meaning falling prices, or inflation, signifying rising prices over time.

Zoning Laws

Zoning laws are statutes that mandate the ways that you are able to utilize your property holdings. Townships, counties, cities, and alternative local governments affect zoning laws so that they are able to create standards for development that benefit all residents in common.

It does not matter how big or how small a property is; it will be impacted by zoning laws. If you contemplate improving your property or purchasing another piece of property, you should be certain that you are fully aware of zoning restrictions that will affect you in advance of making any kind of commitment.

As an example, properties can be zoned according to residential or commercial restrictions. Commercial buildings will never be permitted to be constructed in a residential area, while residential dwellings can not be put up in commercial zones, unless the zoning laws of the area are changed.

Getting the zoning laws for a property altered proves to be extremely difficult. You would first have to give out public notice before getting an approved variance from the responsible government agencies in charge of zoning plans. Many times, neighbors will stalwartly resist your proposed zoning changes.

Zoning laws allow for a variety of different zoning designations and uses. Among these are commercial zoning, residential zoning, industrial zoning, recreational zoning, and agricultural zoning. These categories are generally further subdivided into other categories. Residential zoning might have sub zoning categories under it including multiple family use, for condominiums or apartments, or single family houses.

Zoning laws include a number of limitations to the property and potential improvements. The total size and height of buildings on the property is commonly restricted. The buildings can only be placed so close to each other. There will be limits to the total area percentage that is allowed to have buildings on it. Perhaps most importantly, the types of buildings that can be built on a given land's zone will be mandated.

You can learn about the zoning laws and ordinances simply by getting in touch with the area planning agency. Alternatively, you might go on the Internet to the local and state search engine to learn about your county and city zoning rules. Local planning organizations will tell you what must be done to get a variance to the area zoning.

Zombie Banks

Zombie banks prove to be financial institutions that in reality have literal economic net worths of less than zero. They still keep running because they are able to continue paying their debts using government's real or implied support for their credit and balance sheet. Although this term has come to be heavily used in the financial crises of 2007 to 2010, it did not originate there.

Instead, Edward Kane coined the phrase Zombie Banks back in 1987. He used it to refer to and relate the perils of allowing a great number of banks that were actually insolvent to continue operating. The phrase came to be utilized for the Japanese banking crisis that began in 1993. It once again arose in popularity during the financial crisis of the last few years where hundreds of banks have failed in single years.

Zombie banks have many problems. Among these are bank runs from frightened depositors who are uninsured for their full account values. They also suffer from margin calls from their counter parties in derivatives contracts.

Zombie banks can be deceptive, as on the surface they may look like they are actually healthy and have the necessary level of capital to run. As investors learn the fair value of their assets, then they are suddenly looked at as insolvent institutions. This is to say that Zombie Banks keep operating in a regular manner as if nothing is wrong with their balance sheets. Yet the truth is that they will likely be seized by the Feds when the word becomes wide spread that they do not have the assets and money that everyone believed.

Healthy banks are able to make loans to new borrowers at the same time that they honor their obligations to lenders and share holders. Insolvent banks, or Zombie Banks, are incapable of generating new loans, since they lack the money and capital to make such loans while still performing on their obligations to lenders and share holders.

Comprehending what constitutes a Zombie bank requires that you know the basics of a bank balance sheet. One side of a balance sheet actually contains a bank's assets. The other side is comprised of the bank's liabilities as well as the bank's equity. The two sides are supposed to equal out, which is expressed in the equation assets equal liabilities plus the bank equity.

Zombie banks manage to hide their problems since no one is able to determine how much their assets are really worth. Asset backed securities and collateralized debt obligations are examples of assets whose values can not clearly be determined at any given moment. They might be worth as much as seventy-five cents for every dollar, or they could be valued as low as twenty-five cents per dollar.

The problem comes when Zombie banks have over valued their assets. If they later are forced to revalue them to correct and more appropriate levels, they quickly discover that they no longer have the assets to cover their future liabilities. Admitting to this causes them to become Zombie banks. At this point, the bank share holders are typically wiped out, while the depositors are given their money back by the Federal Deposit Insurance Corporation.

42853676R00153

Made in the USA
San Bernardino, CA
10 December 2016